UK AND IRELAND
CIRCUMNAVIGATOR'S GUIDE

UK AND IRELAND
CIRCUMNAVIGATOR'S GUIDE

3RD EDITION

ESSENTIAL PLANNING ADVICE FOR ALL BOATERS

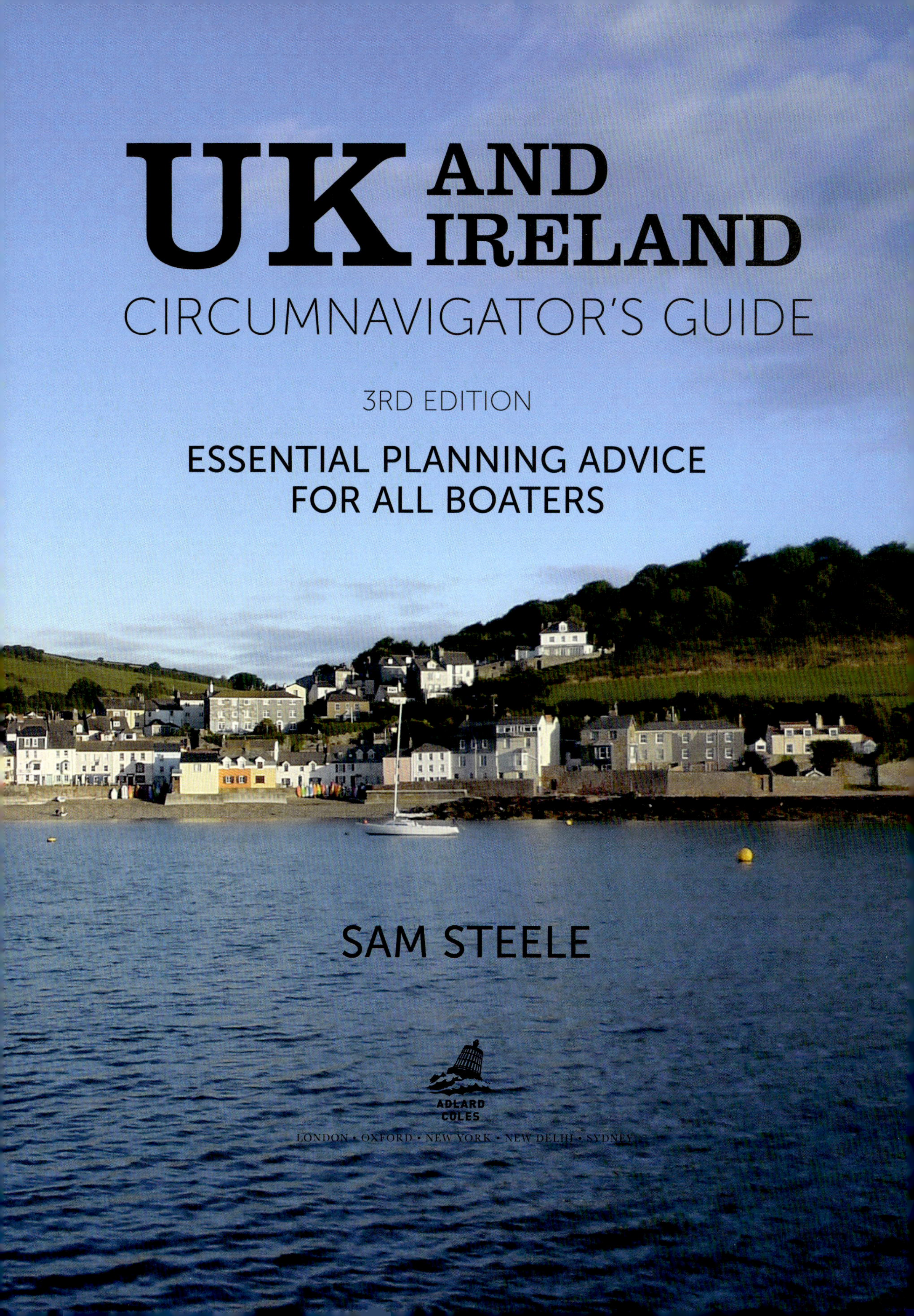

SAM STEELE

ADLARD COLES
LONDON · OXFORD · NEW YORK · NEW DELHI · SYDNEY

In memory of my father, who introduced me to the Arthur Ransome books
and taught me how to sail.

ADLARD COLES
Bloomsbury Publishing Plc
50 Bedford Square, London, WC1B 3DP, UK
29 Earlsfort Terrace, Dublin 2, Ireland

BLOOMSBURY, ADLARD COLES and the Adlard Coles logo are trademarks of Bloomsbury Publishing Plc

First published in Great Britain 2008
Second edition published 2011
This third edition published 2025

Copyright © Sam Steele, 2025

Photographs © Sam Steele, unless otherwise stated

Maps © JP Map Graphics Ltd, 2025

Sam Steele has asserted her right under the Copyright, Designs and Patents Act, 1988,
to be identified as Author of this work

Graphs on pages 21 and 143 © Copyright Met Éireann (www.met.ie). This data is published under a Creative Commons Attribution 4.0 International (CC BY 4.0). Met Éireann does not accept any liability whatsoever for any error or omission in the data, their availability, or for any loss or damage arising from their use. Where applicable, there is an indication if the material has been modified and an indication of previous modifications

This product has been derived in part from material obtained from the UK Hydrographic Office with the permission of the UK Hydrographic Office, Keeper of Public Records © British Crown Copyright, 2025. All rights reserved

THIS PRODUCT IS NOT TO BE USED FOR NAVIGATION

NOTICE: The UK Hydrographic Office (UKHO) and its licensors make no warranties or representations, express or implied, with respect to this product. The UKHO and its licensors have not verified the information within this product or quality assured it

All rights reserved. No part of this publication may be reproduced or transmitted in any form or by any means, electronic or mechanical, including photocopying, recording, or any information storage or retrieval system, without prior permission in writing from the publishers

Bloomsbury Publishing Plc does not have any control over, or responsibility for, any third-party websites referred to or in this book. All internet addresses given in this book were correct at the time of going to press. The author and publisher regret any inconvenience caused if addresses have changed or sites have ceased to exist, but can accept no responsibility for any such changes

A catalogue record for this book is available from the British Library

ISBN: PB: 978-1-3994-1127-1; ePub: 978-1-3994-1126-4; ePDF: 978-1-3994-1129-5

2 4 6 8 10 9 7 5 3 1

Typeset in Museo 300 by carrdesignstudio.com

Printed and bound in India by Repro India Ltd.

To find out more about our authors and books visit www.bloomsbury.com
and sign up for our newsletters

ACKNOWLEDGEMENTS

I would like to thank all the circumnavigators who answered my questions; I enjoyed reliving the trip through their stories and logs. Thanks also go to the people who replied to my questions but did not want their names mentioned.

Yachts

Charlie Tait, David and Mary Trim: *Jemima*, Ovni 385
Gordon Stollard: *Pipe Dream*, Island Packet 420
Sam Kent: *Silverwind*, Hunter Delta 25
Sid and Margaret Hygate: *Kiddet*, Halmatic 30
Clive Anstiss and Les Sutcliffe: *Quintet*, Freeman 30
David Rainsbury: *Piper*, Contessa 26
Geoffrey Palmer: *Shardik*, Contessa 32
John Hill: *Almacantar*, Hustler 38
Carol and Dermot Stewart: *Gemini*, Beneteau 31
Denis Argent: *Dorran*, Rival 34
David Buckpitt: *Nefertiti of St Helier*, 62ft Ketch
Sarah Fagg: *Huffin*, Hurley 22
Steve and Claire Crook: *Touché*, Beneteau 36
Greg, Sue, Kate and Sebastian Hill: *Blue Argolis*, Trewes 41
Bill and Anita Miller: *Marika M*, Westerly Corsair
Stan Lester: *Indalo*, Mirage 2700
Chester Wallace: *Bellini*, Moody 336
Karen Hodges: *Loon at Sea*, Caprice 18
Mike Dixon: *Gellie Fairey*, Atalanta 31
Vince Spooner: *Anita A*, Contessa 26
Iain and Penny Kidson: *Rainbow Catcher*, Gemini 33
Tony Brimble: *Gitana*, Crealock 34
Geoff Holt: *Freethinker*, 15ft Challenger Tri
Mike Fellows: *Kes*, Van de Stadt 28
Jonathan Hutchinson: *Zia Maria*, Moody 31
Irving Benjamin: *Vega*, LM Vitesse 33 (still en route)
Steve Cooksey: *Gamaldansk*, Westerly GK29
Tom Cunliffe: *Hirta*, 50ft Gaff Cutter (completed the trip twice)
Rob Jenkins: *Deerhunter*, Hunter Medina 20
Nico Shipman: *Gothik*, Westerly GK29
Tim and James Mitchell: *Elle*, Sadler 26
Chris Ward: *Snow Leopard*, Cat 39ft (completed the trip twice)

Graeme Hall: *Ceòl Na Mara*, Hallberg Rassy 35
Colin and Elspeth Iskander: *Scarba*, Nicholson 35
Derek and Val Shepherd: *Western Wind*, Sadler 34
Colin Hall: *Boysterous*, Oyster 53
Dick Dyer: *Sunshine*, Sadler 29
Robert Cundall: *Spring Breeze*, One-off Wooden Cutter 43
Ken Marsden: *Picaro*, Vancouver 34
Martin Whitfield: *Knot Telling*, Cornish Crabber 26
Bill Aylward: *Double Vision*, Catana 42
Jonathan & Anne Winter: *Nova*, GT Yachts 35
Jill Rogers: *Vela*, Sadler 25
Charles Cameron: *China Blue*, Maxi 1100
Keith Millay & Glenn Hammet: *Zanzibar*, Moody 346
Jes Bates: *Mwera*, Corribee 21
Mark Ashley Miller: *Good Dog*, Nauticat 331
Mark Edmondson: *Compaen*, Najad 360
Derek Hathaway: *Thalmia*, Westerly Fulmar
Robin & Brigette Matthews: *Ruby Tuesday*, Jeanneau Sun Odyssey 39i
Roger Clark: *Concerto*, Westerly Fulmar

Motor boats

Dominic and Nicola Gribbin: *Jura Pilot*, Hardy Family Pilot 20
Mike, Michelle, Letitia and Michael Perry: *Caribbean Breeze*, Fairline 36 Turbo
Malcolm and Glenda Stennett: *Lady Genevieve*, Broom 39 and Broom 44 (completed the trip three times)
Brian Rhodes: *Limfjord*, Nelson 34

My thanks go to Ali Millward, for her help proof-reading, and Mags, for making the trip possible and for her patience and support when I was writing and updating this book.

CONTENTS

Introduction 9

1. IS THIS THE VOYAGE FOR ME? 11
2. PLANNING THE ROUTE 16
3. FINANCES 53
4. PREPARATIONS 58
5. STORES, EQUIPMENT AND KIT 64
6. PROVISIONING 72
7. A GREENER WAKE 77
8. MOORING AND ANCHORING 84
9. WEATHER 92
10. STAYING IN TOUCH 105
11. NAVIGATION 115
12. LIFE ON BOARD 127
13. SAFETY 135
14. HAZARDS IN COASTAL WATERS 147
15. ENGINE MAINTENANCE 155
16. TEN OF THE BEST! 161
    - Castle anchorages 162
    - Wildlife encouters 166
    - Culinary experience 171
    - Challenging tidal races 176
    - Whisky tasting 183
    - Historical interest 187
    - Taking the ground 192
    - Beautiful rivers and estuaries 197
    - Glorious gardens 201
    - Picturesque marinas 206
    - Remote anchorages 211
    - Tasty treats 216
    - Iconic lighthouses 221
    - Sea shore gems 225
    - Maritime history 229
    - 'Drop-dead gorgeous' places 234
    - Maps 239

Appendices
1. Marinas in north-west Ireland and Scotland 243
2. Fuel availability 245
3. Pilot books and sailing directions 248
4. Books and websites 251

Index 253

Ituna in Puilladobhrain

INTRODUCTION

There are an increasing number of motorboats and yachts circumnavigating Britain and Ireland. To many sailors it is the trip of a lifetime, a real dream, but it can seem daunting. The year before our planned voyage, the weather forecasts seemed to show endless gales sweeping across Scotland; how would we cope in such conditions?

This was to be our first extended cruise, but when we looked for advice we found little available on cruising in home waters. Most books are aimed at sailors preparing for blue water cruising and I avidly read many of them. But there was much relevant information for us missing, which was the reason I was inspired to write this book. It is designed to fill in some of the gaps and I hope it whets your appetite to explore our wonderful coastline.

Whether you own a motorboat or yacht, the planning and preparation are much the same and the aim of this guide is to help you to prepare successfully, so that you can make the most of your circumnavigation. It is surprising how much work has to be done in advance for a trip like this. There is new equipment to fit, stores to buy and stow and charts and pilot books to source, to name just a few of the tasks. Throughout this book, I describe our methods but also explain what we would have done differently. Since 2018, we have been lucky enough to be able to sail throughout the summer, so I have also drawn on our experience of extended cruising.

Since returning from the voyage, I have researched a number of other circumnavigations and obtained information from 85 boatowners: 71 in yachts, 11 in motorboats and 3 in RIBs, which includes an additional 14 yachts for this third edition. The experiences and advice of these sailors, added to my own knowledge, has enabled me to compile this guide for all would-be circumnavigators.

The influence of technology on navigation, weather forecasts and communications over the last decade has been transformational to all aspects of life on a boat. It was only fitting to completely rewrite these chapters for the third edition, and it now reflects how we sail today. The other area that has changed how we cruise, is that we are now more aware of our environmental impact, and we are trying to leave a greener wake. While some of the change needed is behavioural, some we were already doing because it just made sense. We were at a lecture by Mike Golding, when the host was discussing his current projects with him. One of these is finding a replacement material to GRP that is sustainable, and as quick as a flash, the host said 'you could try wood....', we do still have much to learn from the old more sustainable ways. Also in this edition, I have expanded the number of amazing places to visit in the 'Ten of the Best' section, because where to visit is still one of the hardest decisions to make.

The term 'round Britain' can be used to describe many routes, though strictly speaking, Britain includes all the islands out to Rockall and Muckle Flugga but excludes the Channel Islands and Northern Ireland. If you do not include the islands on your route it is 'only' a circumnavigation around mainland Britain. Taking a route through the canals technically cannot be called 'round Britain'; however, in this book I refer to a trip via the Caledonian Canal as 'round Britain' as it is a recognised route.

My wife, Mags, and I sailed our circumnavigation in our Rival 38, *Ituna*, built in 1977. Mags holds the RYA Day Skipper qualification and has gained most of her experience on our short summer cruises around the French coast, the Channel Islands and the south coast. I started sailing on the Norfolk Broads in my home-built Mirror dinghy. I progressed to yachts and gained the RYA Yachtmaster Offshore qualification at the age of 20. I have since cruised around France, the Channel Islands, Canary Islands and the Azores. For the past nine years, we have kept our new boat, *Carra*, in the Baltic, where we have enjoyed cruising among the rocks of the Swedish, Finnish and Estonian archipelagos and Denmark.

One of my greatest rewards for writing the book is meeting people who have read it and hearing that the book has inspired them to make a successful circumnavigation. It has always been my aim to show how this 'Door Step Challenge' is a very realistic option for many. If our stunning coastline, the wildlife or the challenge aren't reasons enough, then the limitations of extended cruising in Europe, post-Brexit, might be a deciding factor. Or if you are working, then one barrier to setting off has always been financial. Up until now, for most people, that has meant waiting for retirement, getting a sabbatical or leaving their job, the latter two having a financial cost. But with remote working becoming more commonplace, this might enable some to cast off their lines without having to cut their income.

When we bought *Ituna*, the idea was to go off cruising for a year, but we quickly discovered that saving money and owning a boat seemed to be incompatible. We managed to arrange four months' leave from our jobs, so sticking to home waters seemed the best plan. Also, Mags suffers from seasickness as soon as the sea state is declared to be 'slight'. Committing to a year, with long passages would really have been her idea of torture. So we decided on a round Britain. This book should give hope to all those who are stuck with the dreaded malaise... you do eventually get your sea-legs!

I grew up with the stories of my heroes, such as Dame Naomi James, and have always wanted to go off on my own adventure but I am, by nature, cautious. This circumnavigation was our big challenge and at the back of my mind was the thought: 'Could we do it?' But on 1 May 2006 we set off from Gosport and sailed clockwise around Britain, arriving back safely on 23 August. If we can do it – so can you!

Sam Steele

CHAPTER ONE

IS THIS THE VOYAGE FOR ME?

How many times have you finished your annual cruise and thought, 'If only I could continue sailing a bit longer?' Or maybe it was after reading an article in a boating magazine that you dreamt of a real adventure in your boat. However, for many the dream never becomes reality because time is limited. To sell up and head off into the blue yonder is a brave step to take. But if you want to try a taster to see if living on your boat appeals to you, then perhaps a cruise around the UK could be the answer, as it offers several advantages:

- You never have to decide at what point to turn back, as you just keep going round.
- With many harbours and anchorages to choose from, you have the ability to coastal hop, with only a few long passages required.
- You are never too far from home, in case of an emergency.
- You don't have to sell your house to complete the voyage.
- You don't need to be as self-sufficient for maintenance as you would on a longer blue water cruise, as most harbours have some skilled mechanics.
- There are no language issues, which does make it much easier to understand the weather forecasts.
- As the cruise is for a relatively short period, you may be able to get a sabbatical from your job. Having a guaranteed job to come back to considerably reduces the financial risks.
- With remote working offering more flexibility, it is possible to work from your boat with the right connectivity, making this an option for some.
- You are not limited by the 90 in 180 days Schengen restriction.

IS OWNING A BOAT ESSENTIAL?

If you don't own a boat you can still circumnavigate. There are several sailing schools that offer a round Britain experience, either as part of a Yachtmaster fast track course or a mile-builder. Their trips last from six weeks to three months. We met one couple who had chartered a boat with a skipper for eight weeks and successfully completed the trip via the Caledonian Canal. They showed an adventurous spirit, as neither of them had much offshore experience prior to their trip; though they did feel that after the trip, they would know what qualities they were looking for in a boat.

RACING OR CRUISING?

I have assumed that most readers will be cruising, but if you are interested in racing there are

NOT JUST A HOLIDAY!

Your circumnavigation is not just a holiday, you will experience:

- Hard work, with lots of early starts to catch the tide.
- Tight schedules. Depending on your time available, you will always be thinking about pressing on, so that you are back home at the right time.
- Challenging tides and navigation.

But the rewards are:

- Awesome scenery – our coastline is truly beautiful.
- Spectacular sunrises – just rewards for those early starts.
- An abundance of wildlife which can be seen at close quarters.
- Many new friendships will be made along the way.
- An incredible sense of achievement.

We now watch the TV weather forecasts and see the map of the UK with a sense of pride – it is great to see exactly where we sailed, recognising each bump on our coastline.

Sunrise over Dover

several races open for motorboats and yachts, however, not all are open to amateur entrants. If you really feel the need for speed then there are many records that have been set. Though you will have to be flying to beat the current ones: in a power boat it is 27 hours 10 minutes for a round Britain voyage. If sailing, you will need to be clocking up an average speed of nearly 24 knots to compete with the 'round Britain and Ireland' record of 3 days 3.5 hours. A new record was set in 2024 by Henry Besley who completed the first circumnavigation of Britain via the Caledonian Canal in an electric-powered RIB in 31 days 20 hours 46 minutes, visiting 43 locations and averaging 8.2 knots, saving 12,858.6kg of CO_2 compared to a motor boat.

WHAT SIZE BOAT DO YOU NEED?

Many sizes of boat have been used to complete the trip (see Acknowledgements for a list of those whose boats are detailed below).

Yachts

The smallest yacht was 18ft (5.5m) and they ranged right up to 62ft (19m). The largest boat to be sailed single-handedly for the whole trip was 33ft (10m), though most boats less than 26ft (8m) were sailed solo. The average size of the yachts was 32ft (9.7m). The smallest yacht to be sailed via Cape Wrath was a 20ft (6m) Hunter Medina 20, *Deerhunter*.

Motor boats

The boats ranged from 20 to 48ft (6 to 14.6m) and the average size was 36ft (11m). The smallest motor boat which made it successfully around via Cape Wrath was a 20ft (6m).

INTRODUCTION 13

RIBs
The RIBs varied in size between 28 and 31ft (8.5 and 9.5m).

Other craft
Most would consider a circumnavigation in a reasonable-sized boat a challenge. For some that is not enough; smaller boats completing the trip included:

Dinghy – Ron Pattenden sailed round Britain in a 13ft (4m) Laser dinghy in 2004; his diary was featured in *Yachts and Yachting*.

Kayak – There have been a few voyages by kayak and many of their stories have been featured in books or on websites; their details can be found at www.sailingwithcarra.com.

Windsurfer – Tim Batstone circumnavigated Britain in 1984 on a 12ft (3.7m) windsurfer.

GOALS
While researching this book, I have come across many different goals which inspired such an adventure:

- To be the fastest circumnavigator.
- To race others.
- To see the scenery and wildlife.
- To experience new places.
- To gain sailing experience and test your seamanship skills.
- To gain a qualification.
- To challenge yourself physically.
- To raise money for charity.
- To find freedom outside your physical boundaries
- And just because the cruise appeals to you.

There are probably many others but, whatever your goal, you need to have a common understanding with your crew if you are going to make the voyage a success. Your goals will help your decision-making process along the way, eg whether to sail, how long to spend in a location etc. Dissimilar goals will lead to friction, as your crew will have different expectations and may not understand or agree with the decisions you make. When Vivien Cherry skippered the Global Challenge boat *Coopers & Lybrand* around the world, friction arose among the crew: the skipper's goal was 'race around the world', while for some of the crew, the aim was to 'sail around the world'. These are conflicting goals; one requires that you constantly drive the boat to maximise your speed, and the other is about enjoying life onboard at a more relaxed pace.

For us, part of the joy of extended cruising was to get away from the stresses of our daily lives. Work is driven by targets, so we wanted to be careful to avoid setting tough targets for our time off. We could have been unlucky and had to turn back due to lack of time because of bad weather. Once people know what your goals are, if you fail to complete them, some may think you have failed, even if you had a great cruise. When people asked us where we were going, we used to say that we are going out of the harbour and turning right. Well, for 51 days we turned right and on three days we turned left!

Sound of Hoy

COURAGE AND DETERMINATION

For most people this trip will be a real adventure, the challenge of a lifetime. However, one group of people have so much courage and determination that they have found freedom, through canoeing or sailing, to overcome their disabilities.

- *Nigel Rogoff*, who lost his leg in a parachuting display, completed a trip round Britain in 2002 in a kayak. His companion *David Abrutat*, paralysed in a car crash, accompanied him on a hand-cycle on the coastal roads.

- *Geoff Holt* was paralysed from the chest down and confined to a wheelchair after a swimming accident. He successfully completed his trip round Britain (via the Caledonian Canal) in his trimaran dinghy *Freethinker* in 109 days, visiting 51 places and spending 51 days at sea. Not only did he sail round Britain in the summer of 2007, which was a challenging year for weather, it was also an impressive logistical exercise. He had a support team of seven, three vehicles and a RIB. Geoff aptly describes this as his personal Everest; you can find out more about his journey in his autobiography *Walking on Water*.

- *Hilary Lister* was quadriplegic and was only able to move her head. In 2005, she sailed into the record books when she went solo across the English Channel by using a 'sip and puff' system of straws to control the sails and tiller. Hilary successfully completed a solo circumnavigation around Britain over the course of two years in an Artemis 20, a 20ft (6.1m) carbon fibre performance keel boat.

Geoff Holt and *Freethinker*. © Andy Cockayne, Personal Everest 2007

Sunset over Mull, from Puilladobhrain

WHAT EXPERIENCE DO YOU NEED?

Good seamanship is essential for this trip. Our coast, while spectacular, is full of dangers: you will experience strong tides (the Orkney Islands see spring tides of 12 knots), treacherous sandbanks (those of the North Sea can uncover 20 miles out to sea), plus navigation between rocks, and that is before you add the weather and other vessels. Clearly, an RYA Yachtmaster or similar qualification and experience will help. However, completing this cruise successfully is about much more than having a certain qualification or a defined number of years' experience. Some of the additional skills you will need are as follows:

- *Maintenance* Using your boat for an extended period means that you need to keep both it and its equipment working. It is important that you are able to carry out basic fault-finding and servicing on your engine.
- *Living on board* Your boat will be your home for an extended period. Conditions can range from primitive camping to a very comfortable caravan, depending on your budget. Whichever you choose, you have to be able to live in the confined space that you have.
- *Cooking* Food is your fuel, and hot food is especially important on those cold wet days. You must be disciplined in order to feed and hydrate your body. After a long tiring passage, it is easy to miss meals because you are too tired to cook. Dehydration can be debilitating, and is a very real danger even in cold climes. Even being slightly dehydrated every day can build up into a problem over time.
- *Crew bonding* A boat is a very small place if you fall out with your fellow sailors; you must choose your crew carefully. If you are going on a trip which is organised by others, you should feel confident that you will get on with the rest of the crew.
- *Management* The whole trip will require good planning and preparation. You can have all the sailing experience in the world but a poorly planned cruise, and an ill-prepared boat, is unlikely to result in a successful trip. Hopefully, the next few chapters will help you to get well organised.

CHAPTER TWO

PLANNING THE ROUTE

HOW MUCH TIME DO YOU NEED?

For most people the length of the cruise is likely to be dictated by factors such as work, finance etc, therefore, it will have to be a balance between the route and the number of stops. There are several options:

- England, Wales and Lowland Scotland via the Forth and Clyde Canal
- England, Ireland and Lowland Scotland via the Forth and Clyde Canal
- Britain via Cape Wrath
- Britain via the Caledonian Canal
- UK and Ireland via Cape Wrath

Obviously, the more time you have, the more places you can visit and the shorter the legs between stops can be; there is also a greater chance that you can pick and choose your weather windows. You may also decide to press on quickly through areas that you know well, or take on additional crew to do some long initial legs to allow you to spend more time cruising new areas. The shorter your time frame, the greater the pressure will be to keep moving. Even with a four-month cruise you will still feel the pressure to move on whenever you can.

If you take the inside route through the Irish Sea up to the Minch, then Ireland and the Outer Hebrides will protect you from the Atlantic swell. Circumnavigating Ireland adds an additional 300 miles to your trip but you also need to take into account the weather and Atlantic swell. You will see from Graphs 1 and 2 (page 21) that Malin Head has the highest number of days with summer gales of all the reference points chosen round the UK and Ireland.

If time is running short, the Caledonian Canal offers a way of saving time. It is 50 nautical miles (nm) long and will save you approximately 250 to 500 miles depending on the number of stops you make. It can be done in two to three days, though your licence allows you seven days in the canal. The benefit comes not only from the shorter distance, the canal is also more sheltered, though the wind can be funnelled down the glens. So the wind will either be with you or against you, and in fresh water the wind can cause quite a chop. There are other options if time is short: England and Lowland Scotland via the Forth and Clyde Canal, or round Ireland, or round Scotland, though strictly speaking it is only part of Scotland. This route is approximately 690nm.

We completed the round Britain trip in 4 months – a total of 114 days. We were at sea for 54 days with an average passage length of 41 miles and

Castle Stalker, Loch Linnhe

we visited 53 places; our route can be found in Appendix 3. We decided to take a 10-day holiday in Orkney, after all, cruising can be hard work! The remaining 50 days in harbour were due to bad weather, needing to catch up with boat tasks or just sightseeing. Yet an identical boat to ours completed a similar route in 20 days, with only 4 stops, on the Round Britain Race. We left northwest Scotland with a feeling that we had just had a taster and that there was still so much to be seen. It was difficult to decide what to miss out on the west coast of Scotland, given the huge choice of islands and anchorages. There were fewer suitable ports on the east coast but it did mean more opportunities for meeting people on similar trips.

Circumnavigation time survey

In a survey I conducted, I found that the length of time spent at sea varied considerably. Greg and Sue Hill (*Blue Argolis*, Trewes 41) completed the same route in the school holidays, in just over 6 weeks, of which 28 days were at sea, they visited 14 places en route. At the other end of the scale, Steve and Claire Crook (*Touché*, Beneteau 36), took 2 summers and visited 133 places, but even they said they had not had time to see everything that they wanted to. When asked what they would do differently, they said 'take three summers'!

For motorboats, the average number of days at sea is relatively high but this is over a small sample of boats. The quickest motorboat was Mike Perry

ROUTE BY YACHT AND NUMBER OF BOATS	AVERAGE				
	Logged (nm)	Passage length (nm)	Cruise duration (days)	Days at sea	Number of places visited
England, Wales and Lowland Scotland via the Forth and Clyde Canal (1)	1,561	27	92	58	47
England, Ireland and Lowland Scotland via the Forth and Clyde Canal (1)	1,700	27	108	64	62
Britain via Cape Wrath (33)	2,281	39	95	55	55
Britain via the Caledonian Canal (26)	1,813	39	86	47	44
UK and Ireland via Cape Wrath (8)	2,444	50	90	51	47
Ireland (4)	1,100	48	33	30	26

and his family (*Caribbean Breeze*, Fairline 36), they completed their trip via the Caledonian Canal in 98 hours, after 21 days at sea and a total cruise length of 38 days with 18 stops. However, when asked what he would do differently he said 'take longer and make more stops'. At the other end of the scale Dominic and Nicola Gribbin (*Jura Pilot*, Hardy Family Pilot 20) cruised for 18 weeks, visiting 57 places and spending a total of 58 days at sea on their trip via Cape Wrath.

Can the trip be done in stages?

If you are not able to take much time off, it is possible to split the trip up and complete it in stages. This also gives you the ability to base your boat in a new location and enjoy exploring

ROUTE BY MOTOR BOAT		AVERAGE				
	Type and number of boats	Logged (nm)	Passage length (nm)	Cruise duration (days)	Days at sea	Number of places visited
Britain via Cape Wrath	Motor boat (6)	2,113	59	64	36	42
	RIB (2)	1,915	101	28	19	17
Britain via the Caledonian Canal	Motor boat (5)	1,597	73	30	22	29
UK and Ireland via Cape Wrath	RIB (1)	2,000	286	8	7	7

the area from that base, before moving on. *Yachting Monthly* featured the story of a couple, John and Sue Chadwick (*Stromboli*, Saltram 36), who completed a trip via the Caledonian Canal. They broke up the route into 13 legs, taking 27 days and 4 nights, spread over a 13-month period. If you have a motorboat, it is very feasible to complete the cruise in stages. *Motor Boat and Yachting* published accounts by Maurice and Wendy Walmsley (*Mors*, Broom 37) and Malcolm and Glenda Stennett (*Lady Genevieve*, Broom 39) about their trip round Britain via Cape Wrath. Splitting the journey up into 6 legs, they completed the trip in 31 days at sea, leaving the boat in Hull, Peterhead, Craobh Haven, Inverkip, Dartmouth and finally returning to Southampton.

If you are planning a trip in stages, there are two things that you need to consider:

- Where you will leave the boat to ensure that it is secure.
- Transport links to and from your boat.

If you are planning to leave the boat in a marina you will find that, in the north-west of Scotland, marinas and pontoons with good transport links are limited. Between Oban and Orkney, marinas are only located at Kerrera (near Oban), Dunstaffnage, Stornoway and Orkney. There are similar challenges in the north-west of Ireland, with only Killybegs marina between Galway and Lough Swilly. You also need to plan transport to and from your boat. A summary of main marina locations, facilities and transport is in Appendix 1.

Sailing towards the Small Isles

When should you leave?

The main factor that will influence your decision is the weather. April to the end of September seems to be the slot that most people pick, and looking at Graphs 1 and 2 opposite, you can see why. Looking at highest wind gusts of 43 knots and over (the Met Office gust definition of a gale), March has twice the number of gales as April, and October has more than twice as many gales as September. The graphs show maximum gusts measured in a day. That doesn't mean there are gale force winds all day, but it is illustrative of when to go. My survey showed that the most common time for yachts to leave was the first two weeks of May; over a third left then and returned in August. The motorboats that were on a longer cruise left in May, but RIBs and those on a quick dash left in mid-July.

WHICH WAY ROUND?

One of the biggest questions is do you go left or right out of harbour? Two main factors will probably affect your decision.

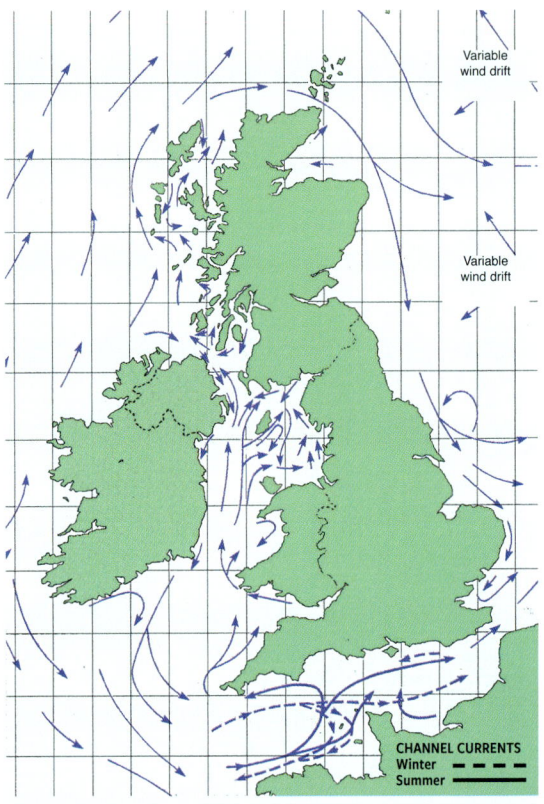

General near-surface pattern of water movement around UK and Ireland from *Atlas of Seas around the British Isles*. © British Crown copyright (MAFF 1981)

Prevailing currents

The prevailing currents are relatively weak, with the rate of travel approximately 1.5nm per day (the apparent passage of an object), and they favour a clockwise direction, with the exception of part of the south coast. On this stretch, you will carry the tide for longer, going anticlockwise. Likewise, from north-east England down to the Wash, there is a noticeably longer tide, favouring a southerly route.

Prevailing wind

There are two critical factors when looking at the prevailing wind: direction and percentage

Whitby, the day after the storm in August

PLANNING THE ROUTE   21

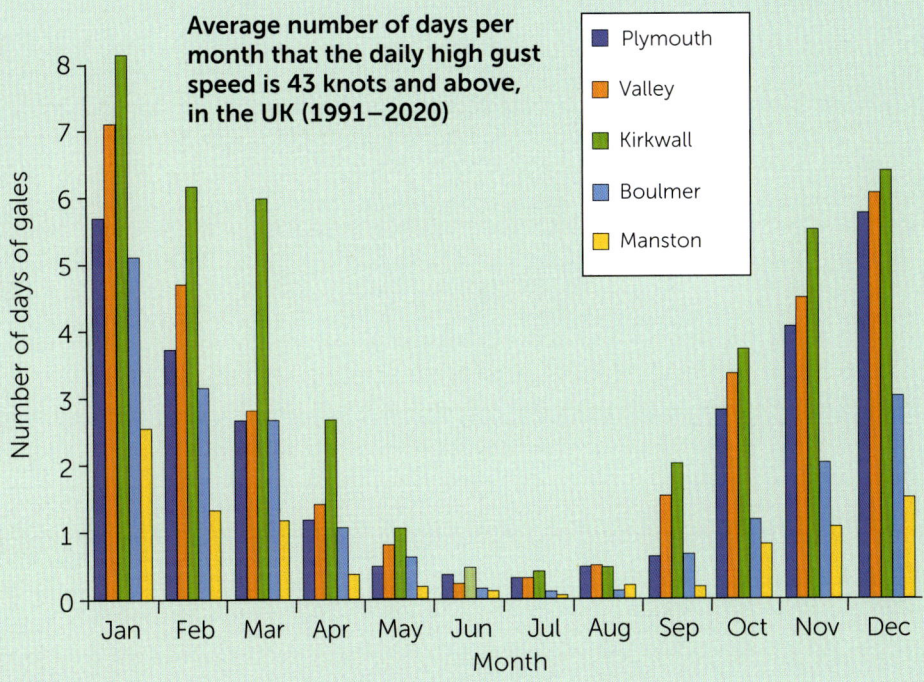

Graph 1: Adapted from © British Crown copyright data supplied by the Met Office

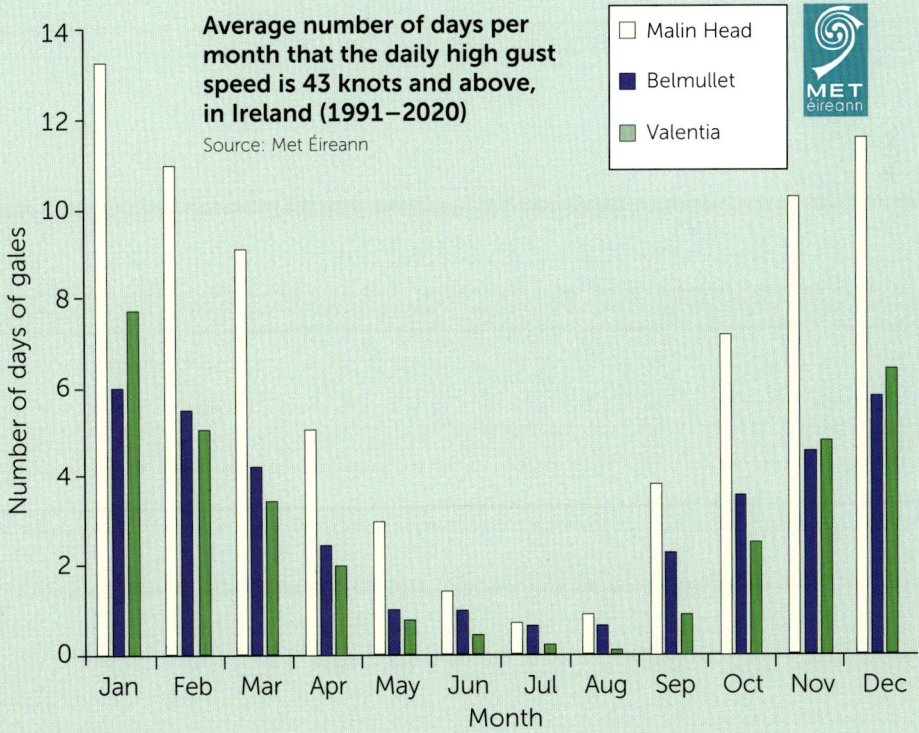

Graph 2: Adapted from data supplied by the Met Éireann (see page 4 for more information)

occurrence. A wind may blow from one direction more frequently than from others; however, if its occurrence is low, it means that it is not consistent from that direction. Some parts of the world never have wind from certain sectors. However, for a circumnavigation, the challenge is that the percentage occurrence from March to October, from any particular sector (45°) is relatively low. In May, when most people leave, the highest occurrence of any particular wind sector in UK and Irish waters is on the Irish west coast, where there is a 21 per cent chance of a westerly wind. This also means that there is a 79 per cent chance that the wind is coming from a different direction! The occurrence increases if you look at a quarter, rather than a sector. The highest in May, is again off the western Irish coast, where the occurrence of a westerly or south-westerly is still only 36 per cent. This does also mean that you have the potential to make progress against the prevailing wind, if you have enough time to wait.

However, here is a word of caution about theoretical calculations. These are averages over many years, but you will just be passing through the area and are very unlikely to spend a month seeing all the wind sectors. Unseasonal weather does happen; you have often heard weather forecasters say that a particular month is the wettest or hottest since records began. Local variation is another factor; the figures used are averages over a large sea area, and coastal areas have more variation due to the effects of the land. Even if the wind is in the right direction, you then need to consider the swell. We were pinned down in Whitby for six days with strong north-easterly winds in August. Yet, according to the figures, this was very unlikely to happen. Once the storm abated, it was another two days before it was safe to leave the harbour because of the swell in the shallow entrance.

Table 1 (page 23) shows the most common wind direction grouped by percentage of likely occurrence. In order to reduce the complexity of the table, I have not included any winds whose occurrence is 10 per cent or less – but that doesn't mean that they don't occur.

Sunset over Hurst Spit © Nick Boxall

	PERCENTAGE OCCURRENCE	APR	MAY	JUN	JUL	AUG	SEP
ENGLAND: EAST COAST	21–25				SW	SW	SW
	16–20	NE	NE, SW	SW		W	
	11–15	E, SW		N, NE	W	NW	W, NW
ENGLAND: SOUTH COAST	21–25				SW, W	W	
	16–20		SW	W		SW	W
	11–15	NE, E, SW, W, NW	W, NW	NE, SW	NW		SW, NW
IRISH SEA	21–25					SW	SW
	16–20					W	W
	11–15	N, NE, SW, NW	N, NE, S, SW, W, NW	SW, W, NW	N, S, SW, W, NW	NW, S	S, NW
IRELAND: SOUTH COAST	21–25					SW, W	
	16–20		SW, W	SW, W	SW, W		SW, W
	11–15	N, NE, S, SW, W	NE, NW	NW	S, NW	S, NW	S, NW
IRELAND: WEST COAST	21–25		W		W	W	
	16–20	N		SW, W	SW	SW	W, SW
	11–15	NE, S, SW, W	N, S, SW, NW	NW	S, NW	S, NW	S, NW
OUTER HEBRIDES	21–25						
	16–20					SW, W	SW
	11–15	E, SW, W, NW	NE, SE, S, SW	SW, W, NW	N, S, SW, W, NW	S, NW	S, W, NW
ORKNEY	21–25						
	16–20				W		S, SW
	11–15	N, SE, S, SW, W, NW	S, SE	N, S	N, SE, S, SW, NW	SE, S, SW, W, NW	SE, W

Table 1: Wind direction and percentage occurrence extracted from the Admiralty Atlantic Routing Charts. Adapted from © British Crown Copyright data supplied by the Met Office

STARTING POINTS			
	START POINT: SOUTH	**START POINT: EAST**	**START POINT: WEST**
PREVAILING WIND	No real advantage to clockwise or anti-clockwise route. There is a 2 per cent advantage* favouring an anticlockwise direction but this is so low as to be considered statistically irrelevant.	There is a slight advantage to an anticlockwise route (6 per cent).	There is no clear advantage either way.
SAILING CLOCKWISE	A shorter distance than the anti-clockwise route to enjoy the best months in Scotland. You will pass the south coast during the off-peak season. Early spring often sees a high-pressure system in control over central and NE Europe, when E to NE winds may persist for several days, occasionally lasting 2–3 weeks.	You will pass the south coast during the off-peak season.	You will arrive early in the west coast of Scotland – in mid-May. Whereas on an anticlockwise route you might not arrive until mid-June.
SAILING ANTICLOCKWISE	See general advantages below.	The higher up the east coast you start, the less distance you have to travel to the west coast of Scotland to arrive in time for the best months.	Nearly 50 per cent chance of a favourable wind along the south coast in July.

*Calculated assuming the average cruise starts in May and takes 90 days to circumnavigate Britain. The wind direction information was taken from the *Atlantic Routing Charts*.

Starting point

Scotland's best months for weather are May, June and early July. Ireland's driest time of the year is spring, and the sunniest month is May. If you want to take advantage of these conditions, your starting point may influence which direction you choose.

CLOCKWISE V ANTICLOCKWISE

These general advantages apply to any round Britain route, regardless of starting point.

General advantages of clockwise

The prevailing current favours a clockwise direction.

General advantages of anticlockwise

- Tacking across the Irish Sea allows good progress against the prevailing S, SW and W winds.
- You will enjoy the east coast first and then be even more impressed by the west coast.
- If a sea breeze forms on the east coast, it is likely to veer parallel to the coast with you during the day.

For a UK and Ireland circumnavigation, most of the factors are the same as round Britain, given that the time frame for cruising is similar. The following factors require additional consideration:

- **Prevailing wind** There was a marginal advantage of 1–2 per cent for clockwise circumnavigations for both east and south coast starting points, but this is so low that it is statistically not significant. For the west coast, there is no advantage either way.
- **Swell** The Atlantic swell on the exposed coasts of Ireland has a big impact on your trip. The size of the swell will at times prevent you from leaving harbour. From June onwards the onshore winds are more frequent and the chances of a large swell increase.

Does the start date affect your route?
In theory, in an average year, you are likely to encounter more headwinds the later you set off whichever way you go.

Clockwise route
The later you set off, the more established the westerly and south-westerly winds will be on the south coast and so you are likely to experience head winds once you have passed Dover.

Anticlockwise route
By August, south-westerly and westerly winds are well established on the west coast and Irish Sea, with the occurrence being around 40 per cent for the quarter and 52 per cent including southerly winds. Therefore, passing through the Irish Sea before August should reduce your chances of meeting adverse winds. However, you may just be lucky and pick up a wind with a northerly element.

The experiences of other circumnavigators
Yachts
Let's now look at the actual experiences of the yachtsmen who have completed a circumnavigation and see how much motoring was involved.

Based on starting point
Most people on the south coast go clockwise. Whereas for those on the east coast, the decision is split, though nine of the twelve boats that went clockwise started from Woodbridge or further south. The percentage of time spent sailing is similar, regardless of starting point or direction travelled, which supports the theoretical prediction.

Based on route
Looking at the direction based on route provided little insight, with the exception of round the UK and Ireland, where six out of seven boats travelled clockwise regardless of their starting point.

	MOST POPULAR DIRECTION	CLOCKWISE		ANTICLOCKWISE	
		Number of yachts	Percentage sailing hours (of total)	Number of yachts	Percentage sailing hours (of total)
East coast	Equal	12	48% (10)	12	47% (7)
South coast	Clockwise	24	51% (14)	13	47% (9)
West coast	Clockwise	2	78% (2)	–	–

Note: not all yachts were able to provide the information to calculate the percentage of time sailing, hence the sample size is in brackets.

	BOAT	MOST POPULAR DIRECTION	CLOCKWISE NUMBER OF BOATS	ANTICLOCKWISE NUMBER OF BOATS
East coast	Motor	Anticlockwise	–	2
South coast	Motor	Anticlockwise	3	5
	RIB	Clockwise	2	1
West coast	Motor	Clockwise	1	–

Motorboats and RIBs

It is difficult to draw conclusions with so little data, but it would appear that anticlockwise is the favoured direction for motorboats and clockwise for RIBs.

Our trip

With a start date of 1 May, we picked a clockwise route to benefit from the better weather on the west coast of Scotland in June. We were hoping for the prevailing SW up the west coast of the UK, but didn't really pick it up until after the Crinan Canal. Yet on the way down the east coast, we met headwinds, or a lack of wind, for much of the way. This meant that we were motor sailing for quite a lot of the time. This was frustrating and we thought it was perhaps just us, until we met a couple on a Beneteau who expressed the same frustration. The surveys showed that this was a common experience; the average time spent motoring or motor sailing was 52 per cent of the total hours taken.

We came back believing that anticlockwise would have been a better direction. But one other skipper who went anticlockwise from the same starting point, at the same time of year, wished they had gone clockwise. When writing this book, I thought that I would find the right answer, either from my research or the surveys. However, I have come to the conclusion that there is no single right answer because there are so many variables – some unpredictable, some conflicting and some that you may be able to overcome by taking on extra crew. So you need to make the decision based on the factors that are important to you.

CREW

You may need to take on additional crew for certain legs or even all the way around. This should be considered in your route planning. John Hill (*Almacantar*, Hustler 38), who successfully completed a sail round Britain voyage via Cape Wrath, broke his trip up into nine fixed legs, with

Laggan Locks on Caledonian Canal

PICKING A CREW

- Only use people you know and have sailed with before, or crew that have been recommended by other skippers.
- Try to balance crews so that you have a group with differing depths of experience on each leg.
- Ensure that you have a mate who can cope without you if necessary.
- Put everything in writing to ensure a commitment; this also gives you a chance to sell the adventure to them.
- Try to arrange for the mate to arrive before the rest of the crew to help with the preparations.
- Put them in touch with each other and let them sort out their own transport arrangements.
- Try to match the crews to the sailing conditions, eg stronger crews for more challenging parts such as the Irish Sea.
- Give all crew a briefing on house and safety rules when they arrive on board.
- Give them an easy first day, if possible.
- Keep them well fed and watered.
- Share the work.
- Allow a few days at each changeover point to allow for arrivals and departures and so that everyone can recharge their batteries.

John's aim was not to make a profit on the expenses:

- **Food** He charged each person a fixed fee per day for food.
- **Drink** He kept a sheet on the bulkhead recording what had been drunk and charged a fixed fee for lager, beer and wine; he then simply shared the total between the crew onboard.
- **Harbour charges** He kept a record of harbour charges etc and divided it between everyone.

different crew on each leg. His voyage involved 44 crew, which was quite a logistical exercise to organise, but he only had two crew members drop out before the start. See the box above for advice on organising the crew.

John had fixed changeover points, which can reduce the flexibility of your schedule. So you might prefer to have variable ones. The advice from David and Mary Trim (*Jemima*, Ovni 385) on variable changeovers is to make sure that your crew know that getting to the boat will be the challenging bit. Their joining instructions read: 'Reaching *Jemima* will probably be the biggest challenge of the trip. As we are uncertain of exact locations, we suggest that you contact us one week before your date of arrival to get an idea of where the sailing party will be. We will then stay in touch over the course of the following week and be able to give you a precise location two to three days beforehand. You will need to be patient and maintain a sense of humour during this time, which will be rewarded on arrival!'

CHARTERING A BOAT AND SKIPPER

If you don't own a boat, it is possible to complete this trip by chartering one. Charterers David and Mary Trim gave me some advice for making a success of this arrangement:

- Go on a taster trip and then ensure that the skipper wants to do it for their own reasons, so check their motivation.
- Work with a named skipper; eight weeks, or however many you have set aside, is a long time, so you need to know the person and be comfortable with them.
- Decide what you can afford and mould the programme around the number of weeks you can pay for.
- Be clear about what's included and what will cost extra. Be very clear about the initial deposit/final payment amounts and dates due.
- Draft a proposal very early on, with objectives and key areas as a basis for shaping an expedition agreement.
- Keep in regular touch with the chartering company; appoint one person who is able to make all financial decisions and co-ordinate planning of the route.
- Arrange cancellation insurance very early.
- During the trip, have a weekly meeting to review how it is going; this can be an opportunity for raising issues.
- Recognise the roles. The skipper is in charge. The charterer has responsibilities too, such as paying for marina fees etc. If some crew members have short fuses, and you recognise potential personality clashes, either limit their participation or make sure that the overall makeup of crew can handle it.
- Decide who is going to do the catering on board. If it is to be shared, make sure this is known in advance.
- Make a very clear business plan for the costs. The Trims' trip was based on a charter rate which covered up to four crew. This was less than the cost of two places on another scheme, plus they had a better skipper and boat, albeit shorter in time than the other 12- or 13-week schemes on offer.

Ituna ghosting past the Spey Bay, Moray Firth
© Klaus Schroeter

ROUTE PLANNING
Schedule

Most people need to be back at their home port by a certain date, therefore, it is important to have a rough schedule so that you can determine whether you are ahead or behind your plan. It helps to break the trip into legs, then you can plan how much time to spend in each area. Our split was:

Month 1 (May)	Gosport to Campbeltown
Month 2 (June)	Campbeltown to Orkney
Month 3 (July)	Orkney to Whitby
Month 4 (August)	Whitby to Gosport

We only spent about 25 per cent (one month) on the west coast of Scotland; this was not enough time. If I were to repeat this trip, I would plan to spend at least six weeks (approximately 40 per cent) on the west coast of Scotland as there is so much to see. Certainly, most of the sailors who contributed to the survey said that the west coast was one of the many highlights of the trip. One couple successfully completed an anticlockwise trip in eight weeks via the Caledonian Canal. Interestingly, they didn't head south after leaving the Canal, they turned right and cruised around the Inner Hebrides visiting Canna, Skye, Rum, Staffa, Iona and Jura. For anyone considering a Caledonian route, if time allows, I would strongly suggest this, otherwise you will miss out on some stunningly beautiful cruising.

Next, you need to work out which ports you want to visit using pilot books, taking into account the draft of your vessel. To build a realistic plan, you must allow for rest days after long passages, bad weather and work days. This will give you a rough idea of your timing. Sometimes you will be ahead of your schedule and sometimes behind. If you are behind you may need to do longer legs to catch up. The spare days also allow you to catch up on your chores, washing, shopping etc, which always take longer without a washing machine and a car.

Yachts

On average, yachts spent 57 per cent of their days at sea, therefore, every week you need to plan two spare days. However, if planning a single-handed trip, give yourself more time for recovery.

Motorboats

If you are in a motor boat you can cover the distance more quickly but you should still allow spare days, as the weather conditions will restrict

NUMBER ON BOARD (NUMBER SAMPLED)	PERCENTAGE OF DAYS AT SEA	AVERAGE CRUISE DURATION (DAYS)
1 (16)	52%	106
2 (26)	52%	95
3 (9)	57%	75
4–5 (7)	77%	69
6+ (2)	87%	54

you more than if you were sailing. On average, the motorboats spent 64 per cent of their days at sea and RIBs spent 76 per cent.

THE ROUTE

For the purposes of describing the route I am assuming here a clockwise circumnavigation starting at Penzance. The four extremities (most northerly etc) of your circumnavigation will provide key milestones and you will pass each with a real sense of achievement. These are Dunnet Head (north), Lowestoft Ness (east), Lizard Point (south) and Ardnamurchan Point (west). Those on mainland Britain and Ireland are shown on the map (above). The Dingle Peninsula is Europe's most westerly point. Stotfield Head is less well known but will be the most northerly point if passing through the Caledonian Canal. Two other important milestones are Land's End and Cape Wrath.

When cruising in familiar waters you know where to find those hidden gems, but on this

Catching the tide
10 May – Penzance to Padstow

Alarm went off at 2:15am and I dragged myself out of bed. Mags was already whirling round the boat making lunch, disconnecting shore power etc, while I was struggling to function at this hour. Up on deck I noticed that there was no sign of the lock keeper and the lock was still closed. 'Great, I can go back to bed and blame the absent lock keeper for delaying our trip.' But within seconds he saw me and asked if we were ready and offered to open the lock gate. 'Damn,' I thought, 'no more sleep.' We left the harbour at 3am and we were on our way.

Planning this leg was quite tricky as there are three tidal gates. One at the start (the lock opening), one at Land's End and a bar to get over at Padstow – most of which is sand when the tide is out. It was impossible to meet all three, so we had to push against the tide round Land's End. The early start was rewarded with the most spectacular sunrise over the cliffs at Land's End. We rounded Longship lighthouse, marking some rather unfriendly rocks and started to head north for the first time.

We carried on motoring, using the mainsail as a steadying sail (as there is always an Atlantic swell, even on a calm day), and I went off watch – we tended to sleep three hours on, three hours off on long trips. Fog came in and visibility was between 0.5–1 mile. Mags fired up the electronic aids (radar etc) and began tracking any targets and the coast. This meant that entering Padstow harbour was less stressful than if we had been navigating without electronics.

---

cruise, you will be passing through unknown areas. It is likely to be a once-in-a-lifetime opportunity and so you don't want to miss out on those special places. One of the biggest challenges is deciding where to go and the fear that you will pass by something special, unaware of its existence. But how do you find out where they are? Cruising guides are full of so many potential places. Through the surveys, and the knowledge of locals, I have compiled ten of the best destinations (see Chapter 16) for: castle anchorages, wildlife encounters, culinary experiences, challenging tidal races, whisky tasting, historical interest, taking the ground, beautiful rivers and estuaries, glorious gardens, picturesque marinas, remote anchorages, tasty treats, iconic lighthouses, sea shore gems, maritime history and drop-dead gorgeous places. In the next few sections, I will look at the most common routes based on those people surveyed.

PENZANCE TO ST DAVID'S HEAD VIA LIZARD POINT
(mainland Britain's most southerly point)

GENERAL DESCRIPTION OF THE AREA

- There are relatively long legs (a couple between 70–80nm) and careful timing is needed to make the tidal gates.
- Dramatic rugged cliffs fringe the coast of Cornwall. Once round Land's End you are exposed to the Atlantic swell. North Cornwall has few useable harbours unless you can take the ground. The Pembrokeshire coast, with its warm red tones, is memorable and there is much bird life around the volcanic islands of Skomer and Grassholm.
- If you have fine weather, try to visit the Isles of Scilly or Lundy.

STANDARD CRUISING ROUTE

- Penzance/Newlyn – Padstow – Milford Haven/Dale – Fishguard/Arklow

Ituna in Padstow (centre boat)

MAJOR TIDAL GATES

- The Lizard, Land's End, Doom Bar, Bishops and Clerks or Ramsey and Jack Sound, depending on your route inside or outside the islands off the Pembrokeshire coast.

The River Camel (looking out towards the Doom Bar) with Padstow nestled on the left

WEST COAST OF IRELAND: CROSSHAVEN TO PORTRUSH VIA GARRAUN POINT, DINGLE PENINSULA

(mainland Ireland's most westerly point)

GENERAL DESCRIPTION OF THE AREA

- It is approximately 42nm across St George's Channel from Wales to Wexford and 140nm from the Isles of Scilly.
- On the exposed west coast, you will encounter the long rolling Atlantic swell. When it meets the reflected waves from the coast, it can cause quite disturbed seas. There are many headlands where the weather can hold you up in their lee. The north coast is also exposed to the swell in westerly and northerly winds.
- Secure harbours are located at convenient intervals (with a couple of exceptions, eg the west coast of County Clare), with a comprehensive network of marinas, public moorings and anchorages. Deep water around the southern and western coasts of Ireland means that the majority of harbours are accessible at any state of the tide. However, while they provide shelter, many harbours on the west coast are unsafe to enter in very bad weather.
- Kinsale to Dingle is Ireland's most popular cruising ground, with impressive coastal scenery. Beautiful anchorages can be found in the rias, which are deep drowned rivers caused by changes in sea level. The west coast has miles of raw, natural beauty interspersed with tiny, quaint villages.
- The wild and dramatic Connemara mountains provide a stunning backdrop to anchorages and harbours on the Galway coast. Donegal is the remotest and least visited part of Ireland's coastline but you are rewarded with spectacularly varied shores: deserted beaches, turquoise waters and rugged cliffs.

STANDARD CRUISING ROUTE

- *Crosshaven* is the usual arrival point if departing from the Isles of Scilly and *Waterford* if leaving from the south Wales coast.

Lot's Wife, which guards the entrance to Baltimore, overlooking Sherkin Island and Cape Clear in the distance

Crosshaven – Kinsale – Glandore – Baltimore – Bantry Bay (Bere Island/Lawrence Cove/Glengarriff) – Sneem/Derryname/Valentia – Dingle – Scraggane Bay/Fenit/Carrigaholt – Kilronan – Roundstone/Clifden – Inishbofin – Blacksod – Broad Haven – Killybegs/Teelin – Aranmore – Tory Island/Sheephaven – Lough Swilly (Portsalon/Rathmullan/Denree Head) – Portrush

MAJOR TIDAL GATES

The many prominent headlands are: Mizen Head, Valentia, Loop Head, Slyne Head, Ennis Head, Rossan Point and Malin Head and the Sounds between the islands and the mainland, eg Dursey Sound and Blasket Sound. Tides are approximately 1–2kt on south and west; close to headlands they can reach 4kt.

EVENTS

Cork Week in mid-July.

PASSAGE THROUGH THE IRISH SEA

GENERAL DESCRIPTION OF THE AREA

If you have good weather to explore the Welsh coast, you will find great variety – from popular resorts with sandy beaches to lush green hills and wooded banks; parts of the coast have the Welsh hills or mountains as their backdrop. However, Cardigan Bay can be a dangerous lee shore in strong onshore winds, with little refuge to be gained from the harbours along the coast due to the bars that guard their entrances. The coast of Ireland may provide a safer passage in strong south-westerlies. The east coast provides contrast from cities to small towns and villages; rolling hills give way to sheer cliffs as you go north towards Ballycastle.

The Isle of Man (IOM) is a very useful refuge in the middle of the Irish Sea.

South Stack

The Solway Firth is a beautiful area but has hazardous sandbanks that east coast sailors would be proud of. Only Kirkcudbright is suitable for visitors to the area but it is worth a visit. Just 20nm separates Ireland from Scotland across the North Channel.

STANDARD CRUISING ROUTE

Fishguard – Holyhead – Isle of Man – Portpatrick – Campbeltown – Milford Haven – Arklow – Dun Laoghaire/Howth – Ardglass – Bangor – Glenarm

If crossing to explore the east coast of Ireland, it is usually from Milford Haven or the Isle of Man. If you are planning to go round the Mull of Kintyre, the north Antrim coast is a popular route, leaving from Glenarm or Ballycastle to avoid the challenges of the tides close to the Mull.

Sunrise over Charles Fort, Kinsale

UK AND IRELAND CIRCUMNAVIGATOR'S GUIDE

MAJOR TIDAL GATES

⏱ At springs there are 4kt through St George's Channel and 5kt through the North Channel.

⏱ Wales: Bardsey Sound, Menai Straits and South Stack.

⏱ IOM: Calf Sound; SW Scotland: Mull of Galloway; N Ireland: Torr Head and Fair Head.

WEST SCOTLAND: MULL OF KINTYRE TO ARDNAMURCHAN POINT

GENERAL DESCRIPTION OF THE AREA

- You will do short day passages, with only short hops across open sea. Unless you get bad weather, you will rarely lose sight of land. Navigation is mainly by eye; ensure that the chart matches the land and use transits and clearing bearings. Whichever way you look when you are sailing, there is a stunning view.
- Firth of Clyde: Many people on a round Britain cruise don't have time to visit the beautiful cruising ground of Lochs Long and Fyne, and the Kyles of Bute.
- ★ You will pass the southern isles of Gigha, Islay and Jura if you round the Mull – the latter two will give you an opportunity to sample a 'wee dram' from their distilleries.
- Puilladobhrain (pronounced 'Pull door en' and meaning 'pool of the otter') was our favourite (see photo on page 8). We were lucky to share it with only one other boat on a sunny day; there was scarcely a ripple on the sea and while anchored there we saw the most spectacular sunset over Mull.
- Although you may plan to follow the standard route, I do recommend that you take advantage of this spectacular cruising ground.

STANDARD CRUISING ROUTE

- Glenarm/Ballycastle – Gigha – Craobh Haven – Kerrera – Tobermory
- Campbeltown – Tarbert – Crinan – Kerrera – Tobermory

MAJOR TIDAL GATES

- Mull of Kintyre, Dorus Mor can run up to 8kt. Sound of Mull, Sound of Luing, Cuan Sound and Ardnamurchan Point.

EVENTS

- Tarbert Bell Lawrie Series, Scotland's equivalent of Cowes, the last week in May.

Tarbert Loch Fyne en route to the Crinan Canal

NORTH WEST SCOTLAND: ARDNAMURCHAN POINT* TO CAPE WRATH (*most westerly point on mainland Britain)

GENERAL DESCRIPTION OF THE AREA

⚠ You will make short day passages until you pass the Inner Sound. When you enter the Minch you start to experience more open water and pass some major headlands. The Outer Hebrides protect the coast from the Atlantic swell until you reach the top of the Minch. But heavy seas can quickly build up on the exposed headlands. There is a lack of navigational aids and many harbours are unlit, but as the nights aren't long it is unlikely that you will sail in the dark. Given the tidal streams of the area, transit lines are very useful.

The mountains of Loch Torridon

Campbeltown

PLANNING THE ROUTE

Tobermory with its colourful quayside houses

- 📷 The raw, awe-inspiring scenery of the west coast is almost beyond adequate description. Its scale, depth and remoteness are best appreciated from the sea.
- ⚠ Outer Hebrides: to explore the west coast you will need some settled weather; the same applies to St Kilda, some 40nm to the west. The beaches of South Harris are incredible: white sand with turquoise waters.

STANDARD CRUISING ROUTE
- ⊕ Sound of Sleat (pronounced 'Slate') (Arisaig/Mallaig/Armdale/Isle Ornsay) – Kyleakin/Kyle of Lochalsh – Loch Gairloch (Flowerdale/Shieldaig/ Badachro) – Lochinver – Kinlochbervie

MAJOR TIDAL GATES
- ⏱ Kyle Rhea (6 to 8kt at springs), Rubha Reidh, Stoerhead and Cape Wrath.

Mainland Orkney

NORTHERN SCOTLAND AND NORTHERN ISLES: CAPE WRATH TO WICK

GENERAL DESCRIPTION OF THE AREA

The long leg to Orkney or Scrabster is made easier by the short nights.

Vast areas of land are totally uninhabited; and it is much easier to access many of these areas from the sea than by road. If conditions allow, pass close by Sandwood Bay, a 2km deserted sandy beach near to Cape Wrath; it is a 6km hike to see it by land. Rounding Cape Wrath is a big milestone and you have the feeling of being a long way from civilisation. The top north-west corner near Cape Wrath is isolated; you sense that many of the communities are on the edge of survival, following the demise of the fishing industry. You expect Orkney to be the same, yet they are vibrant islands, with a real buzz and feel of a community in control of its destiny. The clarity of the light, the lush vegetation, the turquoise colour of the water and the white sandy beaches, make a cruise around Orkney memorable. Although the tides are tricky, good planning, and a healthy respect for them, will ensure safe passage. Their rich history, spanning thousands of years, make a stay very rewarding and if time and money permit, it is worth hiring a car to explore mainland Orkney.

Not many cruisers make it to the Shetlands on this cruise, but a few make the 46nm passage from Westray to Fair Isle. You will meet quite a few yachts en route to and from Norway.

STANDARD CRUISING ROUTE

Kinlochbervie – Stromness – Scapa Flow – Wick/Kinlochbervie – Scrabster – Wick/Kinlochbervie – Stromness – Kirkwall – Wick

MAJOR TIDAL GATES

Cape Wrath; the whole of Orkney. In particular: Eyenhallow Sound, Westray Firth, Hoy Sound and the Pentland Firth.

EVENTS

Orkney Music festival, mid-June.

Grobust Beach, Westray

NORTH-EAST SCOTLAND: WICK TO EYEMOUTH

GENERAL DESCRIPTION OF THE AREA

⚠ The east coast of Scotland is far more exposed and there are few natural harbours; most of them are man-made and are accessed by skinny entrances. This gives you an indication of the power of the seas in the winter months along this coast. Have a look at the picture in the harbourmaster's office in Whitehills if you want to see evidence! Reasonable weather is required to enter many of the ports so if the weather turns bad, you will either be storm-bound or end up making long passages.

🏠 Most harbours were created in the prosperous days of herring fishing, the 'silver darlings'. The active fishing fleet is now concentrated into a few harbours, where pleasure boats are often none too welcome. Eyemouth is one exception; it is a busy fishing port, but very welcoming to all.

📍 The scenery is varied: from the fortress-like cliffs of Sutherland to the golden sands and pine-clad coastline of the Moray Firth. From Wick/Helmsdale, there is always the temptation to cut in a straight line across to Whitehills or Peterhead – though you miss out on the beautiful Moray Firth.

⚠ The Firth of Forth offers many pretty fishing harbours, though in many places you need to take the ground.

STANDARD CRUISING ROUTE
⊕ Wick – Whitehills – Peterhead – Stonehaven – Arbroath – Eyemouth

MAJOR TIDAL GATES
⏱ Chanonry Narrows (from the Caledonian Canal) and Rattray Head.

EVENTS
⏱ Port Soy, a traditional boat weekend in July.

The skinny harbour entrance at Whitehills. There is a sharp 90 degree corner at the end of a narrow entrance

EASTERN ENGLAND: BERWICK-UPON-TWEED TO DOVER VIA LOWESTOFT (Britain's most easterly point)

GENERAL DESCRIPTION OF THE AREA

Northumberland's coastline is memorable for its castles, wild sandy beaches and islands. As you sail south, the landscape becomes more industrial until you get to the Yorkshire Moors. While there is no shortage of harbours along this coast, some have tidal restrictions, such as Hartlepool, Amble and Whitby. Whitby is very atmospheric, particularly in the early morning before the tourists emerge.

The Humber is characterised by sand banks, strong tides, shipping and gas rigs. Spurn Point makes a useful overnight

The busy and friendly fishing port of Eyemouth. We were relieved to see that there are still some fishing boats left in the UK

stay and prevents a long haul up to the Humber marinas, which are governed by locks and so accessible only at certain times of the day. At this point, the chart changes colour, as sandbanks appear everywhere. You have to wind your way through the maze of sandbanks, gats and swatch ways.

Sailing up to Pin Mill

⚠ Wells-next-the-Sea is a beautiful tidal harbour but you need local knowledge (available from the welcoming harbour-master) to enter, due to the shifting sands. Like many harbours on this part of the coast, entry is only safe in good weather.

📍 East coast river cruising is a delight – a different pace of life. If you are lucky you may see a Thames barge in full sail. If you have time, a trip up to London is an experience worth having.

STANDARD CRUISING ROUTE
- Eyemouth – Amble – Blyth – Hartlepool – Whitby – Scarborough/Bridlington – Wells – Lowestoft – River Orwell (Harwich/Shotley) – Ramsgate – Dover.
- Those choosing not to dry out miss out Bridlington and Wells.

MAJOR TIDAL GATES
- The Norfolk coast and the Goodwin Sands.

Whitby Harbour is overlooked by the Abbey

SOUTHERN ENGLAND: DOVER TO LAND'S END VIA THE LIZARD (Britain's most southerly point)

GENERAL DESCRIPTION OF THE AREA

- As you head west, the harbour dues increase dramatically. Don't be surprised when the daily harbour fee can be the equivalent of a week's fee elsewhere.
- Dover is tucked into the base of the impressive White Cliffs; these chalk cliffs will be visible along much of the south coast, all the way along to the Jurassic Dorset coast.
- The naval history is evident immediately as you enter the Solent, with the impressive Napoleonic Forts and the invisible (but very hard) submarine barrier. If you can, avoid visiting the Solent during the weekend, so that you can sample the delights of Newtown Creek, Beaulieu or Yarmouth without seeing masses of other boats and tourists. The historic ships in Portsmouth are worth a visit.
- Once you pass the Needles, the boating density drops considerably. The natural harbour of Poole provides both peaceful anchorages and good facilities in the marinas. There are many charming harbours and anchorages in the west country.

STANDARD CRUISING ROUTE

- Dover – Eastbourne – Brighton – Portsmouth – Yarmouth (Isle of Wight) – Weymouth – Dartmouth – Salcombe – Plymouth – Fowey – Falmouth – Helford

MAJOR TIDAL GATES

- Beachy Head, the Needles, Portland Bill and Start Point.

EVENTS

- Cowes week, during the first week in August. It is a very popular event so expect to raft five deep.

Sunset at Yarmouth

THE CANALS

As well as providing short cuts, canals provide a break, slowing down the pace and allowing you time to relax and enjoy the scenery. Remember that the canals are fresh water, so you need to allow for the increase of your draft by 10cm. The depths of the canals may vary from the minimum depth stated, so it is always advisable to phone ahead to the sea lock keepers in order to confirm. The entry and exit from the sea locks are constrained by the times of the tides.

The Scottish canals have a very useful website www.scottishcanals.co.uk covering all the canals, with a Skipper's Guide for each canal, up to date prices and information about issues on the canals, such as water levels and maintenance work.

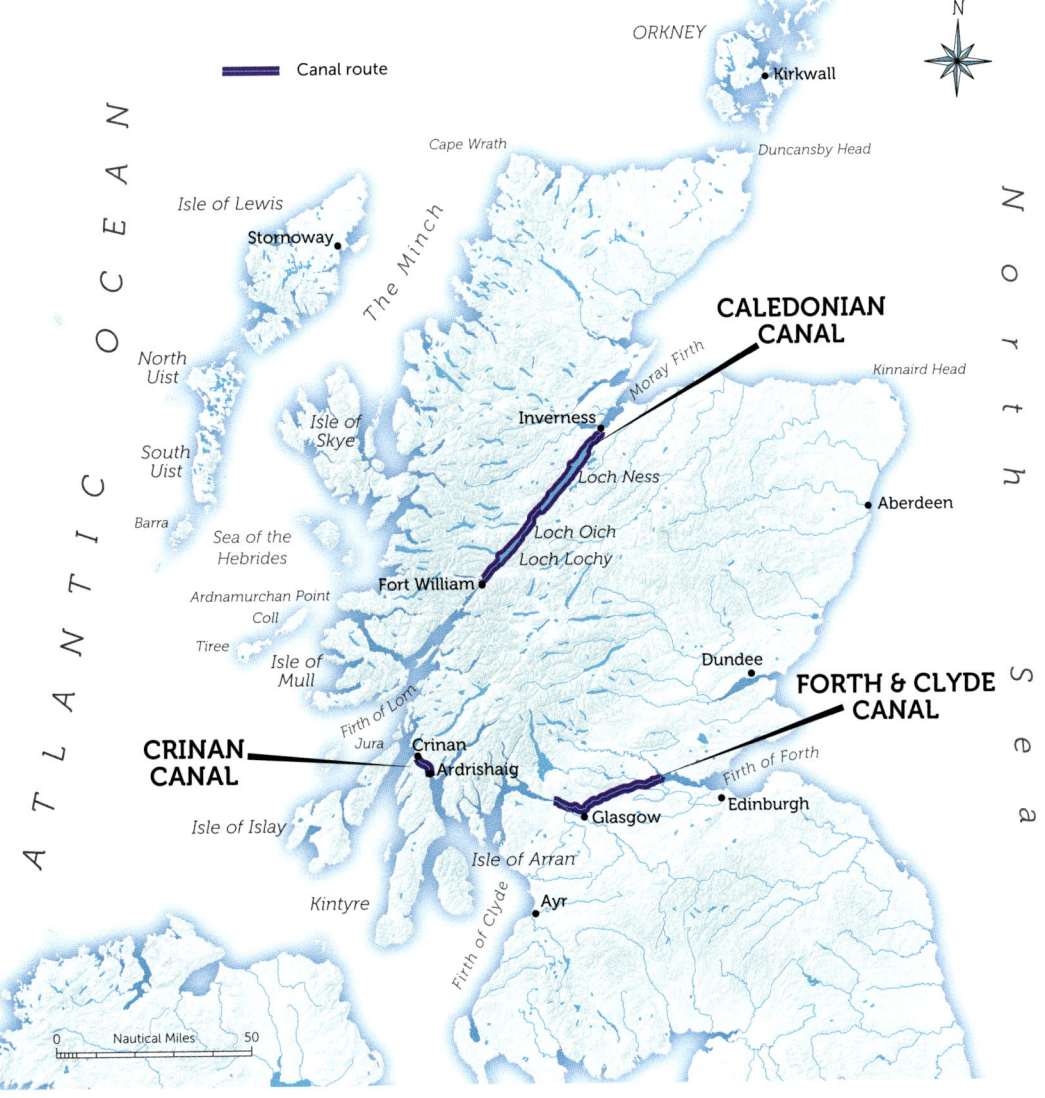

Forth and Clyde Canal

DETAILS	STATISTICS
Length	57km (31nm)
Number of locks	39
Number of self-operated locks	Most of them
Depth of water	1.83m (6ft)
Width of channel	6m (19ft 8in)
Maximum height	3m (9ft 10in) – yachts have to demast at Bowling, Port Edgar or at contractors along the River Carron. Boat crews need to operate the crane at both ends.
Length due to locks/wheel	19.2m (63ft)
Opening hours	0800–1800 during daylight hours, though you need to book passage in advance.
Licences	£19.55 per metre for a 10-day licence (2024).
Transit time	A minimum of 24 hours including the passage from Port Edgar and the negotiation of the River Carron to the sea lock. This excludes unstepping and restepping the mast.

This restored canal, reopened for use in 2001, connects the Firths of Clyde and Forth. This route takes you through large towns with busy areas and also peaceful countryside, and passes the Falkirk wheel, the first rotating boat lift, and The Kelpies, a pair of 98ft/30m-tall horse head sculptures, inspired by the working horses of Scotland's past.

One boat in the survey took three days to transit the canal, spending two nights in the canal and one night at Grangemouth, though it could have been completed more quickly. You can only pass under the new road bridge at certain times, so it may mean an early start.

The Falkirk Wheel © Izzy Campbell

Crinan Canal

DETAILS	STATISTICS
Length	14.5km (8nm)
Number of locks	15 locks and 7 bridges
Number of operated locks	3 and main road bridges
Number of self-operated locks	12
Depth of water	2.89m (9ft 6in)
Width of channel	6.09m (20ft)
Maximum height	28.95m (95ft)
Length due to locks/wheel	26.82m (88ft)
Opening hours	7 days per week
Licences	£15.80 (2024) per metre for a 4-day licence; this gives you berthing free of charge.
Transit time	A minimum of half a day. The average transit time of the 18 boats surveyed passing through the Crinan was 1.7 days.

Described as 'Scotland's prettiest short cut', it meanders just 9 miles from Ardrishaig (pronounced 'ar–drish–ig') at the north-west extremity of the Clyde across mid-Argyll to emerge at Crinan. It allows you to miss out the Mull of Kintyre, which has strong tides; if you look at the weather for Malin Head (Graph 2, page 21), just across the water from the Mull, you will see that it can be stormy in the summer.

You can pre-arrange for assistance for the 12 hand-operated locks if you are shorthanded, though it's not mandatory. We had Hugh's help and it was money well spent. He opened all the locks in advance and he was there to take our lines; plus we got information about the canal. Costing £140 (2024) for a single day transit, at busy times you need to book two weeks in advance. Contact pilots through www.crinanpilots.uk.

Hugh, the lock keeper (right), closing a lock on the Crinan Canal

Caledonian Canal

DETAILS	STATISTICS
Length	93km (50nm)
Number of locks	29 locks and 10 bridges
Number of operated locks	All
Depth of water	4.11m (13ft 6in)
Width of channel	10.67m (35ft)
Maximum height	35m (115ft). Note that Kessock Bridge on Inverness Firth is 27.4m (89ft)
Length due to locks/wheel	45.72m (150ft)
Opening hours	7 days per week, 0800–1800 during the summer months
Licences	£26.15 per metre (2024) for a 7-day transit.
Transit time	A minimum of 2 days. The average transit time of the 18 yachts surveyed passing through the canal was 4 days and 4.3 days for the 3 motorboats surveyed.

Climbing Neptune's Staircase Caledonian Canal

The natural feature known as the Great Glen Fault divides the Highlands, running from Inverness to Fort William, and follows a 60-mile fissure scoured out by glaciers in the last ice age. During the Jacobite rebellions, the Glen had great strategic importance in controlling the Highland clans, enforced through the presence of forts at Fort William, Fort Augustus and Fort George at the mouth of the Moray Firth.

Joining up the lochs of the Great Glen was considered as early as 1726, but work did not start until 1803. It was a huge undertaking, as the 22 miles of man-made canal were cut using only picks, shovels and muscle power. Designed by Thomas Telford, it was Britain's first state-funded transport project, taking 19 years to build at a cost of £840,000 and opening in 1822. However, it was not a commercial success as, at 14ft (4m) deep, it was too shallow to take large shipping. It was only deepened, to Telford's original plans of 20ft (6m), 25 years later. The concept of the canal was not just to create employment and revitalise the Highlands, but it was also designed to be a short

PLANNING THE ROUTE

Fort Augustus Staircase © Mike Perry

cut, missing out the treacherous Pentland Firth. However, by the time the canal was deep enough, sail had given way to steam and the Pentland Firth was not such an obstacle. The canal was used to transport timber and other goods but its use declined from 1880.

The canal climbs 105ft (32m) from sea level and features staircases, flights of interconnected locks, in which the top gates of one lock are the bottom gates of the next. Eight locks make up Neptune's Staircase at Banavie just north of Fort William. With Ben Nevis as a backdrop, it is truly spectacular, as it raises vessels 70ft (21m) above sea level in a distance of 500yd (21m in 457m). There are two other staircases at Muirtown and Fort Augustus. The staircases were more economical to build, but in practice they created bottlenecks for transiting vessels. Passage through the canal is now more relaxing since the 29 locks were mechanised over 30 years ago. The canal survived because of its importance to the local economy and is still widely used by commercial traffic and leisure craft.

Dramatic scenery and places to stop

En route, the Caledonian Canal passes dramatic scenery: the Great Lochs of Lochy and Oich, the infamous Loch Ness and the historic Urquhart Castle. It offers the opportunity to drop anchor in some tranquil spots.

The 'Caley' is made up of four lochs, and all bar Loch Dochfour have recommended anchorages. Despite being 752ft (229m) deep, Loch Ness has few anchorages: at Urquhart Bay, in the shadow of the imposing 13th-century castle, Dores Bay and Foyers Bay. At Dores, there is a good pub, and from Foyers it is just a short walk to the Falls of

Urquhart Castle on the shores of Loch Ness is a beautiful place to stop overnight, either on the buoy placed there or in the tiny harbour. © Mike Perry

Ben Nevis from the Corpach end of the Caledonian Canal

Ardnamurchan Point

Foyers, some very impressive waterfalls. You can anchor in Loch Oich by the River Garry, and Loch Lochy at Achnacarry Bay and the surrounding bays. Gairlochy is very scenic and gives you the opportunity to visit the Commando Memorial, which is close by. At Laggan it is worth visiting the floating pub. If you are looking for isolation, peace and quiet, then stop between Cullochy and Kytra.

VISITING IRELAND

If you are planning to visit Ireland you need to be aware of certain rules:

- **Crew** The Republic of Ireland is not part of Schengen but belongs to the common travel area, which thankfully means the 90/180 restriction doesn't apply. So you can spend as much time in Ireland as you wish. Though you will need your passports.
- **Boat VAT Status** A UK VAT registered boat can only spend 18 months in Ireland, if it was in the UK on 31 Dec 2020.
- **Procedure** On entering Irish waters you must fly a Q flag, and the crew remain onboard until the skipper has completed necessary customs and immigration formalities, then the Q flag can be taken down. You will need the ship's papers, proof of ownership, where your boat was on 31 Dec 2020. Contact Customs and the harbourmaster on arrival. The actual experience appears to be more relaxed, often the Customs response is, they will visit when they are in the area. But always go with the correct procedure.
- **Pets** Entering Ireland with pets in 2024 seems to be more problematic. So please see CA/RYA websites for the latest information.
- **Waste** Food waste from the UK is treated as International Catering Waste (ICW), which requires special disposal. Minimise the amount of food waste you take into Ireland and separate it from your normal rubbish.
- **Red diesel** Is not permitted in Ireland, only unmarked diesel is allowed.
- **Returning to the UK** Re-entering UK waters you need to complete a Pleasure Craft Report (sPCR) either online or posting and fly a Q flag. Departing the UK, you need to complete a pleasure craft report.

CHAPTER THREE

FINANCES

TAKE POSITIVE ACTION TO MAKE IT HAPPEN

Lack of finance is one reason why people don't go on an extended cruise. So put a financial plan in place to make sure that it happens. First calculate how much money you will need. For a short cruise most people will not rent out their house. Therefore, you need to calculate:

- The running costs for your house, including financial commitments such as the mortgage, utility bills etc.
- Pre-trip costs such as charts, pilot books and additional equipment required to prepare the boat.
- Cruising costs such as food, fuel and harbour fees.
- Any additional costs for your return journey home until your first salary payment.
- A contingency fund for unforeseen costs en route or if you have no guaranteed income on your return.

If you find that you don't have enough funds for the trip, then you must take some positive action. The steps we took to make sure our dream became reality were to:

- Set up a regular saving scheme 18 months before our start date.
- Generate money through the auction website eBay. We boosted our cruising budget by £600 through selling old sailing kit; it paid for the electronic charts.

PRE-TRIP COSTS

There are several pre-trip costs:

Boat insurance

Most policies insure from the Elbe to Brest, so this will cover your route. Our insurance company didn't charge us any more than our usual annual premium. Clearly, you should check this with your insurer. Be aware that if you are sailing single handed some insurers limit the passage hours to only 18 or 24 hours, so you might need to shop around.

Charts and pilot books

Charts and pilot books are a major cost of the cruise, particularly as you will need quite a few. Possible costs (2024) are outlined in the table overleaf, discounts aren't included:

ITEM	COST	COMMENTS
CHARTS	£493	Given the approach to carrying paper charts and the scale carried varies, it is impossible to cost. This is a very basic paper chart back up of 19 Imray passage charts – buying in bulk discounts should be possible.
ELECTRONIC CHARTS	£320 £20	Price for Navionics but there are cheaper charts available particularly if they aren't used in a chart plotter Antares Charts for West Coast Scotland
ADMIRALTY TIDAL ATLASES	£112	Try to get a discount if buying in bulk. We negotiated a 19 per cent discount at the Boat Show,
REEDS NAUTICAL ALMANAC	£55	Covers every UK port and harbour.
PILOT BOOKS	£225	Six pilot guides: a mixture of Clyde Cruising Club and Imray pilot guides (excludes pilot guides for the south coast as we already owned these). We obtained a 10 per cent discount on Imray books from the Cruising Association.
TOTAL	£1,225	

Reducing the cost of the charts

There are several ways to reduce the cost of your charts:

Electronic charts

Most main chart producers have regions that cover all of the UK & Ireland. You may want additional detailed charts for certain areas such as Antares Charts.

Paper charts

You may be lucky enough to be able to borrow charts from friends. If this is not possible, then another way to reduce costs is by buying second-hand charts through online sites such as eBay. Always check independently whether you are buying a current or a cancelled version, and make sure that you update them. All the issuers have good websites which makes this easier. We decided to buy new charts where they are issued annually, due to the number of changes.

We sold charts and tidal atlases on eBay after the trip to recoup some of the costs. One way to reduce the cost of charts and pilot books is to return the same way. It might be better to change your goal than not cruise at all. For example, going round Cape Wrath and returning to the west coast via the Caledonian Canal would mean that many of the charts and pilot books could be reused.

TRIP COSTS

Looking at trip costs from the most recent surveys, without food and money spent ashore for leisure activities, the average cost ranges from £12 to £35 a day. Clearly there are lots of variables that impact this, one of the biggest is how much you anchor. Those who reported £12 a day, anchored 45 per cent of the time and the boat that reported £35 a day anchored 3 per cent of the time. Adjusting the costs to make the boats the same size, then the range is between £19 and £35 depending on how much you anchor. This will give you a good planning budget, then you need to add your food and onshore costs, such as sightseeing etc.

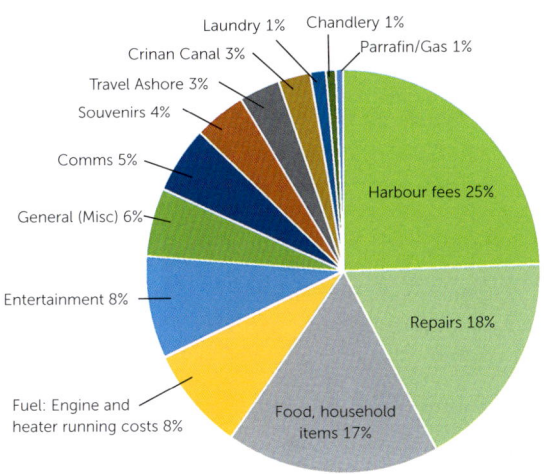

Percentage split of our costs

Loch Gairloch which runs rover tickets with other harbours

While it is no longer relevant to look at our trip costs, the percentage split is still relevant. As time went on, we learnt how to reduce our costs and adapt to life as live-aboards on a limited budget. For example, we stopped having lunches ashore and took sandwiches and drinks, or ate on the boat.

Harbour fees

Harbour fees are a major cost, and they contributed a quarter of our total cruise budget. At 2024 prices, our harbour costs would have been £3841 or £34.12 a day. They can be reduced if you increase the number of nights spent at anchor. We spent only nine nights at anchor, but the highest number of nights at anchor on any cruise surveyed was 60 (representing 54 per cent of their time). Also, reducing the number of nights you spend in south coast harbours will substantially reduce your cost, because on average they are 1.6 times more expensive than elsewhere.

In Scotland, various councils and Orkney marinas run 'rover' tickets allowing you to visit several harbours at a reduced cost. These tickets allow

HARBOUR	NUMBER OF NIGHTS	PRICES UPDATED FOR 2024 FOR 38FT YACHT
Marinas	51	Average cost £36
Pontoon	27	Average cost £34.73
Mooring buoy	13	Average cost £25
Wall	11	Average cost £34.73
Anchor	9	Be aware that if you anchor on the south coast, you are likely to be charged. In Scotland, you will not be charged for anchoring, but if you are in a sea loch (open at one end) the owner can charge you for landing your dinghy above HW; in a sound (open at both ends), charges are not allowed.

you to either spend two days at one marina or you can stay at multiple locations, ie a day in each. For example, a 14-day rover ticket in Orkney costs £403 (2024). *Reeds Nautical Almanac* has a lot of information about rover tickets and the prices of overnight stays. Our split of harbours and the 2024 costs are shown in the table on page 55.

Fuel costs

Clearly, if you are in a motorboat, your fuel costs will be a major part of your budget. Even in a yacht your fuel costs will be higher than you might expect. On average over all the routes, the boats surveyed motored or motor sailed for 52 per cent of their time.

Fuel prices varied enormously; it is always worth finding out from the harbourmaster where the fishing boats or commercial boats fill up. It is often at a different place to where yachties and motorboats refuel and can be cheaper. It was significantly cheaper in the fishing ports of Kirkwall, Tarbert, Campbeltown and Whitby. In some places we were able to get a volume discount when buying quantities over 100 litres. Prices varied dramatically, so we started to phone ahead and plan where we would bunker up.

In a motorboat you will be able to get volume discounts. It is also worth researching a local fuel company and arranging a tanker delivery, which can save you a significant sum depending on the volume taken. However, be warned that the flow rate from a tanker is faster than from the diesel pumps and could cause a problem, depending on the size of your pipes. So only fill your tank to 90 per cent capacity, so that you don't get a blow-back.

Repair costs

Our knowledge of mechanics enables us to do basic fault-finding and servicing such as changing oil and fuel filters, impellers, oil and alternator belts. For anything more complex than this we need to call an engineer. Both time and money can be saved by carrying more spares; see Chapter 15 for details on what we carried. Repairs accounted for 18 per cent of our costs.

RETURNING HOME

It is advisable to leave money in the bank for expenses when returning home such as MOTs, car tax etc. We discovered that we needed to replace the car, an event which we had certainly not planned for!

SPONSORSHIP AND RAISING MONEY FOR CHARITY

The majority of people do not get sponsorship, but if you do, it is more likely to take the form of equipment rather than money, unless it is a donation to a charity. The key question is: what is your unique selling point? What makes your story different to anyone else who is completing the trip? It is unlikely that you will be sponsored unless:

- You are an exciting prospect for a company and will gain media exposure, as in the case of Katie Miller, a young solo sailor raising money for the Ellen MacArthur Trust.
- You intend to raise money for charity.
- You have a connection with the company.

You need to consider what you can offer your sponsor:

- ***TV time*** While this is very attractive you have to have a really exciting story to attract the interest of TV producers.
- ***Press articles*** Targeted at an audience that the company wants to attract.

- **Advertising space** On the boat or on your website. This could take the form of a sticker on the hull, advertising on your sail or a logo on your sail cover.
- **Social media coverage** If you have a large number of followers, you are likely to be more appealing.

You need to be prepared to write many letters and start well in advance. If you do get sponsorship, you need to work hard. John Hill (*Almacantar*, Hustler 38) was raising money for the Lincolnshire Air Ambulance and recounts: 'As part of the deal for getting sponsorship I had to arrange substantial publicity and, to this end, I achieved interviews with local papers at most of the changeover ports. I sent photographs, together with the reports I did for each leg, to the staff of the Air Ambulance, who pushed these out, suitably edited, to many other papers. I carried a sail cover advertising the charity and the company who sponsored me.'

Bill and Anita Miller (*Marika M*, Westerly Corsair) raised an amazing £14,000 for Stroke Research in 2005 by cruising round Britain via Cape Wrath. Bill and Anita wrote approximately 250 letters to friends, business contacts and a few companies. Bill suffered a stroke in 1999 and was in a wheelchair for a year which, as Bill says, 'helped no end' in securing donations. That was his unique story.

Often the charities you are supporting are able to help with publicity. Other sources for contributions are:

- **Friends and family** Probably the easiest solution for managing your donations is by using a website such as www.justgiving.com.

SELLING STORIES?

Perhaps the most awe-inspiring circumnavigation that I have come across and I have surveyed over 80, is Mark Ashley-Miller's in *Good Dog* (Nauticat 331). He departed Dartmouth in March 2019 and sailed round The British Isles (UK & Ireland) and met every harbourmaster. After five years, he had sailed 9,000 nm, visited 310 harbours, met a total of 256 harbourmasters, been helped by 90 different crew and raised over £30,000 for The Seafarers' Charity. The remarkable story of his trip, the harbourmasters and their harbours can be found at www.harbourmastersailingchallenge.co.uk and Mark is currently writing a book, which is due out in 2025.

- **Harbourmasters** Mention the charity to the harbourmaster when you arrive in harbour: they may waive the fees as a donation to your charity, especially if you are raising money for the RNLI.
- **Your home marina or harbour** Bill found that his marina waived 50 per cent of their fee, which went into the pot.

The other advantage for a charity is the contribution to raising awareness. While the trip itself might not instantly generate returns, with a raised profile the charity could raise money in the future in the form of bequests.

CHAPTER FOUR

PREPARATIONS

A chance to explore new and unusual places – the Blinking Bridge, Newcastle upon Tyne

If you don't designate the preparations as a project in itself, your time will run out. Even so, no matter how much time you allow, it will never be enough. You will still have a few late nights before you set off, but a preparation plan should help to reduce some of the stress. The key messages here are: plan, start early and make lists of work.

PROJECT MANAGEMENT

The task of getting the boat ready breaks down into three phases:

1 What equipment and skills will you need?

- Identify new equipment needed
- Do an electrical audit to make sure you have the power to match your needs
- Purchase equipment
- Identify any courses required

2 Getting yourself and the boat ready

- Fit the new equipment
- Test new equipment
- Attend courses

3 Ready to leave

- Sea trials
- Do a 'shake-down' cruise
- Pack the boat
- Victualling
- Leave your house secure

The timing of these phases depends on your circumstances, whether you are working and how much work or equipment is required before you set off. If you have equipment to buy, take the timing of the boat shows into consideration as they are good places to get discounts or just evaluate which items of equipment you want to buy.

From the boats surveyed, the average time taken to plan the trip was just over nine months, but this can be misleading as it really depends on how much of that time is devoted to planning and preparation. Our trip was planned over two years. We were both working and we wanted to fit various bits of equipment to our boat and take a sabbatical. I had to ask for the time off 18 months in advance. The last six months were dedicated to planning the trip around Britain, the rest of the time was used to ensure that we had the equipment we wanted for extended cruising.

1 WHAT WILL YOU NEED?
New equipment for your boat

Identify well in advance any equipment that you require to be fitted.

Electrical audit

Prior to purchasing any electrical or electronic equipment, do an electrical audit to make sure that you have enough current to power your equipment. Identify the current (amps) required and the number of hours that you plan to run the equipment. Run two scenarios: at anchor and at sea, and then calculate the total amp hour requirement for each scenario. Our audit is shown overleaf. Our total daily requirement ranged from a minimum of 77Ah up to a maximum of 156Ah.

If you have any AC equipment that you are planning to charge from a 12-volt system, then you can use an inverter. However, they are inefficient for converting DC to AC, as they lose 20 per cent during the process. So, the amp hours need to be multiplied by 1.2 to calculate the amount required. This should then be added to your total daily requirement. See example on page 61.

A sunny spot in Salcombe

Here is an example of how you calculate your requirements:

Daily requirement of 388 divided by 12 volts = 32Ah x 1.2 = 38.4Ah

With lead acid batteries only about 30 per cent of the battery capacity is usable, therefore to arrive at your required battery capacity, you need to multiply the total daily requirements by three. We needed 231 to 468Ah (3 x 77 and 3 x 156) – but only had 240Ah available from our domestic batteries. Our engine is supported by a separate starting battery. There was just enough domestic battery capacity to cover our minimum requirement. We upgraded the batteries to 320Ah (2 x 160Ah) – but we had to shop around to find batteries to give us the maximum amp hours and fit into the available space. This was still insufficient capacity. In the end we decided to upgrade to AGM batteries, where 50 per cent of the capacity is usable, then we only needed to cover 144 to 312Ah (2 x 77 and 2 x 156), making it an efficient way to reduce our needed battery size, though they were more expensive. This meant we covered our requirement, but on some days we might have to run our engine during the day

DC DEVICE	CURRENT DRAW (AMPS)	AT SEA		AT ANCHOR/HARBOUR WITH NO MAINS POWER	
		HOURS USED	TOTAL AMP HOURS (AH) = AMPS X HOURS USED	HOURS USED	TOTAL AMP HOURS (AH) = AMPS X HOURS USED
REFRIGERATOR	6.0	3	18.0	6	36.0
RADAR TRANSMITTING	4.2	3	12.6		
NAV LIGHTS	0.5	8	4.0		
INSTRUMENTS	0.6	16	9.6		
INSTRUMENTS (NIGHT)	0.9	8	7.2		
COMPASS LIGHT	0.1	8	0.8		
ANCHOR LIGHT	0.3			10	3.0
AUTOPILOT	2.0	20	40.0		
VHF	0.3	24	7.2		
CHART PLOTTER	1.1	24	26.4		
FORWARD-LOOKING ECHO SOUNDER	0.95	1	0.95		
SEA-ME ACTIVE RADAR REFLECTOR	0.4	24	9.6		
NAVTEX	0.1	24	2.4	24	2.4
HEATER	1.5	0		6	9.0
CHART TABLE LIGHTS	0.4	1.5	0.6		
SALOON LIGHTS	1.4	0.5	0.7	3	4.2
GALLEY LIGHTS	1.4	1	1.4	1.5	2.1
CABIN	0.7	1	0.7	1	0.7
RADIO	0.1			8	0.8
MOBILE PHONE CHARGING	0.6			2	1.2
PC CHARGING	2.7			3	8.1
CONTINGENCY (10%)			14		7.0
TOTAL DAILY REQUIREMENT			156		74.5

AC DEVICES	POWER (WATTS)	HOURS USED	TOTAL WATT HOURS = WATT X HOURS USED
Microwave	600	0.5 (30mins)	300
Coffee maker	350	0.25 (15mins)	88
Daily AC requirement			388

when the radar was on and/or use an alternative power source. We chose a wind generator.

You also need to ensure that you have the right alternator to charge your batteries. This is a complicated subject and I would suggest you refer to a specialist book or website.

Electrical independence

There are several strategies you can use to decrease your dependence on shore power:

- *Alternative power sources* Wind, sun or a towed generator can be considered. Given the latitudes, only wind and towed generators are realistic for anything more than a trickle charge. We purposely went for a high-output wind generator, a Duogen D400, and we would get 3.5 amps in 15 knots of wind. It also started turning at 6 knots, which is another important consideration, as is the noise generated.

- *Reduce power consumption* You can reduce your power consumption by the use of efficient appliances. For example, fitting a Lopo LED tricolour navigation light with an all-round anchor light. It only draws 0.3 amps while at anchor, compared to 2 amps with our previous light, a saving of 17 amps for 10 hours overnight. This might not seem much, but if you consider that you need twice as much battery capacity, we would have needed an additional 34Ah of battery to use the conventional anchor light. Or even an LED bulb, with a sensor that turns the light off when it is daylight. If you do fit an LED light, do make sure it is compliant with the regulations. Reducing the number of screens reduces the amps required; rather than having a wind/speed display at the chart table I use the Navtex screen to display that information. The goal of any extended cruising boat's set up should be to reduce power consumption where possible.

- *Reduce the appliances that can only be charged by mains power* We used 12V chargers for both the PC and the mobile phone, as it is a more efficient way of charging than an inverter. That only left us with the camera batteries that needed mains power.

- *Reducing battery charging time using a smart charger* A smart charger, such as an Adverc, optimises your charging regime, which will reduce the time needed to fully charge your batteries.

- *Careful use of appliances* We used to turn on the heating while motoring into the harbour. This ensures that the heavy current draw, when getting the cabin up to temperature, happens while the engine is on. Likewise, we would always turn the fridge on when motoring.

- *Carry a generator if your power demands are high* This is really only an option on larger boats. You may also wish to consider an intelligent energy system such as Victron, to make battery charging as efficient as possible.

Buying equipment

Here are a few tips for reducing the cost of buying equipment:

- Buy equipment in one go if you can; we prepared a long list of all electrical equipment and bought most of it from one supplier and received a substantial discount at a boat show. If you need additional cables or accessories, ask if they will throw them in free of charge.
- Ask for free delivery.
- Consider buying last year's models. With new equipment being launched at the boat shows, there are some real bargains to be had if you are happy to have an older model.
- Always ask for a discount – it doesn't cost you anything to ask!

Your own skills

It is not just the boat that you need to get ready. You need to look at your own skills. Some relevant courses might be:

- Additional RYA theory and practical navigation.
- Own boat tuition: most schools offer tuition on your boat.
- RYA Sea Survival Certificate: hopefully you will never have to use the skills learnt but this one-day course is also very useful if you are looking to update any safety equipment, eg a liferaft.
- DSC VHF – if you have updated your VHF to DSC.
- Weather forecasting course: you may feel that your weather knowledge needs brushing up prior to your trip. I can recommend Weather Consultancy Services Weather School run by Simon Keeling, who has a PhD in Meteorology and is a BBC TV weather presenter. While Simon is not a sailor, he has worked on many courses with Stokey Woodall, a very experienced and well-known sailor. More importantly Simon is a brilliant communicator who teaches weather theory with passion and makes it easier to understand. See www.weatherschool.co.uk.
- RYA Diesel Maintenance Course: to ensure that you can carry out basic maintenance and fault-finding.

2 GETTING YOURSELF AND THE BOAT READY

Fit the equipment

Leave plenty of time to get new equipment fitted. If you need contractors, they are particularly busy just before the season starts. Also, ensure that you leave enough time to test the equipment fully after fitting it.

Reducing the costs

If you do not have the skills to fit electrical and electronic equipment, you can substantially reduce the cost of installation by running the cables through yourself. An electrician can advise you on the sizes of wires. If you are replacing any old equipment that is still serviceable, try selling it on eBay; we sold our old radar and antenna for £385.

Attend courses

Avoid doing this the month before you leave, as you will have many other things to do.

3 READY TO LEAVE

Sea trials

Prior to the trip, carry out sea trials as they allow you to check that all the equipment is working and that you are up to scratch. Those that we carried out were:

- Putting up storm sails
- Putting up the cruising chute
- Putting in all three reefs
- Anchoring overnight
- Using dinghy and outboard
- Using emergency antenna
- Calibration of autopilot/radar
- Fire practice/use of fire extinguisher
- Familiarisation with flares
- Man overboard drills
- Using lifejacket hoods

Shake-down cruise

Once packed, a shake-down cruise will be a good way to check that you haven't forgotten anything.

Sometimes it is good to let the autopilot take over

Leaving your home

Don't underestimate the tasks to be done when you are leaving your home for a couple of months. Also be mindful that your insurance will have a maximum number of days that your house can be left unattended. You might need to ask a friend/neighbour to pop in regularly to check on it.

ITEM	TASK
HOUSE	Arrange for someone to check your house from time to time.
	Check house insurance cover.
	Arrange for someone to look after your front garden to prevent your house looking empty.
	Set up a system for watering the garden or arrange for it to be done.
	Empty freezer and refrigerator.
	Reduce junk mail by using a mail preference service.
	Set up 'mail divert' with Royal Mail.
CAR	Arrange where to park or store your car.
	Check your road tax and MOT – you can register your car off the road at the end of your car tax period.
	Advise your insurers of what arrangements you have made.
GENERAL	Ensure that as much as possible of your financial and admin activities can be managed online.

CHAPTER FIVE

STORES, EQUIPMENT AND KIT

Before our previous summer cruise, we made a list of everything we thought we should take, adding to it throughout the winter. Then when we packed the boat the winter before we left, we bought several large storage boxes and stored everything in them, ticking them off the list. This meant that loading the boat the following year was much easier as we knew where everything was and we knew what still needed to be purchased. The only things that we forgot to take were our thermals; we discovered this at 1:30am, just as we were setting off from Yarmouth, Isle of Wight.

Bear in mind that when you draw up your stores, equipment and kit list, it all has to fit on your boat – weight is a consideration and you may need to make compromises.

GENERAL ITEMS TO TAKE
Clothes
You will be surprised how few clothes you really need. We took enough clothes to last us for three weeks and that was more than ample, as launderette facilities were regularly available. Once the weather improves, you can hang washing outside to reduce the cost of using a dryer in a launderette. A mini drying rack with clothes pegs attached helps to increase the amount you can dry in one go. Take a large zipped bag for laundry; it is amazing how quickly a washing mountain builds up.

Take a pair of waterproof trousers and a jacket for wearing ashore, as there is nothing worse than traipsing around ashore in wet oilies. Along with walking boots, they proved invaluable as they enabled us to make the most of our trips ashore.

We followed the layer principle for sailing clothes: several thin layers are warmer than one thick layer. Breathable oilskins are a good investment, as you may end up living in your oilies and they will help to prevent dehydration.

Good quality boots which keep your feet warm make the world of difference. I lived in my Dubarry boots and at the beginning of the trip, they were fantastic. However, a word of warning about salt: after a while my feet got very cold at night, to the point they were so cold that they kept me awake during my off watch. I noticed that my boots appeared constantly wet, even if they had dried out in front of the heater vent. I realised that so much salt had been absorbed into the leather that when outside, even if it was dry, they would absorb water again. This meant that when I wore the boots, they would draw heat out of my feet as the water evaporated – hence my feet would get really cold. The cure was to soak my boots in warm water several times to get rid of the salt and then they kept my feet snug again.

Bikes

We used our folding bikes three times: a cracking ride along the River Camel in Padstow, we cycled around Westray and along part of the Caledonian Canal. But in those places we could have hired bikes. If you are keen on cycling and do have room make sure your bikes are compact and easy to access. Don't forget to take bike locks, puncture repair kit and pumps etc.

Galley equipment

On a short summer cruise you tend to eat out more as, after all, it is a holiday. But on a four-month cruise you are more likely to eat on board most of the time, so make sure you take the right equipment for regular cooking.

Barbecues

We enjoyed quite a few barbecues on board. We have a Cobb barbecue, which you can place on the deck as the surround does not get hot. Other barbecues that have been recommended are the charcoal type that you can attach to your pushpit.

SOME USEFUL BOAT EQUIPMENT

Heavy weather sails

For yachts, it is advisable to have a main that has three reefs. We carried a storm jib and trysail on board, as they came with the boat, both are orange for visibility, but thankfully we didn't need to use either. The accuracy of weather forecasts does mean that you should be able to avoid weather that would necessitate storm sails.

Much of the time we were in oilies, even on sunny days. Here we are screaming along with only a scrap of jib out with 32 knots of wind, in the Sound of Sleat. As usual the waves look fairly flat, hence we took the picture to coincide with the waves breaking over the ketch

Mast steps

It is essential to be able to climb up the mast. For most, this will mean a bosun's chair and a lot of hard work on a winch. We were lucky that the previous owners had fitted mast steps. They are a real luxury and make getting aloft easy, and are worth any reduction in performance.

Cockpit tent

We didn't have a cockpit tent and regretted it. It provides extra living space when it is raining and an area to hang wet oilies. A tent also provides protection for instruments, and from the elements when you are down below while still allowing ventilation from the hatch.

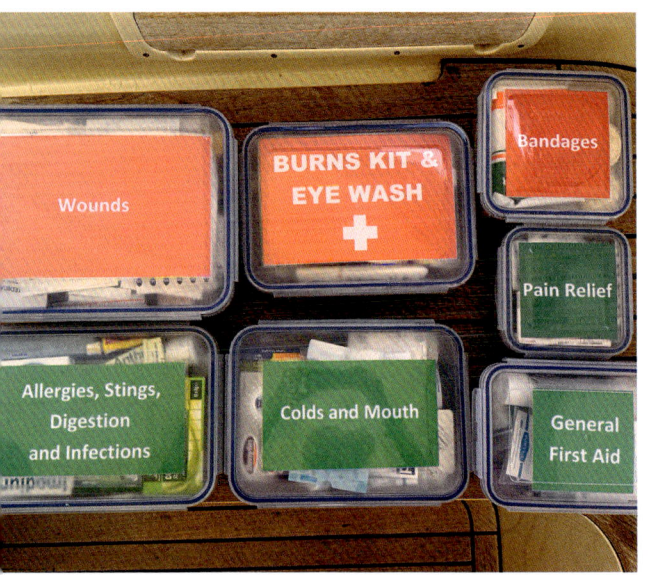

Medicines stored by use

Autopilot

If you are single-handed or even a couple, an autopilot is actually an essential piece of safety equipment, as it allows you to navigate and undertake routines at sea. Even if you have a larger crew, I would say it is essential for your sanity. I love helming and would take the helm for a cracking sail but motoring can be tedious.

Heating

Having heating certainly made a difference for drying wet clothes and for keeping warm. It can be cold in late spring and we had ours on every night up until the end of June! I know of others who have taken a small dehumidifier to improve the environment.

Wetsuit and mask

A wetsuit with hood and a mask are essential pieces of equipment when dealing with fouled propellers (see Chapter 14).

FIRST AID AND MEDICINES

The general assumption on the cruise is that you can get medical assistance within 12 hours. Though it is not just first aid that needs consideration; you also need to look at non-prescription general medicines and any personal medication. We found that chemists were only available in towns. If you are taking prescription medicine, take supplies with you; your doctor may give you a prescription that covers your requirements for the trip or you can arrange to have prescriptions emailed to a chemist en route. If you ever need to receive medical advice over the phone, then a list of medicines that you have on board will be very helpful. Sourcing first aid kits and medicines online will reduce the cost considerably.

We made up our own first aid kit and medicines box, designed to deal with the conditions listed opposite; a pharmacist is a good source of knowledge if you want to do the same. Previously we hadn't carried any dental medicines, but on a recent cruise I was shown the error of our ways, as I ended up with a tooth abscess. We had nothing on board to touch the pain and were two days' sail away from a dentist. In the wilds of Scotland this might happen to anyone. I googled tooth pain, there were all sorts of helpful suggestions, none of which we had on board (we now do). The only one we did have was holding a wet tea bag against the tooth. It is quite disgusting, but it did have a bizarre soothing effect. Thankfully, we had a broad spectrum of antibiotics on board which I took, after consulting with my dentist at home. Although it took 48 hours to start working it was a game changer. We set off with my mouth throbbing, sucking a cold tea bag, then the fog came down.... could my life get any better, I thought!

Note: You should always consult a doctor or pharmacist before taking any medication.

MINIMISING AND MANAGING SPACE REQUIREMENTS

Weeks before leaving, you will make many trips to your boat with your car full to the gunwales and return with an empty one. You are then left with the challenge of being able to fit it all in and to be able to find it again. With limited storage facilities on board, you have to minimise and manage your space requirements. See page 68 for some ideas.

CATEGORY	AILMENT	ITEMS/COMMENTS
GENERAL FIRST AID	Cuts	Plasters, micropore tape, zinc tape, wound closure (steri) strips, crêpe bandage, triangular bandage, fingerstall, first aid dressing (various sizes), Spray plaster
	Sprains	Tubigrip, ice pack, Deep Heat
	Wounds	Savlon, TCP
	Fractures and sprains	Sam Splint, bandages
	Burns	Burnshield hydrogel and various-sized dressings containing hydrogel
	Eye care	Eye washes and eye bath, Optrex
GENERAL MEDICINES	Colds	Beechams Day and Night tablets
	Sore throat	Betadine and throat lozenges
	Constipation	Senokot
	Diarrhoea	Imodium
	Insect bites and stings	Wasp Eaze, antihistamine and Anthisan creams
	Mouth care	Bonjela (mouth ulcer), Blistex (chapped lips) and Zovirax (cold sore)
	Dental care	Oil of cloves, temporary filling kit, wide spectrum antibiotics (if your Dentist/GP will prescribe them)
	Pain	Ibuprofen, co-codamol, paracetamol and hot water bottle
	Dehydration	Dioralyte
PREVENTATIVE	Sunburn	Sunscreen is important even when it is cloudy as you can still get burnt. SPF8, SPF35, aftersun lotion
	Insect bites	An insect repellent is essential to combat the midges on the west coast of Scotland
	Seasickness	Stugeron, sea bands, Scopoderm patches, sea band and seasick bags
EQUIPMENT/GENERAL		Tweezers, thermometer, sterile scissors

Hamster baskets used for fridge storage

Reduce the need for storage space

Manuals – Much of the space on our bookshelves was taken up by instruction manuals. You can minimise this space as most can be found online. However, it is worth downloading, photographing or scanning them so that you don't need to rely on an internet connection.

Music – We connect our phones to our boat radio via a Bluetooth FM transmitter.

FOUR RULES FOR SUCCESSFUL STOWAGE

1. Reduce the need for storage space
   - Start by completely emptying your boat to get rid of the stuff that you don't need; it is amazing how much junk you collect over the years.
   - Use technology to replace some bulky items, such as manuals.
2. Organise your storage
   - Improve accessibility for frequently used items.
   - Try to stow items close to where they are needed.
   - Plan the stowage of heavy items, so that they are balanced in the boat and stowed as low as possible.
   - Group similar items together.
   - Document where you have stowed things.
   - Create more storage space by using the dead space more effectively.
3. Think about safety when planning
   - Any fuels or flammable liquids should be stowed in a locker ventilated to the outside. On no account should they be stowed in lockers that vent to the bilge.
   - Items should be stowed securely, so that they do not fly out and injure someone in a rough sea.
   - If you have a fluxgate compass for your autopilot or radar, check that you don't store anything made of ferrous metal nearby.
4. Protect your kit from the elements
   - Ensure that any kit likely to be affected by moisture is stored in a waterproof container or bag.

Organise your storage

Food lockers – We had one food locker where we kept items that we used regularly eg soups, pasta, food for lunch etc. In this locker we stored food in manageable-sized containers; we bulk-stored the same items in other lockers in the bilge.

Baskets – Lockers can easily turn into caverns where you can never find what you want without having to empty them. We used plastic baskets suspended on wooden rails; this allowed us to minimise the dead space.

Refrigerator – We have a top-opening fridge, which used to be chaotic, as everything wanted was at the bottom. However, our fridge was transformed when we invested in some 'hamster' baskets, which are made to your measurements. These wire baskets stack on top of each other, enabling you to fit more into your fridge. It is also easier to get at items and it keeps your fridge cleaner, as food doesn't get squashed or end up in a primordial swamp in the bottom (see www.hamsterbaskets.co.uk).

Plastic boxes/Bags – You need plenty of plastic boxes for general storage. We chose several different sizes, and while not entirely waterproof, they keep moisture out. One was used to store all the pilot books when they were not needed, and this enabled us to place them low down in the boat. One held all the bike stuff, another had the dinghy and outboard bits (padlock, starting handle etc). Another one contained all the chargers that we had on the boat. We also used plastic bags for storing our clothes, as it prevented them from smelling of 'eau de boat'.

Ship's papers – These were all kept together in one folder.

First aid and medicines – We separated these items into different boxes eg burns, wounds, painkillers, eye washes and general first aid. They were stored altogether and clearly marked so that we could grab the right box.

Tools – Tool boxes are very unwieldy, so we now have all tools stored in various sizes of Tupperware boxes. All screwdrivers in one, all pliers in another etc. That way it is easier to find the right tool quickly, they are easier to stow, plus you can fit more in. Some frequently used tools, such as screwdrivers (flat and cross-headed), and adjustable wrench and pliers, are kept in the companion way. If it is easier to access, then you are more likely to carry out that quick two-minute job when it needs doing.

Emergency tools – We have a set of bolt cutters and a gas-powered Shoot-it on top of the engine box, in case we needed to cut away rigging.

Spares – We grouped spares together by type, trying to keep similar spares together. For small items like screws, fuses etc, we used fly fishing boxes to keep them separate. Those spares that we would need frequently or in an emergency were kept to hand, eg engine emergency spares, such as an impeller.

Pilot books and charts – We were lucky to have a long locker under the chart table for charts, but most people store them under bunk cushions in large plastic wallets to stop them getting damp from condensation. We split the charts into legs in order of use.

Storage for the anchor ball and motoring cone.

'Where is it?' book — Each locker had a number and we noted down the location of everything in a little alphabetical index book. This is particularly useful if you have visitors on board so that they can find things easily themselves. But you do need to be disciplined to keep it up to date. For a while we thought that we had a fatal flaw in the plan, as we lost the 'where is it?' book!

Even though we did all of this, we still needed to use two bunks (a quarter berth and forward bunk) as permanent storage, as the bikes took up quite a bit of space.

Day signals — We stored the anchor ball and motoring cone in netting under the anchor locker lid. Each one had the appropriate length of strop and a carabiner to attach it to the deck.

Views to Hoy over Scappa Flow from Mainland Orkney

POWER CABLES AND OTHER ITEMS

Shore power

Most boats will need a regular dose of shore power. To ensure that you won't be left in the dark, take two shore power cables; in several places it was necessary to have a very long lead. Also, a splitter cable is very useful (ie it allows two cables to be plugged into the same power source) as this will ensure that you get power even when all the sockets are occupied. It is much cheaper to make one up from the various components. Or if you don't want to make them up, they are usually cheaper at a caravan shop. We also took a mains extension lead. On our current boat, we have a polarity checker. If we find a reverse polarity in a marina, then we insert a short cable that we wired especially so that it reverses the polarity. So it enables us to safely plug in, despite the polarity issue.

Batteries

Identify the sizes of all the smaller batteries you need on board and make sure you take spares of each type.

Bike equipment

We needed quite a few items for biking: spare inner tubes and puncture repair kit, helmets, pump, presta adapter, panniers and bike locks.

General items

Other useful items we took were:

- Wetsuit, boots, mask, fins, snorkel, gloves and waterproof torch
- Sewing kit: needles and thread
- Rucksacks
- Laundry bag and drying rack
- Barbecue, charcoal and firelighters

BOOKS AND PUBLICATIONS

Pilot books will be covered in the navigation section (Chapter 11).

Guide books

Much of your time will be spent exploring the mainland; you will find that many harbours in Scotland now have an award-winning heritage museum, but at £9–10 a visit per person, the cost soon adds up. We took the *Rough Guides to Scotland and Great Britain*; these were invaluable as we were able to learn about our new surroundings without paying a fortune.

Wildlife books

You will need some reference books to identify the wildlife, flora and fauna that you will see on your voyage (see Chapter 12).

DOCUMENTS

The documents you need to take:

- Part 1 Ship's Papers or Small Ships Register Certificate (depending on which one you have)
- Passport – In case you decide to go to France or Ireland
- Boat insurance documents
- Driving licence (for hiring a car)
- VHF licence
- Policy number and telephone number of home insurance company
- Names, addresses and phone numbers of doctor and dentist
- National Insurance and NHS numbers

CHAPTER SIX

PROVISIONING

FOOD AND DRINK

Basic provisions are available in all but the most remote locations; there was always a village shop relatively close by. However, if you are at anchor on the west coasts of Ireland or Scotland, there may be no shop, or the nearest one may be a couple of miles away. Don't expect a wide range of products in these shops and you will probably pay high prices. Many bulky non-perishables can be purchased prior to the trip and stored on the boat. This reduces the cost and the amount of shopping to carry without a car. This was also true for staple items like pasta, rice and couscous, which can also be bought in bulk.

In more populated areas there were shops within easy walking distance, though in some of the larger towns a bus ride was needed to get to the big supermarkets. When moored in a town with a supermarket, we would check our route for the following week and, if we were going to be in remote areas, we would stock up with as much as we could carry. Rucksacks are really useful on these occasions.

Basic fresh produce was relatively easy to find, though we did have the luxury of a fridge and so were able to keep food fresh for longer. You also have the opportunity to taste local produce en route. We enjoyed Welsh lamb and mint sausages from local butchers, Grimbister cheese from Orkney, fresh scallops from several fishing villages, and local fishermen sold us lobster cheaply in Whitby. See the box opposite to find out what is a legal-sized lobster if you buy direct from fishermen.

Wine boxes are ideal for a boat, though it is a good idea to keep a couple of bottles for social occasions when invited on board other boats.

Quick meals

We always had a supply of quick meals on board, so when arriving in harbour late at night, instead of having to cook a meal from scratch, we could speedily heat one up. Ready-prepared pasta and sauces were our favourite standbys: a tasty quick solution for hungry sailors. Boil-in-the-bag rice was also popular.

Lunches

Tinned ham and corned beef were useful for sandwiches. Pitta bread makes a good alternative to bread for sandwiches as it lasts for a month, and fresh bread can be difficult to come by in certain areas. Instant soups came in handy for lunches and night watches, and of course the morale boosting sweetie box for long passages or night watches.

FISHING FOR SUPPER

Many people on this cruise supplemented their food with the odd mackerel. Here are their tips for fishing on the move:

- Cruise at about 3–4 knots.
- Use a paravane to keep the hooks below the surface; it takes the place of a lead on a trolling line. Unlike a lead they will not sink rapidly when cornering and will flip and bring the fish to the surface once hooked.
- Use mackerel feathers, preferably barbless hooks so when you bring up the line with all six hooks loaded with mackerel, you can keep the biggest and throw the rest back without injury.
- Don't let them die in the bucket. Rigor mortis sets in and they end up curved and you can't get them into the frying-pan.
- If you bait the hook with mackerel, you may catch bass.

Lobster pot – We caught several crabs in our collapsible lobster pot but, sadly, they were all too small and had to be set free. You need to bait the pot with fish and then place it near rocks but on a sandy bottom.

To be legal, lobsters should be more than 87mm from the eye socket to the back of the head section (carapace). Lobsters are being over-fished, and in order to try to preserve stocks, fishermen cut V notches into the tails of female lobsters. These lobsters are not allowed to be eaten, and must be returned to the sea to help increase the stocks. If you plan to catch legal-sized crabs or lobsters, make sure you have a pan big enough to cook them.

GENERAL PROVISIONS

During the winter prior to your trip, it is worth recording your consumption of non-perishables. This allows you to calculate the quantities you will need for the entire trip. This means that you can buy in bulk, thus reducing your need to shop en route. Here are examples of the usage of some items during the trip:

ITEM	USAGE FOR TWO PEOPLE
KITCHEN TOWELS	2 per week
TOILET ROLLS	1 per week
WASHING UP LIQUID	400ml per month
SHAMPOO	400ml per 6 weeks
TOOTHPASTE	100ml tube per 2 months

FUEL

The availability of clean fuel is an important contributing factor to a successful circumnavigation.

Clean fuel

Prior to the trip I had heard that there could be problems with bad fuel, but of those surveyed only one person came across this. Avoid a bad fill by taking the following precautions.

- Be selective about where you bunker. Don't fill up from anywhere with a low turnover, especially at the beginning of the season, as there will be a higher chance of picking up dirty fuel, or fuel contaminated with water and the diesel bug.
- Change the fuel filter regularly, especially after a bumpy passage if you have had the engine running. Rough seas will stir up any sediment from the bottom of your tank. Fuel filters for our engine cost only £5.50 each (2024 price), so we changed ours a minimum of every 100 hours if we had been motoring in smooth conditions and every 50 hours if it had been a lumpy trip.
- Take a large clear jar, preferably one that can hold half a litre, as a fuel sample jar if you are considering filling up at a dubious refuelling point. The fuel should be left to stand for a short while and then you should check for suspended water or free water that will fall to the bottom.

Petrol

If your main engine runs on petrol, then you will need to plan your resupply points in advance. Appendix 2 shows the availability of petrol at the quayside in 2024. In some places you may be able to arrange a delivery of petrol by tanker.

Also, petrol will be available in some roadside garages but you will need jerry cans to get it to your boat. However, in remote parts of Scotland and the west coast of Ireland, it is likely to be a long trip to find a garage with petrol. One couple reported having to hitchhike with four 20-litre jerry cans, 60 miles there and back, to get petrol in northern Scotland.

If you use petrol in your outboard, make sure you carry enough with you to last between stops. If your petrol outboard is your main engine, then seriously consider changing to a diesel outboard if you can get one to fit your boat. This was the advice of Sam Kent (*Silverwind*, Hunter Delta 25), whose biggest frustration of the trip was finding petrol.

Diesel

The availability of red diesel or green diesel (as it is known in Ireland) is good, but it is not available at every stop, so consult *Reeds Nautical Almanac*.

Managing your fuel

Regardless of the type of fuel you require, you need to ensure that you manage your fuel supply:

- In some places fuel is only available in jerry cans or drums.
- Plan your fuel stops. *Reeds Nautical Almanac* gives the availability of diesel en route, though some of this information was incorrect. It is always worth phoning ahead and asking the harbourmaster if you are unsure of the availability, but also to ask the price as savvy refuelling can save on your budget. Also, check the opening times, as some commercial refuelling points only open during the week. If you are planning to refuel by tanker, you will need to organise this several days in advance, as it is likely that they will only deliver to the port on certain days.

- Monitor your fuel consumption carefully by taking fuel level readings and log the engine hours run when you arrive at your destination. Knowing your hourly usage allows you to work out your motoring range and hence where you need to fill up.
- Always carry some spare fuel. We have fuel tank capacity of 200 litres but always carry 20 litres of fuel in a jerry can.
- If you use an additive, take enough with you for the trip.

FUEL FOR COOKING
Gas

In 2023, Calor Gas announced that they were discontinuing some of the most commonly used gas cylinders, 4.5kg (butane) and 3.9kg (propane), after an unspecified phase out period. However, in January 2024, they announced that they were continuing them. So in theory, at the time of writing, there should be no problem with availability, and those surveyed reported that butane was readily available. Having a spare cylinder will definitely give you flexibility. Gas availability, is shown in *Reeds Nautical Almanac*. Note that in Ireland butane is supplied by Kosan, a sister company of Calor Gas. It has a different connection and is a different size; the smallest bottle is larger than the smallest 4.5kg Calor Gas bottle. Many people reported that getting the UK Calor Gas in Ireland, further west than Kinsale, was difficult. If you are going to Ireland for any length of time, you should plan for using Campingaz as it is more readily available, but is still relatively scarce.

The smaller 2.72kg Campingaz cylinders have a wider base and need a different regulator, so you need a plan to be able to use these.

Propane gas (red bottles) was more difficult to find; you may have to travel quite a distance to source it. One couple developed a little buggy that attached to their bikes to make it easier to transport.

WATER

Water is readily available for refilling your tanks, though you should work out how many days your water supply will last and monitor your usage. Our daily consumption, without a shower on board, was about 18 litres for two people; which was sufficient for 18 days. We filled up with water whenever the tank dropped below half full, or if we knew that we would not be in harbour for a while.

We were able to drink the water directly from the tanks as a Penguin water filter was fitted which removes any chemical tastes. It doesn't remove any bacteria, so you still need water purifying tablets even if you are topping your water up regularly. Do take a hose and adapters, as they are often needed to get water from the taps. In many places water can only be used for filling up water tanks, so you are banned from washing your boat. This was mainly in the west coast of Scotland and in Orkney.

RUBBISH

Disposal of rubbish in Ireland is not as straightforward as you might expect, with many reporting that it was problematic. Many resorted to unpacking their rubbish and posting it through the narrow slots in any public waste bins they could find. Some marinas will take the rubbish for a charge, but on the west coast in rural areas, you are unlikely to find rubbish bins. At some shops you can buy special roadside rubbish bins. A can crusher was recommended as invaluable. See Visiting Ireland (page 52) for the rules on entering Ireland with food waste.

76 UK AND IRELAND CIRCUMNAVIGATOR'S GUIDE

USEFUL EQUIPMENT

Equipment that you may wish to take on board is shown below:

WATER	FUEL	GENERAL
Hose pipe, hose adapter and spray nozzle	Calor Gas including Campingaz regulator if going to Ireland	Fishing lines, hooks and paravane
Distilled water for lead acid batteries	Funnel	
Collapsible water container	Fuel additive	
Water purifying tablets	Spare jerry can	
Water filter cartridges		

Sunrise over Longships, Land's End

CHAPTER SEVEN

A GREENER WAKE

While climate change has been known about for years, it was only when I read about Ellen MacArthur's expedition to South Georgia that I started to be really aware and consider what was my impact on the world. She highlighted the discipline required to manage finite resources on a solo global circumnavigation, illustrating the point with paper towel, the manufacturer defines the amount you use, a pre-determined square, which is often way more than you actually need.

Along with our use of technology, it is the area that has changed most in our cruising, as we have strived to reduce our impact on the world and leave a greener wake. Some of the actions, we had already implemented because they made sense and improved our live aboard experience. However, we have adopted new practices and while some require greater expenditure, many of the options have saved money over time, plus they also have additional benefits. There are four main areas of opportunity to be greener, by reducing:

- Fossil fuels used.
- Contaminants in the water.
- Impact on the marine environment.
- Waste.

REDUCING THE FOSSIL FUELS USED

The main actions here fall into three areas: produce, reduce and change. Produce your own sustainable energy, reduce your requirement and change to more sustainable fuel sources.

Produce your own energy

For the majority, the use of wind generators, solar panels and hydrogenators will only augment your amps. Each has its inherent weakness as a reliable source of power; a wind generator requires enough wind but not too much, and a water hydrogenator is great on long passage making but useless at anchor. Solar panel efficiency can be impacted by the amount and angle of the sun and any shade on the panels. The most effective output is to combine all three. We now have a high output wind generator and a solar panel. The solar panel produces a useful trickle charge but, on most days, the real power comes from the wind generator on passage and at anchor. Currently we have a 70W solar panel whose peak current is just 3.6 amps. Shading and angle of the sun impacts its efficiency, so in our electrical audit for our current boat, I only assume that I will see this current for four hours – resulting in 14 amp hours. Clearly, if you are able to mount them where they avoid shadow for much of the day, then you may get a longer period of peak generation, plus if you have more than one panel you will generate more.

Reduce your requirement
Use less
Any opportunity to use less makes sense for extended cruising, plus it will save you money:

- *Reducing your electrical power needs* See section on electrical independence (page 61).
- *Reduced gas consumption* Through use of alternative cooking methods: pressure cookers, thermal cookers eg Mr D's thermal cooker which claims to save 80 per cent energy. The slow cookers also have the advantage that if you prepare the meal earlier in the day, then after a long hard day at sea, when you can only muster the energy to flop on your saloon berth, a piping hot meal that is ready to eat is a welcome sight.
- *Sail more!* If you have the time, you might be able to pick the days when there is a favourable wind to maximise your sailing. But this is more difficult if you are on a tight timetable.

Improving your fuel efficiency
There are three main actions here: propeller efficiency, motoring sweet spot and cruising weight.

- *Propeller efficiency* When we first bought *Ituna*, the prop had fixed blades and it was undersized, a windless and extremely tedious motor back from St Peter Port, at 3.5 knots, made this all too apparent. A larger prop enables you to achieve more thrust for the same revs, plus a folding prop will reduce the fuel consumption, as it finds the optimum blade angle to drive the boat forward for the boat speed. The drag, while sailing, is less than 0.5 knots. Although it was expensive to upgrade, the long-term reduction in diesel compensates for this. However, if you do fit one, remember to add greasing the prop annually to your maintenance schedule.

Drag as a function of speed for our current boat
© James Collier

- *Motoring sweet spot* Revs versus speed. With the exception of some modern boats, as your speed increases so does your drag and after a certain point your drag goes up exponentially. For our current boat, which is heavy displacement, up to about 4 knots (see graph above of speed versus drag) the drag is relatively minor. An extra knot to get you to 5 knots creates almost as much drag as the first 4 knots. Cruising at 7 knots is double the drag compared to cruising at 5.8 knots. In practice, on a calm day at 1800 rpm, we achieve roughly 6 knots with a fuel consumption of about 2.5 litres per hour. At 2200 rpm, we achieve about 7 knots cruising speed but the fuel consumption dramatically increases to 4.6 litres per hour as a result of the increased drag. In this example, reducing the speed by 1 knot to 6 knots saves 2.1 litres per hour. On a circumnavigation, it could reduce our fuel requirement by 275 litres. It is an easy way to extend your cruising budget, cruising range and reduce your environmental impact. Clearly, all types of boat are subject to other forces: tides, currents, headwinds which all impact the fuel efficiency, but it is worth understanding your fuel consumption at different rpm and then you can make an informed decision about your speed and the impact on your consumption. Some days there might be a tidal gate you need to make, so need to give it some welly, but on other days you might be prepared to sacrifice speed for a greener wake and less impact on the cruising budget.

If your boat doesn't have consumption charts (rpm versus fuel consumption), you can work out some averages at different rpm. Look at a fuel gauge/dip stick to see how much fuel you have in your tank – then for the next 20 hours do most of your motoring at your normal rpm. Note I say majority, as manoeuvring in harbour, different wind, tide and sea conditions will often determine your rpm. After 20 hours work out how much fuel you have used by refuelling. Then repeat the exercise at 1800 rpm. Clearly, the longer you can run this exercise the more accurate it will be, but roughly right is good enough.

- *Cruising Weight* Over the long term, reducing your cruising weight, and ensuring it is distributed evenly on board, will make a difference to your fuel efficiency. Though it tends to be more of a struggle as each year passes, as more 'stuff' gets brought onboard. The trick is, every season identify things that you really don't need and make sure you take them off. While most items make little difference to weight it does mean you get more space back.

Changing fuel sources for more sustainable ones
Going electric where possible

I do appreciate that if the electricity doesn't come from a renewable source, then this is still using fossil fuels, but hopefully the UK's electricity provision will become more sustainable over time.

- *For cooking* Electric marine cookers are available. Remember that they work off 240V, so you will need an inverter. You need to make sure that you have enough battery capacity, as you will lose 20 per cent on the transformation from 12V to AC current. There is a halfway house, to use a portable induction hob when on shore power, which we now do. It saves gas and hence reduces costs, plus it extends the life of your gas. Be warned though, you require pans with magnetic bases. You can also use mini electric ovens like the Remoska or an air fryer.

- *Electric outboard* As well as being greener than petrol, an electric outboard has many other advantages, such as not having to carry gasoline on board, and its reduced weight means it is easier to handle and it is quiet. While they are expensive upfront, they are much cheaper to run. We have operated ours for nine years and not spent a penny on servicing or on fuel. The only maintenance is to wash it at the end of the season!

- *Propulsion* While some new yachts and motor boats are being built that rely solely on electric propulsion, it is early days. It is assumed that most people will be looking for lower cost options that can be retrofitted rather than buying a new boat! Also, to be successful in becoming reliant solely on electric power means that you need to use Lithium (LiFePO4) batteries as this allows you to use more of the battery capacity (up to 90 per cent). However, it appears that insurance companies are not supporting retrofitted lithium batteries for propulsion, only for domestic service batteries.

Using more environmentally friendly diesel

Problematic emissions from the combustion of conventional crude-based diesel are: carbon dioxide (CO_2), sulphur oxides (SOx), nitrogen oxides (NOx) and particulate matter, though yachts don't emit a lot of sulphur. There is no ideal solution; Shell GTL (gas to liquids) which is derived from natural gas, helps reduce nitrogen oxides levels, particulate matter and unburnt hydrogen carbons but doesn't reduce CO_2 emissions. We use this currently in our engine, it doesn't have the same noxious smell that diesel has and seems to have performed well. There are bio-based fuels like HVO (hydrotreated vegetable oils), which are synthetic fuels, which reduce CO_2 and nitrogen oxides, however they are not yet available where most boats fill up in small marinas.

REDUCING THE CONTAMINANTS THAT GO INTO THE WATER

There are many sources of contamination that will degrade the quality of the water. Consider the risks and identify the actions that you can take to minimise what enters the water and, potentially, the food chain.

Fuel and Oil

See the table opposite for the main risks to address and how to minimise their impact.

Waste through outlets

Of the 14 people surveyed in 2023, 12 had black water holding tanks, but only two used a pump out, though not regularly because of the lack of facilities in marinas they stayed at. Most used their tanks but emptied them at sea. Sadly, the UK still lacks the infrastructure of pump out sites that we see in the Baltic, which means that you are unlikely to be able to dispose of your black water waste into a pump station. Grey water is waste water from your fresh water eg washing dishes, showers etc. It is possible to have a grey water system but it is not common due to the space required for a second holding tank (see table opposite).

Antifoul

Underwater growth, comprising of the build-up of marine organisms on hulls, has plagued mariners for millennia. Applying toxic substances to hulls is not a modern-day invention, there are accounts from 412 BC of arsenic and sulphur mixed in tar to coat hulls. Antifouling is toxic, expensive and is an obnoxious concoction to apply. But as it is a biocide, it is also very effective at preventing the fouling. While some harmful biocides have been prohibited, copper-based coatings are still

RISK	ACTIONS TO MINIMISE IMPACT
FUEL SPILLS DURING REFUELLING	• Use a funnel when refuelling • An absorbent mat in the gunwale behind the fuel pipe will catch spills before diesel runs down the scuppers into the sea. • Catch the drips when transferring the nozzle to and from your boat.
CONTAMINATED BILGE WATER BEING PUMPED INTO THE SEA	• Prevent any contamination going into the bilge by catching oil drips with an absorbent mat under the engine in the engine box, which has the added advantage of highlighting any oil leaks you have. If you have a regular problem, use an in-line bilge filter. • Keep the bilge as dry as possible, then should you need to remove any contaminated bilge water it will be a small quantity. Carry an empty 5l plastic container so you can store any contaminated bilge water till you can dispose of its contents safely.

being used. The toxic material leaches out and is ingested by small marine organisms, but it isn't selective, so it affects those that are not even responsible for fouling. The heavy metals affect the fish that feed on the marine organisms and hence the food chain is contaminated. The heavy metals have a long life and easily get reactivated with storms and other such natural disturbances. Take the Baltic, which is almost a captive body of water, as much as 40 per cent of all copper input comes from antifouling paints from ships and leisure yachts.*

However, allowing the fouling to grow unfettered increases the drag and reduces boat speed,

RISK	ACTIONS TO MINIMISE IMPACT
BLACK WATER	• Use a holding tank and pump out stations. If a pump out station is not available, store the black water enabling you to discharge it when you are out at sea, away from harbours, which will help reduce the environmental impact on sensitive areas of coast. • Always use shore facilities when available. • Don't put loo paper down the heads, it also helps to prevent blockages.
GREY WATER	• Using eco-friendly shampoos and dishwashing liquids that don't contain phosphates. • Laundry sheets are eco-friendly and less bulky, so ideal for the laundry runs ashore.
BOAT CLEANERS	• Use eco-friendly products with natural ingredients to clean inside and outside your boat. Avoid products that contain solvents, such as polyethylene, plastic microbeads, bleach (ammonia), chlorine. • Don't use cleaning wipes.
ANTIFREEZE	• Using eco-friendly antifreeze to winterise the heads rather than those based on ethanol glycol. Note: you must use ethanol glycol-based antifreeze in your engine cooling system. • Always dispose of your ethanol glycol-based antifreeze responsibly in designated facilities.

* Håkansson L and Palmgren M, 'Eco-friendly paint most effective against fouling on ships and boats', Chalmers University of Technology blog post, 12 December 2022

and hence, if you are motoring, it reduces your fuel efficiency, requiring you to burn more diesel, which equally has an environmental impact. How to solve this conundrum? The choice used to be simple, between hard or self-polishing antifouling paints. But the hard paints contain high levels of biocides that are released slowly, and the eroding paints contain lower levels but are released at a steadier rate and both have a negative impact on the aquatic environment. Copper based paints cause the most impact, but all have more or less the same result. It is an area which will develop rapidly, as the demand for more environmentally friendly alternatives and increased legislation will drive innovation and change. Given that it is a major issue for shipping, it will be interesting to see if any solutions can be used in the leisure industry.

There are three strategies to minimise your impact either replace, reduce or use it responsibly.

Much will depend on your marine environment as to what solution is appropriate for your boat. On a circumnavigation, your continued motion will help reduce the growth but not stop it completely.

RESPECT THE MARINE ENVIRONMENT

One of the highlights is the wildlife that you will see. However, you should:

- *Anchor with care* Choose anchorages away from sensitive sites to protect the seabed habitats. Use an existing mooring, rather than anchoring if within a seagrass bed. Avoid anchoring in anchor exclusion zones.
- *Mindful interactions with wildlife* Seeing without disturbing, so as not to cause any action that is likely to change their behaviour, whether you are on land or in your boat. Be especially careful during the breeding season.

	USE MORE ENVIRONMENTALLY FRIENDLY (NON-BIOCIDAL) ALTERNATIVES:
REPLACE	Non coating solutions: • Ultrasonic antifouling method, which uses ultrasound (high frequency sound) which either through the high frequency vibrations or small pressure changes, inhibits biofouling by algae or other single celled organisms without harming fish. Remember to take into account the current draw if you leave your boat. Coating solutions: • Use eco-friendly antifoul paints. There are several available now, copper-free coatings and enzyme-based systems. • Non-stick coatings (super sleek polishes) they don't significantly prevent fouling, they just make it easier to wipe off. However, as they rely on a minimum speed of 15 knots for at least 75 per cent of the time, they are not applicable to cruising yachts and are aimed at racing or motorboats.
REDUCE	• Underwater hull cleaning robot/drone which also monitors your hull eg Keelcrab • Boat washes: Using less antifouling and a boat wash. However, regular boat washes can be expensive and the availability of them is mainly only in large yachting centres.
RESPONSIBLE USE	• Use protective clothing, put protection on the ground to capture debris from the removal and drips from the paint. • Dispose of all material responsibly.

REDUCTION OF WASTE

What makes sense for different boat crews will depend on what and how much you consume. These are areas where we have changed our behaviour:

The Green Blue environmental programme produces some useful information leaflets, which give good guidance in many of these areas: www.thegreenblue.org.uk

USE OF RECYCLED PRODUCTS	○ Selling/buying chandlery items on selling platforms: eBay, Marketplace etc or at boat jumbles. ○ Use rope that is made of sustainable material or recycled products.
CARDBOARD RECYCLING	○ Leave as much as possible at the supermarket when doing your shopping. ○ Separate the cardboard from the rubbish. Separating out the dry recyclable materials (like paper/cardboard) is more practical on a boat if you have to store it before you find a recycling bin.
REDUCE SINGLE USE PLASTIC	○ Ditch cling film and use Tupperware boxes, silicon lids, beeswax wraps instead. ○ Sodastream on board: We use the marina water and a SodaStream to make fizzy water, it reduces single use plastic, and it saves us carrying the heavy bottles back from the supermarket.
ELECTRONIC DISTRESS FLARES	○ They last longer than pyrotechnic flares in terms of shelf life and they are effective for longer in duration of use. Plus, pyrotechnic flares are hard to dispose of.

Our electric Torquedo outboard

CHAPTER EIGHT

MOORING AND ANCHORING

One of the pleasures of a circumnavigation is the wide variety of harbours and anchorages that you will visit on your cruise. This is particularly true if you are used to sailing in crowded waters, where marinas dominate and the opportunity to find a quiet anchorage is rare. On this cruise, you will experience everything from bustling fishing ports, where the harbour is still at the heart of the community, to deserted anchorages far from civilisation. The diversity of harbours does mean that you need to be prepared for different mooring situations. The survey showed that you need to be able to cope with anchoring, buoys, pontoons, marinas and walls, though most boats were able to avoid drying out unless they wanted to. The types of mooring used by the boats surveyed is as follows:

Compared to the last survey I did, the average number of marina nights has dramatically increased from 34 to 43 with the highest number of nights spent in marinas going from 76 to 163 nights. This was expected, as the number of marinas has been increasing. But of more interest was that the average number of nights had also increased; the highest being 60 nights at anchor, which represented 55 per cent of their cruise. I suspect this is because the information about good anchorages has improved, along with Antares Charts giving more certainty when exploring. If your route planning is based on maximising the number of nights in a marina; then you will lose out on much of the real essence of a circumnavigation.

MOORING TYPE	YACHTS (42)		MOTOR BOATS (6)	
	AVERAGE NUMBER OF DAYS	MAXIMUM NUMBER OF DAYS	AVERAGE NUMBER OF DAYS	MAXIMUM NUMBER OF DAYS
Anchor	14	60	9	30
Buoys	10	31	10	21
Pontoon	12	32	9	37
Marina	43	163	25	37
Walls (afloat)	8	28	7	13
Drying	3	4	3	6

MOORING
Mooring buoys

There are two aspects to bear in mind when you are using a mooring buoy:

- **Be safe** Make sure you pick a buoy that you know is regularly inspected and is rated for a greater tonnage than your vessel. Chafing of rope is a risk, so have the right equipment to minimise the chance of it being an issue; either moor with two ropes or have a section of chain spliced into your mooring buoy rope, or tie it directly onto the ring with a knot. Also watch out for chafing on the bow roller, so use strong material as a chafe guard, for example, plastic hose pipe (see page 88).

- **Be prepared** Never rely on a visitor's buoy being available, be prepared to anchor. Many buoys have no pick up, so threading a rope through the ring can prove tricky. We have a loop stitched in the end of our buoy mooring rope, which we can pass through the ring and use the boat hook to pick up the loop.

The easiest way to pick up a buoy is to lasso it. Cleat off both ends of the long mooring warp, then coil the rope and split the coils so that you have half in one hand and half in the other. When you are nearly directly over the buoy, throw the coils up and out, so that the big loop goes over the buoy; this then enables you to make a more permanent attachment to the buoy in a more controlled way.

There are still some buoys which are provided free of charge: Bord Failte, Ireland's Department of the Marine and Coastal County Councils, has laid a series of visitor moorings at selected locations. The moorings are large, coloured bright yellow and are labelled 'VISITOR – 15 Tons', though a small daily charge may be levied at some locations.

Walls

One of the challenges of walls is to have enough slack in your lines to cope with the range of tide, but enough tension to stay close to the wall as the tide rises. Weights such as an anchor angel, suspended on the mooring lines, are excellent for this. It is difficult to spring off a wall, especially at low tide. A boat hook is invaluable to push

Tied up alongside Stonehaven quay

off, though make sure that you keep the hook part inboard and push off with the handle. In the worst-case scenario, with the hook against the wall, it could snap or get stuck. We carried a 4ft (1.2m) wooden pole with a diameter of 3in (8cm), for this purpose; it stopped the boat hook getting damaged.

Fender board

If you value your GRP or wooden topsides, then a fender board is a must. On many occasions you will need to use it when mooring against a wall or pilings, or when refuelling. Many of the cheapest refuelling points are designed primarily for fishing boats that are a little more robust than a yacht.

Fender boards are easy to make, but the key is not to make them too heavy, as they become difficult to hold and manoeuvre. Ours is made from pre-treated timber, sanded to remove the rough edges. The dimensions are: 0.9in (2.2cm) thick, 5.4in (13.8cm) wide and 5ft 7in (1.7m) long. By drilling through the thickness of the board as shown in the photo, the board will hang horizontally and, more importantly, the side that faces away from the boat has no rope, ensuring that it will not get chafed through by rough walls. Two short lengths of 0.16in (4mm) cord are permanently attached to the fender board, making it really easy to tie it to the boat for storage along the gunwales.

If you have to moor against piles, it is very difficult to judge where the board needs to be located. Hang three fenders where the distance between each one is not less than the board; this enables you to move it relatively quickly to the right spot.

Mooring in canal locks

In canals, you will be required to moor against walls in the locks, and at designated mooring spots such as fixed pontoons or in marinas. Anchoring is also possible in the great lochs that make up the Caledonian Canal. Since a canal has no tide, as a general rule you don't need springs; just moor with a head and stern line.

The canals are always kept in immaculate condition. Lock keepers maintain them with a real sense of pride and there are well tended gardens – and spotless paint work. We chose an idyllic staging by Bellanoch Bridge on the Crinan Canal, a beautiful spot overlooking the River Add. The mooring posts were shiny black and we found out why – they had just been painted. The paint streaks on our lines now bring back happy memories of that night on the canal.

Entering the lock

Make up both sides so that you can change sides quickly, as you never know what other boats in front of you are going to do. Tie a big bowline in the end of your lines and you can either throw it to the lock keeper or loop it onto an extendable boat hook, so that you can just pass it up. For this you will need two boat hooks on board. This makes getting the rope to the lock keeper much easier, and was recommended to us by the lock staff on the Crinan Canal. It is far more successful than trying to throw the rope to the lock keeper. Make sure that you have long enough ropes, particularly in the sea locks. You may need to tie two ropes together.

MOORING AND ANCHORING **87**

The water rushes in at quite a rate in a sea lock; this is Ardrishaig, Crinan Canal

Rising in a canal

When in a lock, where the water will rise, it is important to keep the head rope tight, as the water will rush in at an alarming rate. Also, keep clear of the underwater paddles at the front of the lock.

Descending in a canal

The water will be dropping, so keep the stern rope tight. Though never cleat off any of the ropes, as you will end up suspended as the water disappears. If you have had to tie two ropes together, watch out for the knot so that it doesn't get stuck at the fairlead. Stay away from the cill at the back of the lock.

Fender cloth

The lock walls are rough stone from which small flakes and grit can embed themselves into your fenders. A fender cloth will protect your topsides from this grit and you can clean off your fenders once you have left the canal. We only had one so always tried to tie up on the side that was protected by the fender cloth. Ideally have two fender cloths if you are planning to use a canal.

GENERAL MOORING EQUIPMENT

Warps

Ensure that you have enough warps for mooring in marinas, canals or alongside walls. In order to make it easy to identify the length of the warp quickly, use different coloured whippings to indicate the length.

WARP TYPE	COMMENTS
2 long shore lines	2–3 x boat length. These are needed for canals (especially sea locks), walls or rafting up. Remember that a wall requires 4 times the range of tide.
2 long warps	At least 1.2 x the length of the boat.
4 warps	At least the length of the boat.
Heavy set of warps	Needed for storm conditions.

Snubbers

Have four snubbers for the shore lines, so that they take the snatching strain rather than your fairleads or deck fittings.

Chafe guards

Chafing can quickly slice through rope and warps, and has been a sailors' nightmare for centuries. Prevent it by the following:

- Use plastic hose or tough webbing covers that make a tube, with Velcro to prevent warps chafing on the fairleads.
- If you moor next to a wall, use chafe guards to protect the rope at the shore end. A few hours rubbing against the stone will cut the rope like a wire cutter through cheese.
- Tying up to a ring on a stone pier can soon chafe lines. A bit of wood or a stick, to lift up the ring, will reduce the friction on the line.

ANCHORING

If you need any more encouragement to anchor, then Holy Island should whet the appetite! Where else would you use two castles as anchor bearings?

Ground tackle

Good anchoring starts with having the right equipment. Each piece of your ground tackle – anchor, chain and shackle – should be sized correctly for the loads expected. You should also use seizing wire to secure the shackle key. Your anchor should be at least the recommended size for your boat, but it is advisable to have an anchor one size larger than this. You should have enough equipment to be able to lay out two anchors if you are caught out in windy weather. There are many good articles in the boating magazines about anchors with the best holding power, and everyone will have their own preference. You need to be able to hold in sand, mud, rock and weed. There will be some situations with rock or weed when only the fisherman anchor will hold. The minimum number of anchors you should carry is two; we took three anchors for a 38ft (11.6m) boat (see page opposite).

Type of rode/cable

There are advantages and disadvantages of chain and line. With chain you prevent chafing, but the snatching is greater, plus the additional weight can be an issue up forward. The snatching can be reduced with the use of an anchor snubber. You can also have a mixture of both; chain with

Anchoring off Holy Island, with Bamburgh Castle on the skyline; you can see the leading beacons clearly

TYPE OF ANCHOR	WEIGHT	COMMENTS
Spade	20kg	Bower anchor attached to 60m (197ft) chain. The convex shape of the spade anchor increases its holding power; we were extremely impressed with its performance, having replaced our old CQR.
Bruce	15kg	Spare 50m (164ft) chain not attached.
Fisherman	18kg	Taken in case we needed to anchor in weed. Stored below.

rope spliced onto the chain and this mitigates some of the disadvantages. The Clyde Cruising Club *Sailing Directions* recommend a 60m (197ft) chain for anchoring in Scotland.

Anchor snubber

An anchor snubber is generally a length of 33ft (10m) to 49ft (15m) nylon rope measuring 0.5in (12mm) in diameter, which is attached to the chain, either with a rolling hitch or anchor hook and made fast to a cleat or Sampson post. This will prevent any of the boat's weight being held on the anchor windlass. It will also act as a shock absorber, to reduce the effect of snatching on the anchor, which could cause it to drag. Hence you should use a rope that stretches easily, such as nylon. In normal conditions, we would let out 9–13ft (3–4m) more in stringer winds. It is important to attach the snubber to the chain with a knot or hook that can be released in a hurry.

Anchor windlass

If you can fit an electric windlass on board, it has one big safety advantage over a manual windlass: you may have to raise your anchor a couple of times to get it to set correctly; it is therefore less stressful to use an electric windlass, as you are more likely to set it correctly. However, this increases your power requirements.

Anchor chum or angel

An anchor chum is a heavy weight that is attached to the anchor chain or rode and lowered down towards the anchor. There seems to be quite a range

Ituna anchored in Puilladobhrain

of opinion as to how effective they are. They are designed to reduce your swinging circle but it also has a dampening effect when the chain is snatching.

Riding sail
While the chances of gales are reduced in the summer, they may still occur. Tony Brimble (*Gitana*, Crealock 34) rode out a force 9 at the end of May at anchor in Loch Ewe. If caught at anchor in a storm a riding sail will help; it reduces the amount and speed that the boat will yaw by reducing the swinging arc, as it keeps the boat's head closer to the wind. This reduces the snatching, which is what causes the anchor to drag. The very small sail is hanked onto the backstay and the tack attached with a strop to a strong point in the cockpit, hoisted on the main halyard and the sheet led forward to a cleat amidship. While not essential, a riding sail will certainly help.

Bow fender
We have a fender that protects the stern when we are anchoring or on a mooring buoy.

Anchor buoy and tripping line
Make sure you mark 'anchor' on the buoy so that other boats don't mistake it for a mooring buoy. If you are anchoring near fish farms, it is advisable to set a trip buoy.

Monitoring your situation
Anchor watch
During the day you obviously need to take anchor bearings, but at night you are unlikely to be able to see any lights in remote anchorages. We now use an app called Anchor on the iPad; on anchoring we press 'set anchor', we then set the alarm zone xm from the anchor. We also make a note of the anchor position. The app records the boat's meanderings around the anchor, which in itself is fascinating! The iPad can then be placed next to you while you sleep, guaranteeing it will wake you should the boat stray outside the limit you set. If it is very windy and you are expecting a wind shift, you should maintain an anchor watch, in which case you are unlikely to be sleeping anyway!

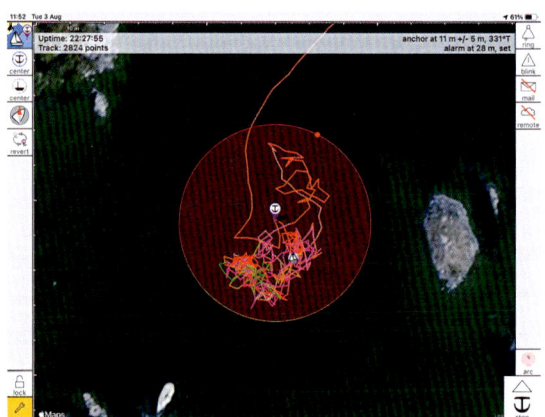
Anchor app in action

DINGHY AND OUTBOARD

A dinghy is an essential bit of kit if you want to explore your surroundings when at anchor or tied up to a mooring buoy. An outboard is strongly recommended, as sometimes you will be quite a distance from the shore. Some landings for dinghies can be crowded, and a long painter will allow you to keep your dinghy out of harm's way. We had a strop and padlock for the dinghy ashore but never felt the need to use it. The strop and padlock were, however, useful to secure our lifejackets in the dinghy to avoid having to carry them around. You won't need to do this everywhere though – many remote communities don't even lock their houses or cars.

If you have davits for a dinghy you are very lucky, because blowing it up and deflating it is a real pain. Many people on the west coast of Scotland towed theirs; we tended not to, preferring to deflate it and tie it to the foredeck. If you choose to stow it, a 10 litre foot pump or a 12 volt electric pump takes some of the effort out of pumping it up each time. A Low Voltage Motor (LVM) pump takes less than a minute to inflate an average-sized dinghy. It uses about 25 amps at 12 volts; if you don't want to power it via crocodile clips and cables to the ship's battery, then it needs a special cable loop and plug. It is a good idea to wire an external deck plug direct to the domestic busbar via a 30 amp circuit breaker; it is sensitive to voltage, and anything more than 12 volts may cause it to burn out, so it comes with a warning not to use it when the alternator is charging.

We used a handy billy to raise and lower the outboard to the waterline. Ours was attached to a cage on the push pit, but I have also seen them on a single davit. It does make the task of lowering the outboard to the dinghy much easier. But now we have an electric outboard which can be picked up with one hand, negating any need for a davit or block and tackle system. We also decided to carry a spare pair of oars, having once had an oar disintegrate. The list of recommended anchoring and mooring equipment we carried is below:

ANCHORING AND MOORING	ALONGSIDE	DINGHY AND OUTBOARD
Bower anchor and 60m (197ft) chain	Fenders	Dinghy
Spare Bruce and fisherman anchors	2 fender cloths	Outboard
Anchor ball	2 boat hooks	Oars
Anchor chum	Heavy duty warps	Spare oars (not essential)
Anchor snubber	Warps	Fuel can
Anchor fender	Snubbers	Starter cord or key
Anchor light if not on mast head light	Chafe guards	Dinghy bag (for keeping things dry when in the dinghy)
Riding sail (not essential)		Small dinghy anchor
50m (164ft) spare chain and 50m (164ft) rope rode		10-litre dinghy pump
Tripping line and buoy		Dinghy boarding ladder
Walkie-talkies		Fuel
Mooring buoy rope		

CHAPTER NINE

WEATHER

Normally, we only really notice whether it is sunny or raining. During this trip we became far more aware of the weather: the cloud formations, their height, the wind strength and its effect on the water and the environment, as it had such a big impact on our everyday existence. It is unlikely that you are going to be at sea for days, unless your time available is very short. You are always trying to work out: should I go today? What will the conditions be like? Will the harbour be sheltered? When is the next weather window? Therefore, you need to be able to:

- Check local weather conditions through local observation.
- Receive short- to medium-term forecasts (the next 6–48 hours).
- Obtain long-term weather forecasts (3–7 days).

Local observation

It is important to check the weather conditions through observation. Do your observations match the forecast? Even though the location where you are moored is sheltered, the weather conditions may be totally different round the next headland. You can get additional information on local conditions from the following sources:

- *Local harbourmaster* For instance, in Newcastle upon Tyne, the marinas are several miles up the river but the harbourmaster will give you information about the conditions at the entrance. This is particularly useful for visibility, especially for your next destination.
- *Observation of surrounding features on land* In Inverness, the marina was sheltered from the wind but there was a tree on the opposite bank of the river. A reading of force 2 in the marina could have misled us but when we saw the tree swaying vigorously, it confirmed a forecast of force 6 out to sea.
- *Observation of the clouds* A forecast of thundery showers while in Dartmouth might have seen us stay in harbour, but the lack of cumulonimbus clouds gave us the confidence to make the three-hour sail to Salcombe.
- *Observation of the barometer* It is invaluable and it will give you an indication of approaching bad weather.

However, you don't always get it right: when we left Helmsdale it appeared relatively calm but we were in the shadow of the mountains of Sutherland, and a few miles out to sea we had 32 knots of apparent wind so we turned around and

WEATHER

Weather to sail
16–17 May – Dale to Holyhead

It was twilight when we raised the anchor. Neither of us had slept well, an uncomfortable swell that affected our anchorage off Dale, but we planned to be in Fishguard by about 1pm. Out past St Anne's Head, the sun was rising but with little wind; we motored. Cutting between the bird sanctuary islands of Grassholm and Skomer we glimpsed comical puffins for the first time. We were unable to take the inside track past the islands, but as it was calm we cut in close to the Bishops and Clerks, some rocky outcrops with fast tidal streams that produce overfalls and whirlpools. Going through was quite dramatic – the sea appeared to boil, but the tidal acceleration sped us quickly round St David's Head, then round to Stumble Head. We dropped the anchor just off Lower Fishguard. We needed some stores, so inflated the dinghy, went ashore and climbed into town (there is a reason it is called Lower Fishguard).

Back on board Mags got some sleep and I pottered and then got the long range forecast… ugh. While we had been expecting strong SW winds on Wednesday/Thursday, the forecast had been upgraded to severe gale 9. Not fun in an anchorage. We had two options: ride out the storm at anchor then make for Holyhead after the storm had passed with disturbed seas, or head to a safer harbour straight away. My heart just wanted an early night and to be tucked up in bed; it had been a tiring day with an early start and not much sleep the previous night. But my head knew that the most sensible option was to run for Holyhead and make it in before the storm. We had a quick bite to eat, and then set sail. Ironically there was very little wind, and by 1am a thick fog descended. For the last hour of our trip to Holyhead, the wind started to blow and the heavens opened – an indication of what was to come. But safely tied up in harbour – albeit resembling drowned rats – we knew we had made the right decision. We listened to the howling wind and did not have to worry about whether the anchor was holding.

---

went back into Helmsdale. After all, we had four months to complete the trip!

Short- to medium-term forecasts

Receiving a short- to medium-term forecast will give you an indication of the weather for your current leg and, coupled with your local observations, will determine whether you should sail. It will also advise you of any changes in the weather once you have set off. With 48-hour visibility, you will have an indication as to whether you will be moving on the next day too.

Long-term weather forecasts

You need to be able to obtain and use long-term weather forecasts (three to seven days) to enable you to plan and pick your weather windows. Careful use of these forecasts will allow you to miss the really bad weather but gives you the opportunity to push on when there is a weather window. It enabled us to avoid some very nasty conditions, as our log entry for 16–17 May (above) shows.

SOURCES OF WEATHER FORECASTS

Weather apps and online forecasts have revolutionised the access to forecasts. Thankfully, you no longer need to wake up at an ungodly hour to catch the shipping forecast. The apps are easier to interpret than manually examining surface pressure charts, plus they provide more granular information. The challenge is that now there is an abundance of them and often conflicting ones, there's a danger that you pick the forecast that you want! So always make sure that the forecast bears a resemblance to what you are observing locally. If you do find that you have lots of conflicting forecasts, it is likely that the forecast confidence is low; hence you should be prepared for changeable weather.

Forecasting models

A hundred years ago, the British mathematician Lewis Fry Richardson modelled the weather by dividing up the atmosphere into boxes, using observations and the laws of physics, and he then calculated separate pressure, temperature, humidity, wind speed and wind direction for each box. Given that his forecast was published 10 years after the initial readings, his work was largely ignored! But the advent of computing, made this approach feasible and is now called Numerical Weather Prediction (NWP).

The models are now more complex, as they take into account the conditions at the boundary between each box, mathematical equations that encapsulate the relationships between speed and wind direction, air temperature, pressure, density and humidity. It also has to represent different processes that occur in each box, as well as processing massive quantities of data of the existing conditions from a variety of sources: satellites, aeroplanes, radiosondes, buoy and ground stations to name a few. When you consider that global models can contain 10 million boxes, it requires an extraordinary amount of computing power.

Resolution

Like pixels in a photo, the more boxes you have in the model, the more detail you will see. But this detail requires more computer memory and processing power. There is always a compromise between the number of boxes, usually described as the 'resolution' of the model, and the computing resources available to run the model in time for the next forecast. A model with fewer larger boxes (lower resolution) permits more rapid model calculations, but may misrepresent important weather features at smaller scales.

Scale

There are weather organisations that run their own models at various scales, covering different sized areas, and hence relate to a time frame for which the forecast is valid. Thus, a global forecast is used to issue predictions such as 'it will be a barbecue summer'.

Limited Area Models (LAMs), which are a mesoscale, are often run by national weather

	MICROSCALE	MESOSCALE	SYNOPTIC	GLOBAL
HORIZONTAL LENGTH	1km and smaller	1km to 250km	250km to 2,000km	2,000km to planet-encircling
TIMESCALE	Minutes	Hours	Days	Weeks to season
EXAMPLE	Cumulus clouds	Sea breeze	Weather system	Jet stream

services but the increased computational demands of a high-resolution model mean that these forecasts only cover a couple days ahead, and are limited to a small area, for example DWD ICON-EU. It has the advantage over some other LAMs covering the UK and Ireland, as its area projects further into the Atlantic than those whose western boundaries are close to Ireland.

FORECASTS

The traditional providers, UK Met Office and Met Éireann, forecasts still provide the backbone of most circumnavigators' weather information. Forecasts are available online and broadcast on VHF.

UK Meteorological (Met) Office

- **Inshore forecast** This is for 19 areas up to 12 miles offshore for the next 24 and 48 hours for the UK. You will track your progress as you enter each new sea area which is bounded by a prominent headland. Some of the radio forecasts contain observations from 20 UK coastal stations.
- **Shipping forecast** Provided for the offshore sea areas for the next 24 hours, these cover much larger sea areas and rarely include the variations that occur near land, so the inshore forecast is more helpful.
- **Strong wind and gale warnings** A strong wind warning is issued for the yachtsman's gale: a force 6. One advantage of the inshore forecast over the shipping forecast is that winds over force 6 are monitored and strong wind warnings are issued.
- **Latest marine observations** There are 28 marine observation points on the coast with hourly updated information, including some Irish coastal information. There are an additional eight useful coastal waters observation points.
- **Rainfall Radar** Forecasts up to five days in advance.
- **Surface pressure maps** Either static or animated pressure maps issued every 12 hours for first three days, then every day for the next two days.

Met Éireann

Met Éireann provides forecasts for Ireland, including Northern Ireland, and covers:

- **Inshore weather forecasts** These are covered by two areas for Ireland for up to 30 miles offshore, and are valid for 24 hours, with a further forecast for the next 24 hours but for the whole area.
- **Hourly readings from buoys round the Irish coast** Locations and current readings can be found at www.met.ie/forecasts/marine-inland-lakes/buoys
- **Small craft warnings** These are issued if winds are forecast to be force 6 or above and are expected up to 10nm offshore.
- **Atlantic charts** These show surface pressure, rainfall, temperature and cloud for the current day at midday and 24 hours later.

Apps and online forecasts

When choosing which apps you will use, it is helpful to understand which model is behind the app, what is the resolution, scale and what area is covered by the model, so that you can appreciate any limitations. LuckGrib (www.luckgrib.com) is a useful reference, as it displays the area that the different models cover. Many apps have the same models behind them, yet they can look very different, with alternative ways of representing the same information. Some of these are more

FORECAST MODEL	RESOLUTION AND RANGE	UPDATES PER DAY	APPS	COMMENT
ECMWF (EUROPEAN)	9km 10 days	2	PredictWind, Windy.com, Windy.app	Best resolution for a global model
UKMO	15km 7 days	2	PredictWind	
UKV	1.5 to 4km 5 days	8	Windy.com PredictWind	Input from UKMO UK and Ireland
GFS (US)	27km 13km grid 10 days	4	PocketGrib, XC weather Windguru, Passage weather, Windfinder, Weather4D	Doesn't consider topography – so not good inshore, but good for oceans
WRF	12km & 6.5km 5 days	1	Windguru, Passage weather	Model doesn't cover north Scotland
DWD ICON7-EU (EUROPEAN)	7km 5 days	8	Windy.com, Ventusky Windy.app, Windguru Weather4D	Excellent LAM for UK and Ireland
SPIRE	12km 10 days	2	PredictWind	Good in remote sensing of atmosphere use changes in radio signals hence good for offshore
PWE	1km 7 days	2	PredictWind	PredictWind's own coastal model Input from on ECMWF

effective than others, so it can be a matter of personal choice. While there is much that is free, you might need to pay a subscription to access more information, greater resolutions, increased time frames, no delays before the forecasts are published and a choice of models. The table above shows all the relevant models to a circumnavigation and popular apps that use them.

Blended forecasts

These are forecasts that are generated by a model but then have a forecaster's input. Weather web (www.premium.weatherweb.net) gives you access to such forecasts under a subscription model. Sailing forecasts can be obtained online or emailed to you. The site has a learning zone with videos, where you can expand your weather knowledge, and videos about the upcoming weather conditions; they also run a weather school.

Forecasts requiring specialist software

A GRIB file is a compressed digital data file that enables weather data to be transmitted effectively across mobile networks (GSM, GPRS and 3G), HF or satellite. When loaded into appropriate software, it can produce weather maps with coastlines, latitude and longitude grid lines and isobars are displayed. Once the GRIB files are loaded it can be viewed offline. Some software is free and others chargeable; the differences are seen in the ease of data access, the presentation format and ease of use, and the data available. GRIB files are also used in some charting software (see Chapter 11), fronts usually aren't shown but it does show sea state. Areas can be zoomed in on, however, you need to be aware of the resolution of the model used. Zooming in on a low-resolution model doesn't increase the detail. Beware, the program will generate smooth interpolation of the nearby data points, that is fill in the gaps; a good program will indicate which ones are generated by the model.

LuckGrib was created by a sailor who was frustrated with what was available. They charge a very reasonable fixed price, rather than a subscription, but sadly only for iOS; it can be viewed on an iPad or a Mac. Their main application displays animated weather files, visually showing different parameters, such as wind, rain and swell, plus you can select the forecasting model you want to use. As well as the routing software application, they have some interesting material weather tutorials. Bill Aylward (*Picaro*, Vancouver 34) is a fan of LuckGrib because it's as close to the original source information, as it's possible to get without the 'interpretation' that many weather apps add.

Jet stream

The polar jet stream, with its strong winds concentrated into narrow bands in the tropopause (approximate altitude of 10,000m), flows round the Earth from west to east, but it also meanders in loops north to south. It is this north/south position that has a profound impact on the UK weather and marks the greatest contrast in surface temperature, between the cold air to the north and warmer air to the south. If the jet stream loops further south than usual, across the North Atlantic and the UK, then it will steer depressions across the UK. But likewise, if it passes well to the north of the UK in the summer, this will result in warm air covering the country, the Azores high may then extend northwards and eastwards, bringing settled weather. Consequently, knowing where the jet stream is in relation to the UK is a good indication of the weather to come. In the photo below the south of England saw temperatures of 24°C in October and Scotland had torrential rain.

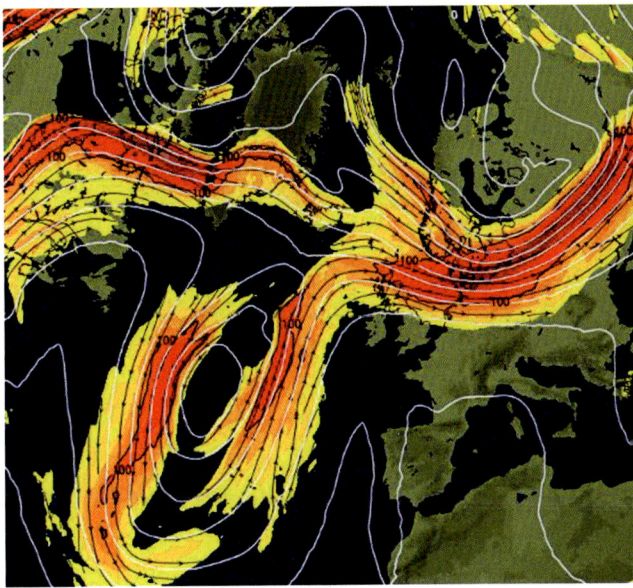

Jet stream © Netweather

In reality the jet stream forecast will give you little information that will impact daily passages. However, it might give you clues that the current weather pattern will change. If you see a dramatic movement in the jet stream it can give you hope, if you are having a series of depressions funnelled over the UK. A 14-day Jet stream forecast can be found here: www.netweather.tv/charts-and-data/jetstream.

Sea conditions in the Sound of Hoy, with wind over tide

Sea conditions

Traditional forecasts just forecast the sea state, but apps are able to display more rich data, the height, direction and even wavelength of the swell. This can make a real difference to your progress and your comfort on board. Heading directly into the large, short chop, will see your speed drain away, along with your enjoyment. But bear away 30 degrees and you can make reasonable progress and morale is restored. Consequently, it is key information for route planning. One other factor to be aware of is wind driven current. According to Penny Haire from the Royal Institute of Navigation, wind drives current at 3 per cent, so 20 knots of wind will create a current of 0.6 knots – useful planning information.

Accuracy

With enhanced models and increased computing power, weather forecasts are improving but they will never be perfect. Also, the time frame of a model could be in one or three hour time intervals, so trying to sum up wind strength at best in two figures: winds and gusts, is a tall order. In the words of Frank Singleton, sailor and weather guru 'always assume that, on some stage on a passage, you will encounter winds greater or less, by one Beaufort force, than predicted.'

RECEIVING

Connectivity to the internet is essential for most of these apps, as they don't have an offline capability. However, mobile connectivity is not guaranteed, particularly in some parts of your route, such as the more remote parts of the west coast of Scotland. It is worth taking a screenshot of the forecast to ensure that you can see it even when there is no connectivity. When internet coverage is limited, VHF can still prove invaluable for receiving the inshore weather forecasts from the coastguard.

NAVTEX

NAVTEX is transmitted over the Global Maritime Distress and Safety System (GMDSS) and provides maritime information: the weather forecast, Subfacts (submarine information), Gunfacts (gunnery range firing information) and other safety information such as navigational warnings. It is broadcast on two frequencies; both are needed to receive the inshore (490Hz) and offshore (518Hz) forecasts. You select the stations and type of information required. Interestingly, no one surveyed after 2018 used NAVTEX on their cruise.

SURVEY RESULTS FOR FORECASTING

The last few years have seen dramatic changes in the field of weather forecasts, so I am only using the results of the most recent surveys for this section, hence it is based on 14 circumnavigations.

Accessing the forecast

All used a combination of methods to access forecasts, but all used the internet as their primary source of obtaining a forecast, GRIB files and specialist software being the next most common way of accessing them.

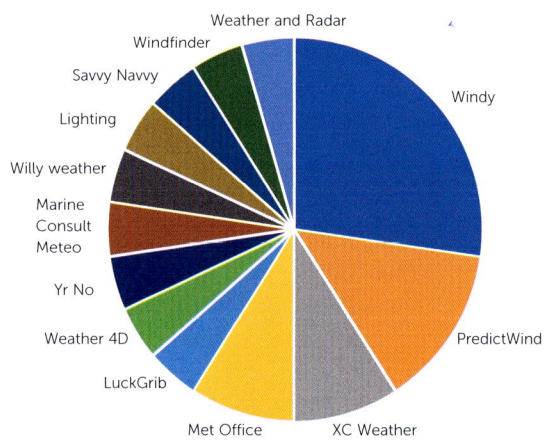

Weather Apps used, based on 14 surveys

Castletownshend to the right

Which forecast?

All bar one surveyed used the Met Office Inshore forecast daily, and 50 per cent of those surveyed used surface pressure charts every couple of days. When it came to apps, 30 per cent used just one app, while the remainder used multiple apps. The most common app used was Windy (note this is windy.com) followed by PredictWind; both using the key forecasting models for the UK and Ireland. Note Met Office in the pie chart is the app for land-based weather.

COASTAL CRUISING

The real challenge for any forecast is that the winds close to the coast are influenced by the shape of the land, the differential of land and sea temperatures, the different frictional forces over land and sea, and the state of the tide. As the majority of your cruise is spent in coastal waters, you will encounter many of these effects.

Sea breezes

Sea breezes are caused by the imbalance in heating between the land and the sea, when the land heats faster than the sea. A sea breeze usually starts to develop on cloudless summer mornings. As the land heats up, the air above it rises. To replace this rising air, cooler air is drawn in from the sea and an on-shore breeze develops, known as a 'sea breeze'. On a hot summer's day, a typical sea breeze can extend about 15 miles out to sea and may add 10 knots to the overall speed of the wind. The sea breeze tends to reach its peak in the late afternoon and early evening, before dying away at dusk, as the land loses its heat. Accompanying the sea breeze may be a line of cumulus cloud along the coastline, on what would otherwise be a cloudless day.

Sea breezes don't always form. One of the reasons for this may be that the wind is blowing off-shore and the on-shore sea breeze needs to

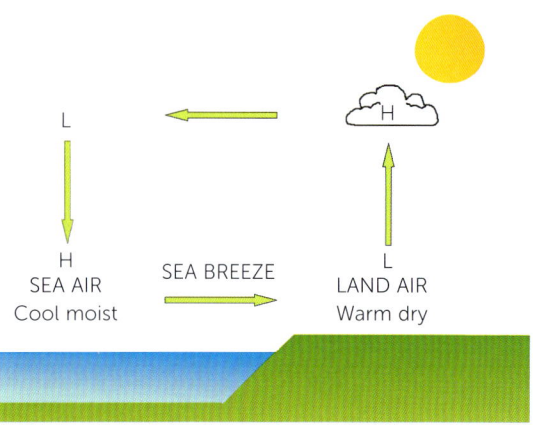

Diagram showing how the sea breeze forms

overcome this competing flow. There are days when this effect simply delays the onset of the breeze, but other days where it can disrupt it altogether.

Initially the sea breeze will be blowing directly on-shore, but during the day the winds gradually veer, eventually blowing parallel to the shore. If you are on a clockwise circuit, this can be very frustrating as you have head winds on many afternoons along the North Sea. I know this from bitter experience.

Headlands, bays and islands complicate the picture when predicting the direction and strength of the sea breeze. A headland will strengthen a sea breeze, while a peninsula will see the wind blowing towards the main land mass and this can lead to a build-up of air over the land mass, perhaps triggering showers or thunderstorms. A bay, however, will see a weakening of a sea breeze.

Land or offshore breeze

The land, while it heats up faster than the sea, also cools down faster. Given certain conditions, such as a clear sky at night, calm conditions and sea temperatures at their maximum, as in autumn, then the sea can be warmer than the land. You then have the reverse situation to a sea breeze. An off-shore breeze can establish itself in the early hours, when the air from the land fills the space of the air that is rising over the sea. It can be felt up to 10 miles out to sea; it reaches its peak at 3am and dies away at dawn.

Katabatic winds

Katabatic comes from the Greek *katabaino* – to go down. This word is used to describe those winds that descend from mountains to the area below. In Scotland and Wales, on clear nights in the high mountains and hills, the land loses heat quickly, a large pool of cold, dense air builds up and is trapped until it eventually spills over the side of the mountain, and rushes down the glens and valleys producing katabatic winds. They can be strengthened by the shape of the surrounding landscape. It can catch you out at anchor, when the wind can increase by two levels on the

DEW POINT HEIGHT	FOG TYPE
Dew point of air above the sea is very high and generally the sea temperature is lower	Extensive or widespread fog
Dew point of the air a little above sea temperature and in some places not above it	Fog banks
Dew point of air is only just above sea temperatures in some patches	Fog patches

Beaufort Scale and then return to a gentle breeze later on.

The effect of the landscape

As a river changes direction and speed when in contact with rocks and banks, so does the wind round headlands and valleys. A gentle breeze can bend more than 90° round a headland. A slightly stronger breeze may bend slightly less, around 25°. A force 7 wind will only change direction marginally around a headland. However, it also accelerates around headlands, sometimes by up to 30 per cent. Islands will also disrupt the wind, so be ready for changes in direction and strength.

Land exerts more drag on the wind than the sea and so when the wind blows parallel to the coast, it causes changes in direction. Winds will converge or diverge depending on which side of the wind the land is. If there is an east wind on the south coast of England, or a west wind on the north coast of Scotland, then they will converge with the shoreline (up to about 20 to 30°). This results in a stronger band of wind within about 3 miles of the coast – an increase of wind strength by up to 10 knots – and it veers towards the coast. When winds are blowing in the opposite direction they diverge, which may result in lighter winds near the coast, unless affected by land and sea breezes. When the wind blows at right angles to the shore, there is little convergence or divergence. However, an offshore wind can veer by 15° over the sea.

Sea fog

Sea, or advection, fog is a real hazard. Fog forms when the warm air is cooled from below, until it can no longer 'hold' the moisture that was previously contained within, so some of this vapour condenses. When the air cools to its dew point, the moisture held in it condenses into very small droplets. The dew point indicates the amount of moisture in the air. The higher the dew point, the higher the moisture content of the air at a given temperature.

The conditions for fog can occur when moist warm air passes over cold water, and so usually occurs between April and September. It is important to note that sea fog can occur at any time of day accompanied by quite strong winds. With winds above force 4–5, the result may be low cloud and poor visibility rather than fog.

North Sea Haar – On the east coast of Scotland, sea fog is known locally as a haar or North Sea Haar, and no doubt you will come across it. It is most likely to occur on the east coast, or over the Northern Isles, during early summer, before the notoriously cold North Sea has started to warm up. With an easterly or south-easterly wind, a haar is possible as the warm air from the Continent passes over the middle of the North Sea (where temperatures are warmer) and so the air becomes warm and moist. It then arrives at the east coast

North Sea Haar, taken by RU1005 Dundee satellite receiving station © Archive Services, University of Dundee

of Scotland where the temperatures are colder. The east coast of England is also affected but here it tends to be known as a sea fret.

South coast

A warm and moist south-westerly wind from the Atlantic in late spring and early to mid-summer can result in sea fog before the inshore water temperatures have increased.

When will it disperse?

Inland, the fog is likely to disperse as the land is warm. So, if you are stuck in a harbour, it is worth venturing inland for a day's exploring and you are likely to find a glorious sunny day. Also, the fog is likely to disperse if you can go up river or into a pool of trapped water, as the water temperature is warmer. Sunshine is needed to burn off the fog; it warms the air and allows the condensed water to be turned back into vapour. However, if the fog is very thick, the sun is unlikely to burn through it.

Fog drifting in from the sea up the River Dart

CHAPTER TEN

STAYING IN TOUCH

The internet has become an essential part of our daily lives, both on land and on water. Online weather forecasts and navigation apps now sit comfortably alongside traditional sources of information and techniques and are now part of any cruise. There are a myriad of reasons to stay in touch: working from your boat, social media, email, face to face calls and a plethora of other demands. However, they all mean that you need to consider how you will keep this digital umbilical cord healthy while away from home. It is clear that the direction of travel is towards cheaper 'Internet at Sea', through new low-orbit satellites such as, Starlink and OneWeb, though satellite-based internet is currently too expensive for the coastal cruiser.

CONNECTIVITY
Mobile
The majority of your internet connection will be over the mobile network; everything from 2G through to 5G depending on your phone and where you are. However, some of your time will be spent at the edge of a network operator's coverage, where you will find areas with no reception, especially if you are visiting remote islands and anchorages. If you ask the locals, they will tell you the exact spot on the island where you can get coverage. Though, if there is a connection it is likely to be a slow speed. It is difficult to know who has the best coverage in remote areas. Of those surveyed since 2018, more than half used EE, with Three being the next most common, though it is unclear how much was driven by the price of data rather than coverage. Just over 40 per cent had two SIM cards from different operators. If you are using data in the Republic of Ireland, check with your operator for any roaming charges or fair usage limits.

Wi-Fi
When I was learning to moor a boat, I was taught to consider the effects of wind and tide. I now realise there is a third dimension – distance to the free Wi-Fi! Being close to the marina facilities not only means a shorter dash to the loo, it can sometimes also mean free internet. While it is the cheapest option, speeds are sometimes unusable due to low bandwidth at popular times. We have frequently had to take our laptop to a café to update our blog and send emails, despite there being 'free marina internet.'

Managing your data consumption
There may be little opportunity to be on Wi-Fi, so if you don't have an unlimited data package, you need a data health warning. At home, most of

your internet use is usually on Wi-Fi, so you are blissfully unaware of data hungry apps. Even if you are on an unlimited data package, slimming down your data requirement will help improve your speeds in poor reception areas. While cruising, I was horrified to see 11GB of data had been guzzled overnight due to OneDrive uploading photos. Mercifully, our contract doesn't have data roaming charges! I am now paranoid about hunting out these data guzzlers. To reduce your data usage that is quietly killing your data plan try to:

- Turn off online storage solutions – particularly for photos.
- Turn your hotspot off when not using it.
- Switch off automatic updating of apps or system updates.
- Unsubscribe from podcasts, otherwise they download automatically.
- Turn on 'Wi-Fi only' for automatic downloads and embedded videos.
- Turn off mobile access for non-essential apps.
- Set a daily data limit warning notification.
- Use apps in an offline mode, then update when on Wi-Fi, such as blog posts.
- Find the data guzzlers by looking at the data usage of each app in Settings.

IMPROVING YOUR CONNECTIVITY

When we were in Eyemouth, we had to wait for high tide to get reception. But now there are other more effective ways to improve your connectivity. This is particularly important if you are considering working from your boat, where you need a stable connection for applications required in the modern workplace.

Mobile

There are several ways to improve your mobile access. However, if you don't have unlimited data, and you haven't choked your data usage, then improving the connectivity will add to your data anxiety and you may just end up turning off your antenna. You can always take the emergency/DIY approach used by Bill Aylward (*Double Vision*, Catana 42), who was holed up in Loch Ewe sheltering from a summer 50kn gale. He managed to get the internet by hoisting his iPhone in a waterproof case to the top of the mast and using it as a hot spot. If you want a more permanent solution, here are some options:

Mi-Fi router

This is a Wi-Fi router with a SIM card and a trailing antenna, it is the easiest and cheapest option to implement. We have used an unlocked Huawei Mi-Fi box in the past, placed near an open hatch with the antenna threaded out of the hatch and raised as high as possible. You can connect several devices to the Mi-Fi box, via its Wi-Fi. The SIM card can be a monthly contract or pay as you go. If the antenna is on deck, it does marginally increase your chance of getting a signal, compared to a phone down in the cabin.

Wideband omni-directional antenna

To improve your chances of obtaining a strong mobile signal, with good data speeds and adequate bandwidth, to enable streaming and reasonable download/upload capability, you would need a high gain antenna, streaming also requires access to a 4G network. Several companies, such as Digital Yacht and MailASail, have 4G and some 3G solutions. Some units are fitted below decks, with an internal antenna, others have two external high gain antennas for optimum speed and range, mounted on your pushpit. Multiple devices can then connect to the router's Wi-Fi. Digital Yacht 4G Connect Pro claims a maximum range of 20 miles from shore. Jonathan and Anne Winter (*Nova*, GT Yachts (GT35)) used a pushpit mounted Poynting 402 omni directional antenna, plugged into a Wi-Fi router below decks, connected to the 12V system. Jonathan's excellent blog post, where he reports the comparative tests that he performed between the antenna and his phone in various locations is definitely worth looking at. https://novaroundbritain.home.blog/2019/10/18/internet/.

Wi-Fi

A high gain antenna, also called a Wi-Fi extender or signal enhancer, is used to sniff out a Wi-Fi signal at a longer distance. Though in more remote areas, where there is no Wi-Fi, you need to rely on cellular. There are two types of Wi-Fi antenna:

- Smart booster antennas which have the software built into the base of the antenna with a cable that uses an ethernet connector. They often require a Power over Ethernet (PoE) adapter.
- Wi-Fi antenna and smart box have their software fitted in a separate box mounted below deck, rather than in the antenna.

When the antenna is connected to a router, establishing a Wi-Fi network, then multiple devices can be connected. Ranges depend on the power output of the transmitter, the sensitivity of the receiver and the presence of obstacles. Ranges up to 10 miles (MailASail Wi-Fi Bat antenna) are claimed in ideal conditions with no obstructions; expect less in real life situations, as line of sight is important and they often have to operate amongst a forest of masts. Other manufacturers are Digital Yacht, Wave and Wi-Fi Onboard.

Our Wi-Fi antenna

Rather than buy a ready-made system, I put together a smart booster antenna with a router system, following the instructions from Steve Neal, who set up Wi-Fi on his boat. I am not a computer geek, but his instructions made it achievable and it was much cheaper than a ready-made system. The instructions are here: https://sailingyachtamalia.wordpress.com/2015/05/11/Wi-Fi-internet-access-on-board/. It has an Ubiquiti bullet (the smart bit) at the bottom of an 8dBI omni-directional antenna, a PoE adapter and is connected to a standard domestic TP link router.

Once moored, I will turn the system on to see what networks are visible. Many networks will be password protected, so with a bit of detective work hopefully we will locate the relevant network in a café/pub. After a drink, we leave with the password in our pockets. Depending on the conditions, we get a range of between 1–3 miles. Before the era of reasonably priced unlimited data packages, this was our preferred method.

Combined Wi-Fi and cellular

A popular solution is to have a combined system, which can switch automatically between Wi-Fi and 4G/5G. Both the Digital and MailASail solutions can have a Wi-Fi antenna added into their cellular solutions.

Siting your antenna

Line of sight without obstructions such as buildings, trees and masts is key. But putting it at the top of your mast comes at a cost of signal loss, due to the length of the cable. Many locate them on their pushpit, where they are easier to access.

Experience of others

Only 20 per cent of recent circumnavigators used an antenna to boost their connectivity. Therefore, it is by no means regarded as essential unless you are working from the boat. Provided you are prepared to be on a digital diet for a few days, when in remote areas, it might be a better use of a limited budget to pay for an unlimited data package, rather than invest money in improving your connectivity.

Working from your boat

Attitudes to working remotely, post the COVID-19 pandemic, have changed dramatically and it is now widely accepted. Enabled by technology, more affordable unlimited data packages and the increased bandwidth that 4G and 5G affords, it does mean that working from your boat may well be feasible. A game changer for some, making this trip a realistic possibility. However, accessing a 4G network around the coast is not a given, yet it is needed for the modern working environment. Your best chance is to use a combined Wi-Fi and cellular option.

In practice, if I have an important meeting, I will plan to be in a location where the 4G mobile signal is good. I use the network provider coverage map as I have a postcode to search on, or failing that, I will contact the harbourmaster to get their opinion of coverage. Coupled with unlimited data, I can work unhindered. I have used this solution to work from the boat, using applications such as Zoom and Slack. If you are planning to work from your boat:

- Purchase an unlimited data package especially if you use applications like Slack or need to have many conference calls using Zoom/Skype etc.
- Improve your connectivity to Wi-Fi networks and cellular networks.
- Ensure you have a comfortable position for working at a laptop.
- Enable voice calls over broadband (VoIP) on your phone.

Complete flexibility to be able to work anywhere in the UK, including remote anchorages, will need an Internet at Sea solution, which is currently very costly, but prices will decrease in time.

SHARING YOUR STORY

You will be surprised at how many people will be interested in hearing about your adventures – family, friends and even total strangers. Social media platforms make it easy to share your cruise. We created our own website, so that we could share our journey daily. It proved very popular, but to our surprise not only with friends and family. We had about 775 different people following us, with an average of 250 hits a day. Which before the days of influencers, was considered to be a big hit! Plus, it is a great record once you have returned.

Blogs

The content of your website will depend on your skill level, but platforms like WordPress and Wix have demystified the black art of HTML coding, so we mere mortals can produce them. Their templates enable you to choose the look of your site, and price depends on the templates used and whether you allow adverts. It is also easy to link your blog to some social media platforms, so that when you publish it automatically goes to your social media feed. They will automatically assign you a web address, though if you want to choose your own, you will need to purchase a domain name from a company, such as Namecheap, for an annual fee. A typical blog might include:

- A chart showing your current location/ daily track.
- Photos and video clips.
- Posts with a catchy title to capture the interest of the reader.
- Information about the boat and crew.
- Itinerary, where you are planning to go.
- Contact form, so you don't need to publish your personal contact details.

Maps

Most people will have no clue where you are and will appreciate a map. There are several easy ways of showing your location and track, which can be embedded into your blog without having to worry about copyright of maps. Both these give the HTML code to paste into the source code of your page:

- Google Maps: My Maps where you can add pin and create tracks.
- Marine traffic will show your live position, provided you have an MMSI number.

Social networking

If you want a less time-consuming solution, and are prepared to sacrifice some flexibility in the format, then there are numerous other platforms to share your journey: Facebook, Instagram and X to name a few. Based on those surveyed recently, by far the most popular way to share the voyages was via a blog.

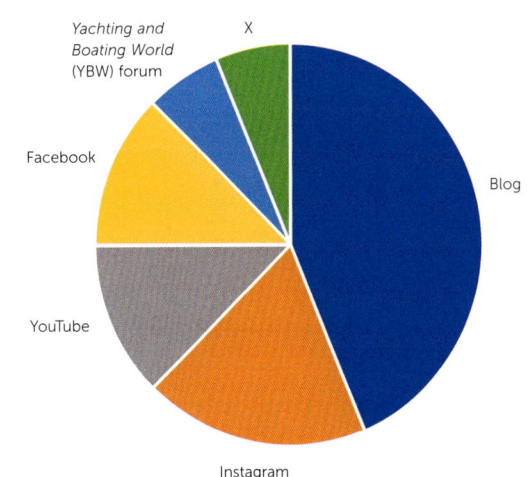

Sharing online, based on 14 surveys

Making decisions
26–27 May – Kirkcudbright to Campbeltown

The engineer had real problems in removing the seized bolt from the alternator; he eventually drilled it out in his workshop. By the time it was fixed, we had missed the morning tide. A blow was expected on Monday, so if we wanted to get to Campbeltown before the windy weather, we needed to leave sooner rather than later. But that meant the evening tide, which was after dark. It had been interesting coming in through the winding river in the daylight, in a flat calm, so a night exit would be very tricky and it was already F5 gusting 6. We went for a walk round the town to contemplate our decision: to stay until after the windy weather or head out on the night tide.

Kirkcudbright is an attractive town; brightly coloured houses line the streets and in the centre is an old 16th-century fortified house. In almost every street there is a gallery. It is also known as the Artists' Town through its connection to the 'Glasgow Boys', a group of 19th-century impressionist painters.

We decided to 'go for it'. As it is tidal, we couldn't leave until 10:15pm. So, we had to sit around waiting. We always felt apprehensive prior to a big passage; in this instance the prospect of navigating out of Kirkcudbright at night, then sailing round the Mull of Galloway, which has a fearsome reputation. It is the anticipation which is worse – why were we leaving a nice secure berth and venturing out on a windy night?

We eventually set off, counting the flashing buoys as we passed them; all went well until the light on the depth sounder stopped working. A depth sounder is essential on this shallow river. Mags grabbed a torch and, apart from two buoys that weren't lit, which gave us a heart-stopping moment as we narrowly missed one, we made it out safely. In the bay, we had 27 knots of wind so we needed three reefs in the mainsail; we settled the boat on course and Mags went off watch. We were sailing into the wind (typical), the tide changed and was now with us. However, the wind was now in the opposite direction to the tide, and raised quite a sea, with sharp steep waves which knocked the boat back. By now we should have been well on our way to the Mull, but our progress was painfully slow. It became obvious that we wouldn't make it past the Mull before the tide changed. With a spring tide against us, we would be lucky not to go backwards. I started to question my decision to leave Kirkcudbright. I considered the options: we could go back to Kirkcudbright – but we would have to get back in time for the next high tide; go to Douglas on the Isle of Man – but that meant going back; or soldier on and accept that for the next six hours we would be looking at the same view of the Mull. We decided on the latter. I headed off watch, and three hours later when I got up, the view was still the same. But the tide was with the wind, and the sea had calmed down considerably, so I cut inside close to the Mull to pick up a back eddy and we started going forward at

> last. But when we turned right to go up the North Channel, so did the wind, so we were sailing into it again.
>
> The next weather forecast was showing N5–7. We would be heading north, bang into the wind, so again we would make little progress. Portpatrick, a small fishing village, was an option, but on a falling tide and with a strong onshore wind, it was not a sensible one. Thankfully, we made good progress up the North Channel with the tide, and when we got to the top of the Mull, the northerly wind had not yet set in, so we decided to make for Campbeltown. We still had three reefs, and at 30 knots of wind, we were steaming along despite the tide being against us. We passed the Ailsa Craig (Paddy's Milestone), a distinctive lump of rock, Mags was back in familiar waters, and before long it was 'Land Ahoy' as we spotted the Mull of Kintyre. Mags did a kind-of rendition of 'Campbeltown Loch, I wish you were whisky, for I would drink you dry'. It was not long before we picked up the light on Daavar Island, which guards the seaward end of the loch. By the time we passed the island it was dark, which was a shame, as we would have sailed right past Mags' parents' house. By 2am, some 30 hours later, we were tied up safe and sound. Getting there gave us a huge sense of achievement; we had seen some awesome scenery and we had a great sail… that's why we do it.

Everyone will have their own writing style, but whatever medium you use, your story will be more engaging and authentic if you are able to:

- Communicate your emotions, not just the facts of the day. Understanding the emotional highs and lows is more effective at conveying the challenge that this trip presents.
- Write a full disclosure blog, by covering what went wrong, as well as what went well. There is a tendency to gloss over it, for fear of denting your pride even further than the original incident managed to do!

One of the most enjoyable blogs that I have read, is 'Solo Sailing round Britain in a little red boat with a supply of gin – what could possibly go wrong' by a friend of mine, Jill Rogers (*Vela*, Sadler 25). Her witty writing style, and her honest full disclosure blog, made for entertaining reading. It also meant that she was able to convey the real achievement of a solo circumnavigation to both sailors and non-sailors alike. www.velatour.home.blog.

PHOTOGRAPHY

Your cruise will pass all too quickly, and to capture your adventure, whether it is to share your experiences or to remember it once home, photography will be a key aspect that you need to consider. You will have no shortage of opportunities to take hundreds of photos and video clips, so hopefully you are more likely to get that 'picture in a million'! The picture quality on phones for both photos and video can be impressive, though depending on its battery life, you may want to consider not relying on this as your main way to capture the moment, or have a portable battery charger on standby. Some other areas to think about:

- **Protection** Use a waterproof pocket or box so that you can keep your camera within easy reach.
- **Storage** Take several large memory cards. If you don't have unlimited data, then try to store your media in two places, so you don't need to use cloud storage.
- **Handsfree photography** Not only can you get unusual camera angles, but also you can leave it running to capture events when you don't have the time to concentrate on photography. We now have a GoPro camera permanently attached on a strut at the back of the boat, controlled by a remote.
- **Power** Carry a spare camera battery.

Photos

You will be cruising with some amazing backdrops; the sheer scale of the beauty of the coastlines are not only breathtaking but a real challenge to do justice to it in a photo. Having a compact camera with the widest angle or a SLR with a lens of 12 or 18mm will improve your chances. At sea, it will also mean that you can capture more of your boat in your frame. If you have the ability to attach a filter, then a polarising filter really helps to capture the beautiful colour of the turquoise water that you will see in some places.

Video

A video will enable you to convey the magnificence of the scenery, the magic of the dolphins playing effortlessly around your bow or the emotions and different aspects of your trip. We have too many photos of an empty sea when trying to take a picture of a dolphin. Adding small video clips to your blog or social media feed will enrich your audience's understanding of your voyage, without the time consuming need to edit a Spielberg blockbuster.

See Instagram and YouTube @sailingwithcarra to see examples of some of my reels. Most of mine are below 40 seconds to keep people's interest, and each tries to tell a micro story. Long clips of you sailing are unlikely to entertain your audience.

Editing

However, if you do have the time to produce an edited video, though it is the most time-consuming way of sharing your journey, it can really show the scenery and experiences of the voyage. However, if your time is limited, it might be a task you undertake on your return. There are a variety of styles out there, Derek Hathaway (*Thalmia*, Westerly Fulmar), whose videos 'Voyages of *Thalmia*' are on YouTube, advised to: 'scan a range of the current well-subscribed channels, decide which you like best, then consider what skills, equipment, time you have underway and in later editing. Also think about whether you intend to make money from it, which is a major commitment, or just share and enjoy creating.' His 10-minute video:'My Round Britain in days sails', has been his most popular. In terms of getting people to watch it on YouTube, his other advice was that: 'it is all about the subject and adding a specific angle, eg "my challenging sail from Scillies". Good editing software will allow you to edit your footage; however, it is often a choice between simple editing software, such as iOS iMovie, which makes a lot of decisions for you, or one that gives you more flexibility but has a higher level of complexity, such as DaVinci Resolve'. I tend to use iMovie, as I get enough flexibility without the complexity, and I can edit video clips/reels quickly on my phone.

Music

Royalty-free music is available, often within your editing package, though it can sound bland

and wouldn't seem out of place in your local shopping centre. If you are using Instagram or Facebook, you can add your favourite artists' tracks through the platform's tools, which ensures that the musicians receive a royalty.

Video sharing platforms
Once you have crafted your epic, you can post it on a video sharing platform, such as YouTube, Facebook or Instagram, depending on the length of their clips.

Drones
The footage from drones can be spectacular, a unique perspective on the world around you, whether stills or a video, it adds an extra dimension. The latest drones are compact and easier to fly, making them more practical to use, though anyone who can land one on a moving boat has my total respect! Roger Clark (*Concerto*, Westerly Fulmar) covered his circumnavigation in 'Fulmar *Concerto* Sail Round Britain' on YouTube using a DJI Mini 2 combi set, as this was under the 250g limit requiring full registration. He said the 'biggest problem of drone flying from a boat is the movement of the boat and avoiding the rigging'. Derek Hathaway (*Thalmia*, Westerly Fulmar) used a DJI mini3 pro; this drone has to be hand caught which as he says 'takes some practice.' They mostly fly them when at anchor or from the shore. Their advice:

- Practise catching on land many times before trying from the cockpit.
- Disable the collision technology if you are planning to land it on your boat.
- Some add a short cord under the drone with a ping pong ball on the end so you can grab the drone or use a net hammock across the foredeck for landing.

- Taking off, you must ensure there is nothing behind the drone, as it will rise up and when the boat moves forward it is likely to collide.
- Avoid flying towards the sun, as it causes the lens to bloom and you get fuzzy images for several hours until it settles.
- If you are unsure of flying the drone from your boat, having a dinghy astern is a good emergency landing zone.

I have also heard that some people fly it back onto the boat backwards, as a way of overcoming the collision avoidance technology.

Cameras for maintenance
While moored up, we have used a GoPro attached to a pole to look at the prop, without having to get the wetsuit out. We have also used an endoscope camera, a camera at the end of a flexible wire, whose picture is displayed on a mobile phone, to look at an issue located in a space we couldn't get at; costing less than £30 (2024), it was good value.

PRINTER
Not all our friends and family could access the internet, so we printed off our blog on a small A4 colour printer. These 'snail mail' versions were very much appreciated. Also, a printer may be useful if working from your boat.

ON YOUR RETURN
Presenting your trip
Once you have completed your circumnavigation, you may want to give a talk about your trip. You will then be presented with the challenge of compressing several months' cruising into a limited time slot and reducing the number of photos to a manageable selection. Here are some hints for preparing a professional presentation:

- Use several photos on a slide rather than one, this allows you to show more photos, though limit this to a maximum of five photos per slide.
- Embedded videos can help the audience visualise the experience.
- Include chartlets showing your track, to help your audience place where you were.
- Create a standard header for your slides, which is the same font and size on each slide.
- Allow approximately three minutes per slide.
- Write your script, practise at least three times, time it, then turn it into bullet points.
- Remember, talk to the audience not the screen!

Turn your blog into a book

If you have a blog, a company such as Pixie Books can convert your blog into a book. The online software makes it an easy task, allowing you to customise the front cover and chose which posts you want to include.

MAIL

While away from home, you will need to consider how you will deal with your postal mail. Prior to departing, try to cut down the amount that arrives by setting up as much online as possible. We have used these methods to handle mail during long term cruising:

A sample of our PowerPoint slide presentation

- Postal redirection service to someone who can forward items that need your attention. Provided the harbourmaster agrees, they can be forwarded to a future planned port. Marking it with the name of the boat and 'please keep for visitor'. Be warned that in the Highlands and Islands you need to allow an extra day for mail to arrive.
- Get someone to open your mail and send you a picture of the mail and that way you can deal with it, without needing to have it forwarded. This is the method we use now.

A summary of communications equipment:

COMPUTER	PHONE	WRITING	CAMERA
Computer	Mobile phone	Paper and memo pads	Camera/Drone/GoPro
12V charger	12V charger	Envelopes and stamps	Camera battery charger
Printer and paper	Portable battery	Pens	Spare battery
SD card reader			Spare memory cards

CHAPTER ELEVEN

NAVIGATION

In 1869, Empson Middleton was the first person to sail single-handed around England and Lowland Scotland via what is now called the Forth and Clyde Canal – a voyage which he recounts in *The Cruise of the Kate*. This was a feat of endurance, because his engine-less yacht's only form of propulsion, apart from the sails, was oars. The *Kate*, according to Lloyd's Register, was a 25ft (7.6m) wooden yacht with an iron keel; so Middleton would find himself rowing to the point of utter exhaustion to reach a harbour entrance or to round a headland in order to beat an adverse tidal stream. Though it wasn't until 1892 that the first circumnavigation of the British Isles was achieved by Frank Cowper, over three years and mostly single-handed in *Lady Harvey*, a 44ft (13m) yawl. Navigation provided its own challenges during that period. Middleton describes passing through Hurst Narrows against the flood tide: 'I kept as close as I could to Hurst, feeling the depth as I went along with a boat hook, which is much handier than the lead.' He complains that the charts were drawn for the commercial coasters, so sometimes lacked some details: 'the headlands are not sufficiently defined; but, worse than that the bays are not properly indented.'

Thankfully, navigation today has become much simpler with the advent of GPS, chart plotters, radar and more accurate charts. However, that doesn't detract from the challenges and the sense of achievement when you have completed your trip. This cruise will test your navigation skills; there are strong tides, tidal gates, rocks and sand banks, all to be negotiated in varying degrees of visibility.

Of the 65 skippers surveyed, whose qualifications were known, 51 per cent were qualified to at least RYA Yachtmaster Offshore practical level. This doesn't mean that you need this qualification to do the cruise; 49 per cent successfully completed the circumnavigation without it. In the first surveys, 25 per cent were extremely well qualified, as they were Yachtmaster Ocean or higher, but in recent

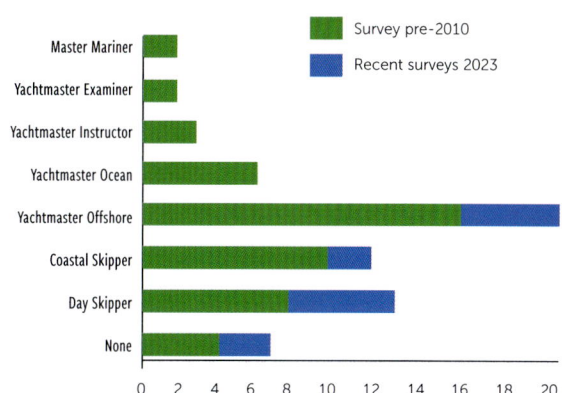

Highest practical qualification held by those surveyed

surveys, no one had this level of qualification, which hopefully is perhaps more reassuring. Seven skippers had no qualifications but they had a great deal of experience. The important point is that you should have the knowledge that is covered by the Yachtmaster syllabus, backed up by practical sailing experience.

NIGHT SAILING

From our survey, we found that on average, most yachts only spent three full nights at sea; no motor boats spent a whole night at sea. However, there were many late nights and early starts. While we only had two nights at sea, we did 44-night hours. If you are around the north of Scotland in June, you will benefit from twilight all night (TAN); the sun does not reach an altitude of 12 degrees, so it never gets truly dark.

ESSENTIAL INFORMATION

Much of the essential information you need is now available digitally, either in apps, on websites or in eBooks. It will be a matter of choice as to how much you want to rely on digital information versus paper. If you go digital:

- Be sure that you understand that the data is from a reliable source. Just because the app looks pretty, that doesn't mean it is accurate!
- Be realistic about using it on the high seas – when you are cold and damp, accessing information on a small touchscreen can be challenging.
- Ensure the information you need is available offline.

Almanac

Almanacs are invaluable for information because of the incredible amount of detail contained within them. We used the loose-leaf *Reeds Nautical Almanac*, rather than the individual area almanacs, in order to reduce the cost. The main disadvantage, not surprisingly, is its size. Some suggestions to make it easier to use:

- Ditch all the countries that you won't be visiting, though if you have the Reeve-Fowkes tidal atlases keep Cherbourg, as it is the standard port for the Channel.
- Take plastic hole reinforcers or frequently used pages will fall out.
- Laminate the key standard ports tidal information beforehand, so that the pages can withstand life on the chart table.
- Use stick on/Post-it type paper flags, so that key information is easier to find quickly; for example, flag up the standard port you are using, the port you are entering and leaving, and sunrise and sunset times.

Digital options

Reed's Nautical Almanac is also available digitally, either as a PDF, on Kindle or ePub. Free tidal height apps are readily available, but you might need to pay a fee to ensure that you are able to interrogate the tidal height curves, such as setting a horizontal line for your minimum depth. You need to be able to view it offline and ahead of time, plus ensure that it is clear whether it is UTC or local time. Also check that it can cope with unusual tidal scenarios, such as the double stand in the Solent. Imray produce an app that does this but there are many others too.

Pilot books

Reeds Nautical Almanac could easily replace pilot books; it contains excellent passage information around the major tidal gates, often better than some pilot books, which tend to focus on the harbours. Pilot books provide valuable information

NAVIGATION

and chartlets about entering anchorages and harbours. I tend to keep the pilot book in a plastic cover, at the relevant page, on deck, for a quick refresh before entering a harbour. There is one other book which is worth mentioning: David Rainsbury's *Fearsome Passages*; it provides some useful advice for many of the infamous stretches of water that you will meet.

Digital options

Most pilot guides appear to be in printed format only. There are some online pilot guides eg Explore with Imray, but currently it is not available offline, though plans exist to address this. www.visitmyharbour.com does have a downloadable PDF but a limited number of harbours. www.eoceanic.com provides detailed online information for Ireland and the South coast of England covering havens and invaluable passage information. Both sites also provide tidal information.

Tidal atlases

We used a combination of Reeve-Fowkes and the Admiralty tidal atlases, and then cut out the pages, laminated them and had them wire-bound. Indelible markers were then used to write the times on the pages and nail varnish remover to clean them afterwards. This meant they didn't get into a soggy mess and it would last for years!

Tides in Orkney and the Shetland Islands

Twice a day, the tide surges from the Atlantic to the North Sea and back again, with the flow being concentrated by the archipelago of 170 islands that make up Orkney and the Shetland Islands. This results in the strongest tides in the British Isles, which can reach up to 12 knots. It is therefore no surprise that Orkney has a wave and tide power generation site. If you are just going through the Pentland Firth then the Admiralty tidal atlas NP209 gives detailed tidal information. However, if you are planning to

Arisaig

spend time in the islands, then NP209 does not give you enough information, as the arrows are too general, given the strengths of the tides. The excellent Clyde Cruising Club (CCC) *Sailing Directions for the North and North-east Coasts of Scotland and Orkney Islands* provide local tidal rates and directions to enable detailed planning. If you speak to any of the harbourmasters in the area, they will give you information and advice about crossing the Pentland Firth.

Orkney was our favourite place on the trip, but do plan the tides carefully. For example, Eyenhallow Sound is meek at slack water, but as Orcadian Willie Tulloch, and the former Master of the Northern Lighthouses Vessel said to us, 'it can be an evil piece of water'. We saw it at springs with a slight (F2) wind over tide and it looked positively scary... and that was from the safety of the land.

Digital options

There are stand-alone apps that cover tidal streams. At the basic level, they give the tidal flow at a given time. The next level, which usually comes for an additional cost, gives you the ability to determine course to steer and set, for example iStreams. The further level is when it is integrated with charting software, as discussed later in this chapter.

Like weather forecasts, tidal stream modelling has improved dramatically with tidal numerical modelling and huge computational power. It is now dynamic, taking into account more environmental

The rewards of rock hopping
9 June – Tobermory to Arisaig

Topped up with fuel, as this was likely to be the last fuel stop for a while, we set off from Tobermory, but noticed that the rev counter was going haywire. So we headed back in and picked up a buoy again and checked out the alternator, which seemed fine. So we set off once more and it seemed to settle down. There were 20 knots of wind and we cruised along at 7 knots downwind, which was great, as we could make up the lost time. We rounded Ardnamurchan point, the UK mainland's most westerly point, with the customary bunch of white heather tied to the pulpit. There was blue sky and a good wind – we were incredibly lucky. Arisaig has a difficult entrance, with very rocky outcrops and a winding route through – 'not for the faint hearted' as the pilot book says. It was tempting just to keep sailing and miss it out and go for an easier harbour. We decided to go for it and pick our way past the rocks and follow the poles. There were brilliant white beaches between the rocks surrounded by turquoise pools of water. We successfully navigated our way in under engine and felt very pleased with ourselves; then a boat the same size as ours sailed out – nothing like making us feel like amateurs! We had dinner in the cockpit and watched a stunning sunset over the Isles of Rum and Eigg – another amazing day.

conditions, and hence is more accurate. Tidetech (www.tidetechmarinedata.com) has a subscription model to access such info as high-resolution tidal models.

CHARTS

There is now a spectrum of chart usage from those that use paper charts as their primary source, through to those that use 100 per cent electronic charts, and there are different combinations in between. Depending where you are on the spectrum will impact what charts you take. If I look at my own use over time, I started at 100 per cent paper and am moving towards the electronic side of the spectrum. With the demand for paper charts falling, the Admiralty decided to stop printing paper charts in 2030, so it is clear that the direction of travel is towards digital.

Which charts do you need?

Having decided on the places you are going to visit; you can start to work out which paper and electronic charts you will need. Your charts need to cover where you are planning to go, your emergency ports, and any alternative routes, for example the Caledonian Canal, if you are planning to use it as a potential short cut.

Charts are one of the major expenses of the trip, so it is worth choosing them carefully. With paper charts, you have the choice of Imray and Admiralty small craft charts. The latter are only available on print to order, with discounts for bulk buys, now that they have discontinued their leisure folios. Imray charts represent good value for money, given the inclusion of harbour plans (1:20000 and lower) in their C series small scale coastal planning charts (1:120000 to 1:240000). If you are going to be in an area for some time, rather than just making passage through an area, then it might be worth investing in some of their ten chart folios. In the most recent circumnavigations, many used the Imray C charts augmented with Antares Charts (see later in this chapter).

Chart datums

If using second-hand charts, and transferring your route from a chart into a chart plotter, you must ensure that the same positional datum WGS 84

Sunset over Eigg and Rum from Arisaig

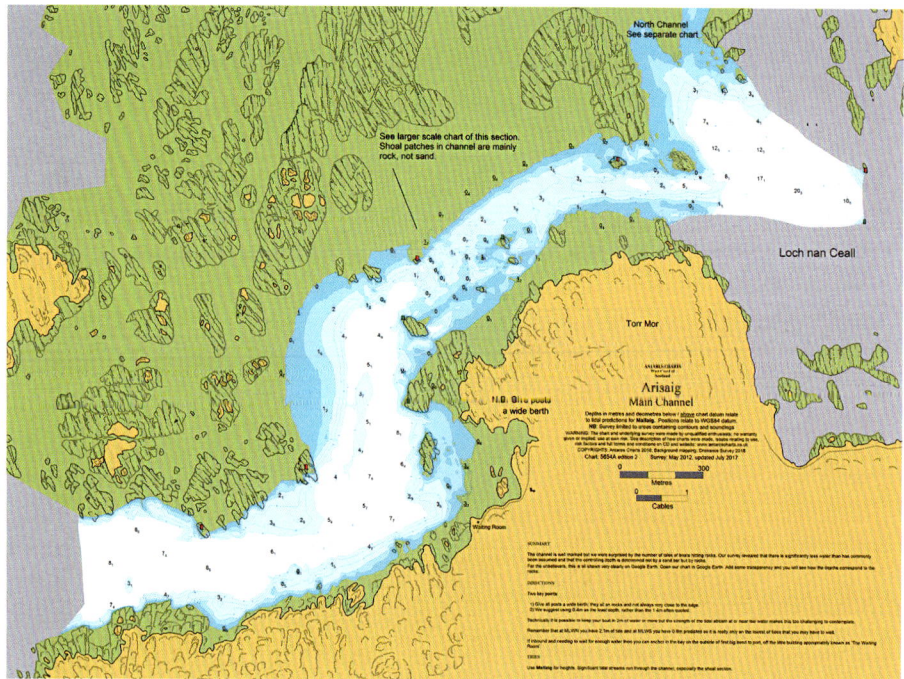

Antares Chart showing accurate detail of Arisaig's entrance © Antares Charts (background mapping © Ordnance Survey)

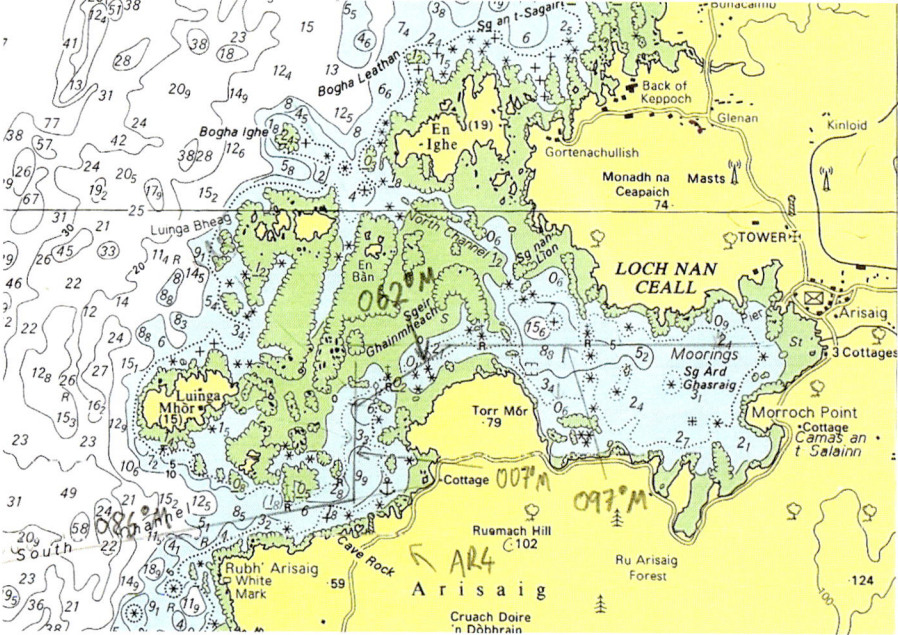

Rocky entrance to Arisaig. Leisure pilots provide valuable information for entry into small anchorages.
© British Crown Copyright

NAVIGATION

is used. You will still find some charts referencing *Ordnance Survey of Great Britain 1936*.

Electronic raster and vector charts

Raster charts are images of paper charts, they have just one layer and are static, hence not so easy to update. The benefits of raster charts are that they show all the hazards that are on the paper chart and have landmarks relevant to mariners. Vector charts are computer generated charts, saved in many layers and are dynamic, so can be updated easily. This has enabled vector charts to compile sonar charts, which are crowd sourced data from echo sounders, which have been used to improve the accuracy of the chart. However, there is one serious limitation of a vector chart; not all detail is shown at all layers of the chart. Some key features may only be shown when you zoom in; be warned these can be fairly fundamental ones, like rocks that would ruin your day if you hit one, as the Volvo Ocean *Vestas Wind* can attest to, after they hit a reef in the Indian Ocean. So, if you have vector charts, be sure to zoom in to identify any hazards on your route.

Accuracy of charts

The expectation of accuracy that can be achieved from today's navigational equipment is now just a few metres. This assumes that the charts are accurate and can lead to a false sense of security as to your location. Many charts on the west coast of Scotland were surveyed by Admiral Henry Otter between 1852 and 1863.

Antares Charts

Bob Bradfield, who himself completed a circum-navigation of Britain, set about addressing his frustration with the inaccuracy of the charts of the west coast of Scotland. With the advent of satellite positioning, Bob has been surveying and publishing large scale charts that are essential for safely exploring the anchorages of this cruising area. Antares Charts (as of 2024) have 693 charts, covering over 685 locations on the west coast of Scotland. They can run with UKHO-type charts on PCs, and all iOS and Android devices. There are a wide range of free apps/software available, while 'the best' setup costs less than £50, including their charts and all UKHO-type charts for the UK and Ireland. www.antarescharts.co.uk.

HARDWARE

Chart plotter

Dedicated chart plotters have the advantage of using less power and being designed for operating in marine conditions, hence they can be on deck. They integrate easily with other systems eg AIS, radar from the same manufacturer and with others if they are based on the same language (a data standard such as NMEA 2000) but consequently tend to be more expensive, as are their dedicated charts. They principally operate with vector charts. However, with a chart plotter, you can't access the innovation of small agile software companies.

PC/laptop

A common solution in the racing world is a PC or laptop by the chart table running charting software. This offers a more flexible solution with access to a wider range of raster and vector charts. This innovation in the racing world has trickled into the cruising market: routing programs which allow the optimisation of routes with weather, tides and some also include your boat's polar diagrams too.

A boat is an unforgiving environment, with exposure to sea air and vibration/shock typically caused by engine operation and rough passages. Ruggedised PCs/laptops are available but that

Across the Pentland Firth towards Duncansby Head

adds to the cost. There is also an increased power requirement, as most boats are 12V DC and PCs are set up for a 240V AC power supply. Therefore, you will need an inverter to convert DC to AC, which is inefficient, with a loss of about 20 per cent of power in the process. The other disadvantage is that the information is usually visible at the chart table rather than on deck.

A healthy respect is needed for the rost in Eyenhallow Sound

Mobile device (tablet or phone)

This has been a game changer in digital navigation for the cruising market; it has dramatically reduced costs as the apps are based on the iOS and Android platforms. A wider choice of raster and vector charts, and a larger number of innovative apps, has led to more competition and lower costs. If there is no GPS in your tablet, as is usually the case with Wi-Fi only tablets which use Wi-Fi to provide a location, then you will need an external GPS such as a Bad Elf, which is connected to your tablet via Bluetooth. In the latest survey, 92 per cent used a chart plotter and tablet for navigation. Nearly 50 per cent used a chart plotter in conjunction with their phone. Only one used a tablet and a PC only solution ie no chart plotter, a compact solution for his Corribee 21.

London Chart Plotters (www.londonchartplotters.com) and Visit My Harbour (www.visitmyharbour.com) offer industrial grade tablets, which are IP68 certified, and therefore protected against ingress of water and dust. The case also provides protection if dropped. Charging a tablet is easier, as you can have USB charging direct from your 12V system. Both use Marine Navigator software, which is basic but functional. Jes Bates (*Mwera*, Corribee 21) uses their system, and had a tablet holder that hinged out into the companionway with a nearby USB C charging socket where it was plugged in all the time unless it was very wet. His main advice was to have 'some sort of waterproof case, as tablet touchscreens don't work when they have water on them. Be careful of charging when there's water around'. Jes speaks from experience, as he fried the charging port on a tablet and phone when they got wet while charging. Be aware of visibility challenges in sunlight and keeping the tablet cool. Many tablets don't like to get hot and can shut down.

Other software providers are Navionics, iNavx, Open CPN, TimeZero Navigator and Weather4D

Navigation and Routing, some of which are compatible with both raster and vector charts. This list is by no means exhaustive. Software exists for phones, though the screen size is often the limiting factor.

There is also the ability to mirror your chart plotter onto a tablet, using the manufacturer app, if your chart plotter has Wi-Fi. Your tablet then acts as a dumb terminal, and it will display your data but you can't control or change it. If your boat electronic backbone is not connected to Wi-Fi, you can add in a NMEA2000 Wi-Fi gateway.

On our current set-up we have a small 5.7" screen by the helm, which is ideal when helming. We then have the main chart plotter, with a 9" hybrid touchscreen, on the companionway, which is where we sit on longer passages. We don't have anything at the chart table as this would mean another screen and more power consumption. Here we use a tablet with a Raymarine app that mirrors the chart plotter. I plan on a tablet with Navionics and transfer the route to the chart plotter.

Martin Whitfield (*Knot Telling*, Cornish Crabber 26) took his lessons from using a tablet on his circumnavigation, and has now connected a wireless radar, wind, depth, AIS, position, speed etc on an iPad. I had assumed he was a computer whizz kid, but it was a local marine electronic systems company that set it up for him. So don't assume they just implement traditional chart plotter solutions.

Whatever system/set up you use, it is important that you:

- Eliminate wasted effort, such as needing to enter the same waypoints on different systems.
- Make sure you have access to the information when and wherever you need it; such as having chart visibility at the helm, or an anchor alarm that you can hear in your cabin, and also have essential information available offline.

DIGITAL NAVIGATION

The combination of digital charts and paper charts provides resilience, as you still have the ability to manually plot your position. If you decide to go 100 per cent digital, it is wise to think about resilience of your systems. You need to identify potential points of failure and how to mitigate the risk.

RISK	MITIGATION
LOSS OF SYSTEM	- Have two systems, eg a chart plotter and a tablet both with digital charts. - If you are using a tablet, you need to be able to charge from 12V but it would be wise to have a separate portable battery. - Ideally use a ruggedised tablet or have protection from the elements and being knocked.
LOSS OF GPS FROM YOUR NETWORK	- Have a Bad Elf device that will provide GPS from satellites and can be connected to a tablet - Your chart plotter will have its own GPS, so if your GPS fails your chart plotter will use its own.
CARDS NOT READING	- Test your digital charts before setting off.

Look up! It is important to check the chart plotter against the actual coastline to see that the information you see electronically makes sense, I have seen our Raymarine plotter freeze several times, and it was only by comparing it to what I could see around me that I realised the chart plotter needed rebooting. As with all electronic navigation aids, it is easy to get mesmerised and believe they are the source of all truth.

AngelNav app

This app allows you to use and maintain your traditional navigational skills: plotting fixes, your dead reckoning and estimated position, on an electronic raster chart. On long passages, there is something rather satisfying about seeing your progress towards your destination. AngelNav can take its navigational data from the device's stand-alone GPS, the boat's NMEA over Wi-Fi, and SignalK. By using raster charts, which show relevant land features, you can plot fixes on the chart. Plus, it works with Antares charts. With the move to 100 per cent digital navigation over time, you would have retained the skills to know where you are, should the global GPS system fail!

Experience of others

Below you can see the spread of those who have circumnavigated since 2014, where they are on the paper chart – electronic spectrum. Interestingly, no one used paper or electronic charts exclusively.

I would now make very different decisions on charts that we took. In our current boat, we have a chart plotter close to the helm, so when approaching harbours, I use electronic charts and pilot guides, using a paper chart only as a backup. When passage making, I have in the past plotted my position hourly on a paper chart, so the small-scale Imray C charts are ideal, as they also have the harbour plans as a backup. However, with the advent of the AngelNav, I would move to electronic plotting, so paper charts would be purely for backup. Rather than invest in the number of paper charts that we took for our circumnavigation, I would now

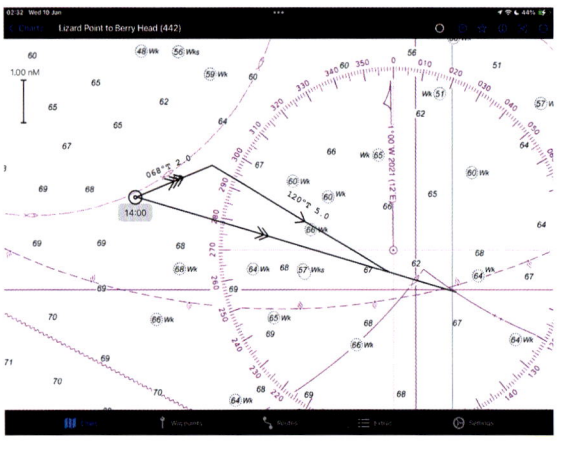

A digital plot using AngelNav app © British Crown Copyright

Paper	Paper charts only	Electronic charts, paper for planning			Electronic charts only	Electronic charts only	Electronic
		Back up: Paper charts			Back up: Paper charts	Back up: Electronic	
	Regular plotting	Regular plotting	Longer passages only	No plotting	No plotting	No plotting	
	0	4	1	2	7	0	

Spectrum of use of electronic charts by those surveyed who have completed a circumnavigation since 2014

invest in more pilot guides and Antares charts for Scotland.

ROUTE PLANNING

Most people have limited time, so one of the challenges is knowing where to go and which harbours and areas you have to miss. The chapter Ten of the Best will help you to find the unmissable ones. You will also get much invaluable information by talking to crews from other boats and to the locals.

Solas V regulations dictate prior passage planning, and anybody considering this trip should plan each leg very carefully. Clearly, everyone will have their own preferred format. We used an A4 book to plan all routes. A double-page, was used for logging tidal information, weather, radio channels, contingency ports, times to be at tidal gates etc. We used our rest days to plan the waypoints for a couple of days in advance, making rough notes about tidal streams but leaving the detailed tidal planning until you are certain of the day you are leaving, otherwise much time is wasted doing tidal calculations that are never used. We used A4 white boards and indelible marker pens for essential passage information, such as key lights, buoys, rocks, and courses for entry and leaving, tidal heights expected at given times for anchoring.

Harbour planning

En route you will want to know more granular information about where you are going: key harbour information, facilities available, top tips on the harbour or anchorage etc, and this is where digital resources and crowd sourcing come into their own. CAptain's Mate is an app available to Cruising Association members which lists over 1,000 harbours and anchorages in the UK and Ireland, and thousands more locations globally. It

Stromness at 11pm with Hoy in the background

CAptain's Mate © Cruising Association

provides information about the location, facilities, what to do when there, things to do in the area, and photos. It is an invaluable source of information with the advantage of being able to filter the search results eg look for a harbour with a laundry or chandlery. Other apps are Navily, Savvy Navvy, Explore with Imray, Visitmyharbour, Eoceanic, which have similar information though the number of locations and detail varies with each.

Routing Programs

There are several levels of routing software, often it is the same software but with a different level of subscription service. Some examples are: Savvy Navvy, PredictWind, iNavx, Open CPN, TimeZero Navigator, Navionics, Marine Navigator, some of which are compatible with both raster and vector charts.

- *Basic* You create the route by entering waypoints. You may or may not be able to transfer it to your chart plotter depending on compatibility.
- *Semi-automated* You enter the start and end point, it will formulate the route, but it doesn't take into account variables such as tidal streams or weather. But you must check the route is viable eg tidal height, height under bridges etc.
- *Advanced* Those that use variables such as tides, weather, your boat's polar diagrams to give you the course to steer allowing for tides and the optimal time to set off. These programs really come into their own if you are going across the tide eg crossing the channel and want to know the optimum time to leave or are going a long distance and are looking to avoid weather systems. For most of this trip, you will either be going with the tide or against it, so the benefit is less obvious.

Digital log

We maintain a written ship's log but our NAVTEX unit maintains a digital log, recording our NMEA data every 15 minutes: position, COG, SOG, heading, water speed, wind direction, wind speed, depth and distance. There are Apps such as Nebo that can track your route and with a subscription allows you to share it with your friends, add photos etc. PredictWind has also developed a datalogger to record NMEA data, track your boat on GPS and put it all together in log files or blog posts.

ADDITIONAL NAVIGATION EQUIPMENT

We found the following items very useful:

GENERAL	
Dividers, Breton plotter	Binoculars
Pencils, pens, pencil sharpener, eraser, ruler and map correction pen	Hand-held compass
Log book	Route planning A4 book
Hole reinforcers and Post-it notes for flagging almanac	Calculator
Admiralty symbols *5011*	Hand-held GPS (back-up)
Green, red, blue, black, purple indelible fine marker pens and nail polish remover + two A4 white boards	Tablet, protective case, external battery

CHAPTER TWELVE

LIFE ON BOARD

WATCHKEEPING

It always surprises me how many skippers, when doing a long trip like crossing the Channel, will stay awake for the entire passage. If you try and do the same on this cruise you will end up shattered, and increase the likelihood of making unsafe decisions due to tiredness. You need to organise regular watchkeeping to pace yourself, and ensure you are adequately rested. Clearly, if you are single-handed this is not a luxury you have, so careful consideration must be given to length of legs and proper recovery time after a long leg.

For any passages over four hours, we set up a watchkeeping routine. Three hours on, three hours off during the day, and two hours on, two hours off at night. Though at times this was flexible; if the person on watch felt wide awake, they would often allow the 'off watch' to sleep an hour longer. For legs shorter than four hours, we used to do joint watches but we would always be clear as to whose watchkeeping responsibility it was. If there was fog, and we were in an area where there was a lot of shipping or hazards, we would do joint watches.

It is important to set up good watchkeeping routines from day one:

- Brief the crew as to what to expect on the leg.
- Make sure they know in what circumstances they should wake the skipper.
- Have a clear handover at change of watch.

SEASICKNESS

When the sea state goes from smooth to slight, Mags generally starts to be 'stomach aware' – the first stage of seasickness. For those fellow sufferers, you will be pleased to know that you do get your sea legs. Mags managed to do the entire trip without being seasick, though there was the odd time when she felt grim. Here are her top tips:

- Minimise the amount of time that you need to spend performing tasks down below:
  - Prepare lunch in advance before leaving the harbour.
  - Use food flasks, which would be filled with hot food if sailing overnight and if we were expecting a rough sea.
  - Prior to a trip, we would fill a flask with boiling water. Our flask dispenses through a push button on top. This means that when you are heeling you don't have to

The relief band or cattle prodder as we call it

defy gravity when filling up a cup, as you can take the cup to the flask and not the flask to the cup. This is very useful even if you don't suffer from seasickness.

- A chart plotter in the cockpit enabled Mags to run a watch without having to go below.
- Use a combination of relief band (see above) and/or medicines.
- Take medication regularly as per the instructions.
- Keep warm.
- Pick your battles: if we knew there was going to be a rough sea, and we had enough time in our schedule to stay in harbour, we did.
- Keep a stack of ginger biscuits to nibble when you become stomach aware.
- Make sure you keep drinking.

Since our circumnavigation, Mags has discovered the relief band (www.reliefband.co.uk) or the cattle prodder as I call it. It stimulates the median nerve under the wrist with very small electrical impulses, and has been very successful for Mags, such as that she can now even cook down below while at sea, and it has transformed her enjoyment of sailing. It was originally designed for sufferers of morning sickness and chemotherapy-related nausea. If you decide to buy one, do be sure to get the version with batteries that can be replaced. If you would rather use medicines, then Stugeron and Scopoderm (Scopolamine) patches are popular. The patches are invaluable because they can be administered even when you are unable to keep any food down. As with any medicine/medical equipment, do check any contra-indications before use.

EATING AND DRINKING

It is important to make sure that you eat and drink properly while at sea; it is easy to become dehydrated. The hot water flask, described above, meant that hot drinks were always readily available. Not only does it help to reduce the time spent below but it reduces the effort required to make a hot drink, which means you are more likely to have one. The quick tasty pasta meals that we carried also ensured that a hot dinner was always available, no matter how late we arrived.

We kept a Tupperware box in a cockpit locker filled with sweets and biscuits, which helped to pass the night watch and gave a sugar boost to keep us awake, though it is not good for the hips!

Mini flasks, made by Life Adventure, which have screw-on tops, were invaluable. They would keep a cup of tea warm for a couple of hours so, if we were leaving in the early morning, we could make cups of tea and enjoy a few sips at a time for the next couple of hours. Thermo mugs lost their heat by the time we had cast off the warps and were just out of the harbour.

Eating out

Our budget didn't stretch to eating out in restaurants, so we made do with the occasional treats of fish and chips and ice creams. Beware, you will come across lots of award-winning fish and chip shops! We did conduct our own national ice cream survey; the best was in Lossiemouth, from the Italian shop just opposite the old harbour.

If your budget does stretch to eating out, then Tripadvisor is an invaluable resource. However, in some places the choice can be limited. For example, we were in the tourist office of Kyle of Lochalsh, a village in Scotland with one main street, whose claim to fame was that it used to be the departure point for the ferry to Skye prior to the bridge being built. When a tourist asked the manager for a recommendation of a good restaurant, he explained that 'being the Tourist Board we are not allowed to recommend any'. The tourist enquired 'can you tell me where the bulk of the restaurants are?' After the manager stopped laughing, he replied 'if we have one of anything here, we are lucky, let alone a concentration'.

ENTERTAINMENT

Socialising

We always made a point of inviting other sailors moored near to us over for drinks. We had some great evenings and made some good friends; this is one of the pleasures of cruising. However, according to one seasoned sailor we met, it was, surprisingly, quite rare to be invited over for drinks; he said people tended to stay on their boats.

On several occasions, we pooled our food with neighbouring boats and had a big slap-up feast. Socialising is also a good way of finding out about places to visit. We also invited local people on board for a drink if they were interested in our boat. After one such occasion, we were then invited back for a meal at their home.

A boat business card is invaluable when you want to exchange details. We had one printed with our names, boat name, email, mobile numbers and web address and a photo of our boat on it. We didn't include our home address, so as not to advertise the fact that we are away from home for an extended period, in case the card fell into the wrong hands. One couple created a bookmark, which also had the details of the charity that they were raising money for. A visitors' book is a nice memento of each such event, and also a useful way to remember everyone's names!

Games

Take along some games to pass the evenings: travel Scrabble and backgammon occupied the odd hour for us. Two boat crews we surveyed took along golf clubs, one anchoring off St Andrews to make a quick trip ashore for a round at the home of golf.

Watching wildlife

One of the highlights on our trip was being able to see wildlife at such close quarters. I now realise that our normal cruising ground, on the south coast of England, is relatively devoid of wildlife in comparison to the rest of the UK waters. So

Puffin on Westray

a book on birdlife and mammals of the sea is essential to help with identification.

The birdlife was plentiful and a few were our companions: fulmars seemed to love 'playing chicken' with the forestay, razorbills did very good impressions of penguins, guillemots would fly in formation and always looked purposeful. When we got further north, skuas and great skuas appeared. These large sinister-looking birds are the bullies of the air, chasing other birds until their victims vomit up their food through sheer exhaustion, which the skua then eats. A special mention should go to the comical puffins, who appear to have missed out on the skills of landing on land and water. As they approach, they lower their orange feet, which have the aerodynamic properties of blocks of concrete, resulting in a crash landing.

You will see them on the water, but you will rarely get a photo of them; they dive just as you get your camera ready. However, if you visit Westray (Orkney), ask the harbourmaster about the puffins' roosting site at Castle O'Burrian and you will see them landing two feet away from you as they come in to roost at dusk.

In anchorages, we would suddenly realise we were being watched by two big brown eyes, as an inquisitive seal had popped up. Then there were the dolphins and porpoises, which make everyone smile. They love to play in your bow wave and they genuinely seem interested in watching you when they surface. On one night watch, Mags heard a wave breaking and was convinced we were about to hit something but it turned out to be dolphins. She was then treated to a spectacular display, with the phosphorescence illuminating their tracks, as they sped around the boat like friendly torpedoes. It was like a Disney film, with sparkles following their twists and turns.

Basking sharks are occasionally seen, though one couple reported seeing 25 off the coast near Padstow. Several boats reported seeing minke and orca whales en route. If you are very lucky you may see a giant turtle; they have been spotted off the Dingle Peninsula on the west coast of Ireland.

Diving

Several crews went diving en route. All credit to Sarah Fagg (*Huffin*, Hurley 22) and her stowing abilities – she sailed around Britain via Cape Wrath, and managed to fit two full sets of diving kit in a 22ft (6.7m) yacht and still had room for another crew member!

DVDs/Downloaded Films

We bought a few DVDs on eBay prior to the trip; they were well worth it, especially as we then sold them on return for more than we paid. Downloading films onto your tablet when on Wi-Fi is a great source of entertainment. We have been guilty of binge watching a box set at anchor on a miserable day.

Skara Brae, Orkney – perhaps inspiration for the first version of IKEA's flat pack furniture

Memberships

We decided that being a member of the National Trust would be a good idea for the trip, allowing free access to some attractions. Sadly, all buildings and monuments we wanted to visit belonged either to English or Scottish Heritage. Membership of one of these organisations would have saved us money.

Books

Swapping books is a good way to keep your library refreshed. A few marinas had book swaps. Kindles are a great way of reducing your storage requirements. Puzzle books are always good to while away the hours when storm bound.

Podcasts

Podcasts are a good source of entertainment as you can download them while on Wi-Fi and listen to them when you chose. Being an avid *The Archers* fan my highlight is a cracking good sail listening to the omnibus of *The Archers*. Sad, I know!

SHOWER FACILITIES

We were generally able to get a shower either at the harbour facilities, youth hostels or Fishermen's Missions. At Kinlochbervie, we had to decide between a shower or the famous fish and chips, as we arrived just as it was about to close. However, they did stay open longer to allow us to get our shower; an example of one of the many kindnesses that we experienced en route. To improve your showering experience in marina and municipal showers, take a shower mat with you. Also a pair of flip flops minimises the contact your feet have with the floors, which can at times be somewhat unpleasant.

The best shower facility award has to go to Crinan Canal (the landing stage at Bellanoch

Warkworth Castle, near Amble

Bridge). Here we had our own private shower and loo in a former lock keeper's building and, like all things on the canal, it was immaculate. A special mention should go to Amble Marina, which used to have a bath. Sadly, no more!

KEEPING A HAPPY SHIP

A trip like this should be an experience of a lifetime, one to treasure, especially if you are a couple. If you and your crew are to make a success of the cruise, a good atmosphere is vitally important. Sailing together worked really well for us, so we decided to look in detail at why:

- Don't embark on this trip unless you and your crew already get on well with each other ashore.

- There is only one skipper on a boat, so it is important to designate a skipper who has ultimate responsibility.

- Good communications are essential to prevent misunderstandings and frustration building up. It is also important to share concerns and not let them bottle up. For example, I can, at times, be too risk averse when in a harbour. The longer I am storm bound, the more apprehensive I seem to get. Mags was always a good sounding board, bringing me back to reality.

Looking down the Kyle of Loch Alsh

- Play to your strengths and split the tasks based on what you enjoy and are usually more skilled at, rather than on gender-related lines. I never understand why men always tend to helm the boat when anchoring and leave the woman to manhandle the anchor, despite the man usually being the stronger of the two. Being two women, we weren't bound by boy jobs and girl jobs! Even though we had our preferred tasks, we still knew how to do each other's as a back-up.
- Ensure that you plan everything together, so that both have an equal say in the important decisions. You may have one skipper but it is joint ownership of the cruise that makes it a success. This doesn't stop you splitting the tasks in order to make best use of time. This holds true for both pre-trip planning and during the cruise.
- While I am the skipper and hold the Yachtmaster® Offshore qualification, I had confidence in Mags' ability as a Day Skipper to run a watch without me. She also knows her limitations and knew when to call me and ask for advice when I was off watch. I know of many crews where their skipper very rarely went to sleep. The 'superman' concept will lead to exhaustion.
- If you are responsible for one task, then make sure the other crew is kept informed. For example, I would do the detailed route planning and then would brief Mags on the planning, the logic, tidal gates etc.
- Common tasks are a good way of building a strong team. We would carry out joint pilotage coming into harbours; not only is it a good sanity check but it also gave us a joint sense of achievement. In fog, or close to hazards, I would be up on deck and Mags would man the radar.
- Understand each other's weaknesses and be prepared to compromise. I am not very good at relaxing, so I am always busy doing things, tweaking sails, helming etc. Mags can easily switch off and would happily set the sails, the autohelm and do a puzzle book on watch, looking up regularly, of course, to keep watch. There was no point in me getting frustrated that we were not going as fast as we possibly could; it wasn't a race.
- The trip is a challenge and will be hard work, so you need commonly agreed goals. If your goals are different from the start, then it will not be a rewarding challenge. I mentioned this in the introduction but can't stress it enough. So spend time getting a common understanding of what you want to achieve to make this trip memorable for the right reasons.

SAILING WITH CHILDREN

A circumnavigation can be a rich and rewarding adventure, with real quality time for any family. Those who have read Libby Purves' excellent book *One Summer's Grace* will also know that it can have its challenges. Greg and Sue Hill (*Blue Argolis*, Trewes 41) completed the trip via Cape Wrath during the summer holidays with their children Kate and Sebastian (10 and 12 respectively). While much depends on your children (and you know them best), the Hills offered the following advice:

- Too much time spent at sea can be boring for children, so make sure that you have allowed for enough shore days and that you plan your route to have fun activities ashore. They said that 'London and St Katharine's Dock were a great hit; how else can a family of four stay in the centre of London for £40?' (£137.50 as at 2024 prices). Too many deserted anchorages will not give the children a chance to get ashore easily or the opportunity to meet children from other boats.
- Involve the children in activities like navigation, watch keeping etc.

Here is some advice from Mike and Michelle Perry (*Caribbean Breeze*, Fairline 36 Turbo), who completed a circumnavigation of Britain via the Caledonian Canal with their children Letitia and Michael (10 and 9 respectively), also in the school holidays:

- A DVD player or tablet can be quite a boon for young children.
- Impose strict rules about the wearing of lifejackets whenever the kids are outside, whether at sea or not.

A memorable day's sail
14 June – Kyleakin to Loch Gairloch

We set off at a civilised time (8.30am) and passed under the controversial bridge to Skye, behind which was the most sublime view of Loch Alsh and the surrounding mountains, which appeared as layers on a canvas, with each layer of mountains being a different colour, lightening as they regressed into the background. Despite the gloomy forecast, it was actually a lovely warm day and we donned our shorts. We headed northwards, up the Inner Sound and on the way saw dolphins, puffins, (who managed to evade Mags' 500 attempts to capture them on camera) and seals. It was blowing about F2, we had the cruising chute up as we glided along at a gentle pace up the length of Skye, with the Cuillins framing the backdrop behind us. We arrived early in Loch Gairloch, which allowed us time to explore the area and we walked up to some local waterfalls. We decided to treat ourselves and go to the local pub for a meal (the first meal out of the trip). It was another excellent day…one of many.

134 UK AND IRELAND CIRCUMNAVIGATOR'S GUIDE

YOUR BOAT WILL BE YOUR HOME

One of the greatest compliments we received was when people came on board and they said how homely it was. Extended cruising doesn't need to mean really basic conditions. We cruised in comfort by adding a few extras, though it does increase the weight, but as our boat is already eight tonnes in the water, we could live with a little more:

- A picture on the wall and scatter cushions (made of fire-retardant material) gives a homely feel to the saloon. We ban anyone from sitting on saloon cushions wearing sailing clothing, because once you have salt on your cushions, they will just absorb water and you will always have that damp feeling in the fabric.
- Proper china mugs and plates (they never broke) make us feel that we aren't camping, though we do have plastic bowls with lids for when eating at sea.
- Proper glasses for wine and the odd dram; again, we have plastic ones for use at sea.
- Proper bedding such as a duvet, sheet and memory foam mattress can make a bunk seem civilised. We have sleeping bags that we use when at sea.
- Scented nappy sacks to place your used loo paper in.

FLAGS

En route you will have the opportunity to fly several flags, some of which you may want to buy in advance:

- **Courtesy flags** Depending on your route and nationality you may need the Irish or British courtesy flag. You may also like to consider optional courtesy flags: for example, the Scottish Saltire or Welsh Baner Cymru, or regional flags such as those of Orkney, Devon or Cornwall.
- **Q flag** For visiting Ireland.

Dressing overall

This trip is a great excuse to dress overall, either at the beginning or end of the cruise. Note that it is much easier to fly the flags if you have sewn them onto a 5 or 6mm line or buy them made up. The flag order is as follows:

From the bow: E, Q, p3, G, p8, Z, p4, W, p6, P, p1, I, Code, T, Y, B, X, 1st Sub, H, 3rd Sub, D, F, 2nd Sub, U, A, O, M, R, p2, J, p0, N, p9, K, p7, V, p5, L, C, S. The size of flags should be appropriate to the size of the boat and for a single masted boat the break at the mast should come between the 3rd substitute and the D.

CHAPTER THIRTEEN

SAFETY

Thankfully, accidents involving the loss of life at sea seldom happen, so it is easy to become complacent. On the last day of our cruise, we heard the mayday call during the search, to the south of the Isle of Wight, for the yacht *Ouzo* and her crew members. A Marine Accident Investigation concluded that the *Ouzo* had been in a collision with a cross-Channel passenger ferry, resulting in the tragic deaths of the three crew. This is a grim reminder of how important safety afloat is, especially with regard to watchkeeping.

The aim should be to minimise the chance of an incident happening, but if it does, then to ensure that you and your crew have the skills and equipment to deal with it. This is particularly important on a circumnavigation; while you may never be too far from land, much of the coast is remote and far from civilisation.

Therefore, when selecting your equipment, you should treat this as an offshore cruise as opposed to a coastal one. Prior to your trip, try to attend the RYA Sea Survival course, if you haven't already done so. Not only because of the invaluable information that you learn about emergency situations but also because you can discuss the merits of different types of safety equipment. A good course provider will have examples on show of all the different types of

Righting a liferaft

safety equipment and will know the advantages and disadvantages of each.

EMERGENCY SITUATIONS AND EQUIPMENT

We considered all the risks, then planned what safety equipment we would need to have on board. It is also a balance between cost and the space that you have available. The good news is that you should have many of these items already. This is our list (updated to include what we now carry):

EMERGENCY SITUATION	EQUIPMENT	LOCATION/COMMENT
MAN OVERBOARD	Lifejackets fitted with lights, hoods, AIS beacons, crotch straps and integrated harnesses. Automatic release	Worn
	MOB block and tackle recovery system	Wet locker
	Long swim ladder (reaching 0.5m below water line)	Cockpit locker
	Danbuoy with light	Cockpit
	Life ring	Cockpit
	Throwing line	Cockpit
	Life sling	Pushpit
ABANDON SHIP	Liferaft in canister	Foredeck/Pushpit
	Grab bag in floating waterproof container	Companionway. It has a mini drogue on it
	RORC flares/Odeo flares in floating waterproof container	Companionway. It has a mini drogue on it
	Water in floating container	Companionway
	EPIRB 406Hz	Companionway
FIRE	Engine fire extinguisher HFC-227EA/FE36 – a clean gaseous agent	Engine compartment
	Powder fire extinguishers	2kg: saloon; cockpit locker. FFS50 50s Fire safety sticks for all cabins
	Fire blanket	Near galley and aft cabin, as no secondary escape from the aft cabin
	Smoke and gas detector	Aft cabin
COLLISION	Sea-me active radar reflector	
	3 bilge pumps	1 operated below deck, 1 operated above deck and 1 for emergency use
	White flares/Odeo Flares	Companionway reachable from cockpit
	Steamer scarer	Cockpit – plugged in when on night watches
	Hole repair kit	Below decks but above water line
LOSS OF RIG	Shoot-it gas-powered wire cutter	Companionway
	Bolt cutters	Behind companionway steps
	Emergency radar reflector	Chart table
	Emergency antenna	Chart table
FOULED PROPELLER	Full diving suit including hood, gloves, boots, mask, waterproof torch, fins and snorkel	In locker below deck
	Rope cutter	On shaft by propeller
	Folding propeller	Main propeller on shaft
ELECTRICAL FAILURE	Emergency navigation lights	Companionway
	Handheld VHF radio	Below deck in grab bag
	Handheld GPS	Chart table
LOSS OF STEERING	Emergency steering	Cockpit locker
SEACOCK FAILURE	Seacock plugs (tapered wooden plugs) that fit into the seacock in case of failure	Attached by lanyard to the seacock, so it is ready to use
ROPE WRAPPED ROUND LIMB	Emergency knife	In protective cover in mast halyard bag
GENERAL	DSC radio	
	Laminated mayday procedure	Near the radio

Emergency Position Indicating Radio Beacon (EPIRB)

The EPIRB, when activated, allows the rescue co-ordination centre to find your boat in an emergency, by sending off a distress signal via the COPAS/SARSAT satellites. There are several differences between types of EPIRBs, including the accuracy which determines the size of the search area and the time taken to detect the signal:

406MHz beacon	3nm radius: 28 sq miles area Approximately 1–2 hours for signal to be picked up
406MHz beacon with GPS	0.1nm radius: 0.03 sq miles area Under 30 minutes for signal to be picked up
406MHz beacon with GPS	As above but also sending out an AIS message to AIS equipped vessels

There is a cheaper version that allows your EPIRB to interface with your boat's GPS, though the majority have their own GPS. It is important to register 406MHz beacons to ensure that a search operation is initiated when the EPIRB is activated. There are also differences between how EPIRBs are released: a category 1 EPIRBs float free and switch on automatically; category 2 is deployed manually but can still be activated by water, once it has been freed from the bracket. EPIRBs are battery operated and they have a 3–5 year lifespan; they usually operate for 48 hours once activated. As they contain internal batteries, you will need to ensure that they do not need replacing during your trip.

Search and Rescue Transponder (SART)

Although we did not carry a SART, you may consider doing so. This is a radar transceiver, which transmits a distinctive emergency signal that any ship can pick up on its radar. The advantage is that the signal can also be picked up by other vessels, rather than just the search and rescue craft.

Personal Locator Beacon (PLB)

This is personal EPIRB, registered to you, not your boat, that sends the distress message on the 406MHz distress frequency. Available with or without a GPS, it is manually activated with a battery life of a minimum of 24 hours. With a GPS, it will identify your location to within 100m.

Automatic Identification System (AIS) Beacon, or AIS Man Overboard (MOB) devices

This transmits a MOB message to AIS-equipped vessels within the vicinity (4-5 miles). The built in GPS ensures that your exact position is also sent and displayed on nearby vessels' chart plotters. We now have these on our lifejackets. If the bladder inflates it automatically triggers the device and sends a distress message. When we anchor, the person at the bow wears a non-AIS lifejacket, because the AIS ones are sensitive and the mechanism can be triggered accidentally when leaning over the pulpit. Once we had lots of concerned people coming to our yacht both at sea and when moored. We were at a loss to know where the distress message was coming from, till we discovered it was the lifejacket AIS.

Liferaft

You should not undertake this trip without a liferaft. You can either buy or rent one for the period. The RYA Sea Survival course allows you to practise getting in and out of one, and once dressed in full

Storm crashes over Stonehaven harbour walls © Victoria Park

kit with a lifejacket, it makes you really appreciate what you are looking for in a liferaft.

The tragic end to the 1979 Fastnet race, where 15 yachtsmen drowned, and the 1998 Sydney to Hobart Race where a further 6 yachtsmen lost their lives, resulted in the ISO 9650 standard. Type 1 (group A) liferafts are designed for open ocean and ideal for long distance cruising, offshore voyages and racing yachts. There is a SOLAS standard, but these are really only suitable for commercial vessels. You can upgrade your liferaft by the addition of different SOLAS packs – either A (Offshore) or B (Coastal). Many of the newer liferafts have servicing intervals of every three years, as opposed to annually, which can help in the justification for upgrading to a newer model.

Your liferaft should be stowed where it is easily accessible and protected from heavy weather. You can choose to have your liferaft released automatically using a hydro-static release unit (HRU), which activates when submerged under 1–4m of water; the liferaft will then float to the surface.

Loss of rig

Cutting through wire rigging is extremely difficult in calm conditions, let alone at sea in a storm. Neither of us felt confident about being able to cut rigging with just a pair of bolt cutters so we decided to buy the gas-powered Shootit, which cuts the wire once the trigger is pulled.

Man overboard – prevention is better than cure

As you will read in the log entry in the next chapter (see page 148), Mags had to go into the water to cut a rope off our propeller. Even in a wetsuit, the cold made her breathing difficult, and after 15 minutes in the water, getting back on the boat unaided was a real effort. Most people who do this trip, like us, are short-handed. One person has to be able to stop the boat, throw over danbuoys, press the MOB button etc, all while keeping an eye on the location of the casualty and then getting the person back on board. All this reinforced our view that the best way to handle a MOB situation, was for the other person

SAFETY **139**

to stay on board. A single-hander has little chance of rescue, so staying on board is imperative. This should reinforce your decisions about when you need to clip on. You may also consider a transom ladder, which can be released from sea level.

Make sure that you have planned and tested how you will get someone back on board, as they are unlikely to be able to help you.

You should try to support the casualty horizontally when you lift them from the water. If you lift them vertically out of the water, the blood drains from the head and a rapid drop in blood pressure can result in a heart attack. Systems such as the Jon Buoy are designed to keep the casualty in a horizontal position. If you are in a motor boat, you will not have the height to rig up a recovery system such as the one in the diagram. You may consider fitting a mini crane, which is the advice of Malcolm and Glenda Stennett (*Lady Genevieve*, Broom 39). If not, you will need to use the bathing platform or the tender, if the sea is not rough. It is recommended to have a long line attached at one end to a stanchion and the other to an electric windlass, via a strong point such as a cleat. It

assumes the casualty can stand on the line which is then winched in.

One fear, if there are just two of you on board, is how would the off-watch person know that the other person has gone overboard, especially if they are asleep? There are several options:

- **Low-cost solution** Set an alarm every 15 minutes and the person on watch must reset the alarm before it sounds. French Solo sailor Florence Arthaud winner of the 1990 Route du Rhum, was able to call her mother when she fell overboard, because she had her phone encased in a waterproof cover and could hold it out of the water. Her mother alerted the rescue services and the phone's GPS helped locate her.

- **High-cost solution** There are several electronic systems such as Raymarine LifeTag and Mobi-lert, which will set off an alarm if you fall outside the guard zone of the base unit. Your position, when the signal is lost, is plotted on your chart plotter.

Grab bag

Your grab bag needs to reflect that you will be in colder climes but that you are not expected to be at sea for an unlimited time. Also, take into account what you already have in your liferaft. We planned ours to keep two people alive for two days. In an ideal world, you would have absolutely everything ready in your grab bag, though this would mean that you would have to have duplicate items, eg EPIRB and handheld VHF radio. However, budget and space are limiting factors. So we had a spare dry bag kept next to the grab bag for additional items. We had a laminated list of all these items, also kept next to the grab bag:

Make sure once you pack your grab bag that it floats. In the liferaft, we had such items as a

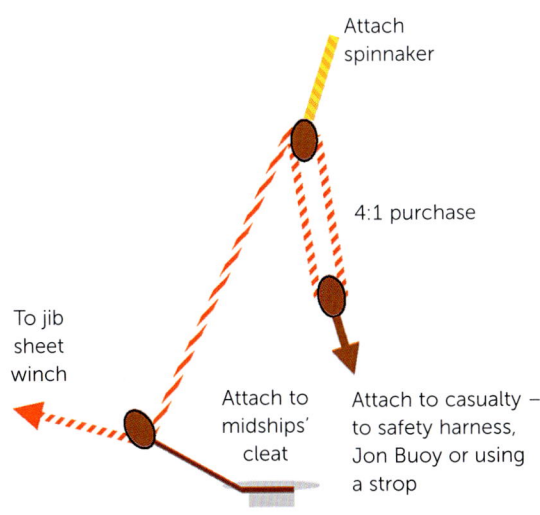

MOB-hoisting block and tackle

ITEM		GRAB BAG	FLARE BAG	ADDITIONAL ITEMS	WATER BAG
COMMUNICATIONS	Handheld VHF			•	
	VHF battery holder and spare batteries	•			
	Waterproof bag for VHF	•			
	RORC flare pack and welding glove/Odeo Flares		•		
	Whistle	•			
	Strobe light and signal mirror	•			
	Fog horn			•	
	EPIRB			•	
	Emergency radar reflector			•	
RATIONS	Water (3 litres)				•
	Snap light stick (2)	•			
	Cereal bars, chocolate bars	•			
	Small plastic drinking bottle	•			
CLOTHING	Fleece hat (2) and gloves (2 pairs)	•			
	Spare clothing			•	
MEDICAL	First aid kit			•	
	Survival blanket	•			
	Petroleum jelly	•			
	Sunburn cream	•			
	Seasickness tablets and seasickness bags	•			
GENERAL	Hand warmers (8 chemical heat packs)	•			
	Plastic bags	•			
	Waterproof torch and spare batteries	•			
	Safety knife with blunt end and cutting board	•			
	Nylon string and duct tape	•			
	Camera in waterproof box			•	
	Compass			•	
	The Liferaft Survival Guide (see Appendix 4)	•			
	Credit card/money/yacht papers			•	

Grab bag contents – things you may need at a moment's notice.

sea anchor, hand air pump, paddles, bailer and sponges. Check that the glue in your repair kit is suitable for use in a damp environment – some aren't! If not, include swimming pool glue.

Flares

Ensure that your flares are easy to access and that you know how to use them without having to read the instructions; you may need to use them at night and with very little notice. Handheld flares become very hot when they are burning, therefore you should carry a pair of welding gloves to protect your hand. On our current boat, we have dispensed with pyrotechnic flares and use electronic Odeo flares, which are safer to use, last for longer when in use and don't have the same disposal issues as with the traditional flares. Admittedly they are not so visible, as there is no rocket, but in conjunction with other electronic safety equipment such as EPIRB and AIS beacons, it is less of an issue.

Lifejacket

There are several factors to consider when buying lifejackets:

- *How do they inflate?* There are several options: manual (by pulling a lanyard), auto release (on contact with water) and hydrostatic release (releases on water pressure). Always check the condition of the gas cylinder and inflation system.
- *What buoyancy?* We made the mistake of buying 275 Newton (N) lifejackets, thinking that the extra buoyancy would make them safer. However, during a test in a swimming pool they nearly killed us; it was impossible to breathe in them and so we needed to let out air. Jackets of 275N are designed for people wearing heavy equipment; hence the extra buoyancy is required. We now have 150N jackets.
- *What features should the lifejacket have?* A lifejacket hood is essential for keeping the spray and water off your face if you are in the water. The best hoods are those already fitted. A light should also be fitted. Fit and use crotch straps to prevent your lifejacket riding up.
- *When should you wear a lifejacket?* This is subject to much debate and you need to decide this for yourselves, unless of course you are in Irish waters, where it is compulsory to wear lifejackets in all vessels larger than 7m. We chose to wear them all the time while at sea.
- *Is it comfortable?* You will be wearing your lifejacket for long periods of time, so do make sure it is comfortable.

Lee cloths

You should have adequate passage-making berths on board with lee cloths to enable you to defy gravity while sleeping.

Boat rules

If you were to do a risk assessment, you would probably never leave the harbour. However, considering the worst things that can happen, then developing routines to reduce the likelihood of them occurring is a sound approach. Our boat rules were:

- Store all flammable liquids in sealed lockers in the cockpit, so they could not leak into the bilge.
- Heave-to when reefing, as you then have a stable platform to work on.
- Wear oilskin bottoms when cooking at sea.

- Clip on in winds above 14 knots during the day, and always at night or any time when you deem it necessary.
- Always wear a lifejacket.
- When manually handling the anchor or anchor chain, disconnect the remote control so that it could not be accidentally pushed or stood on.
- Don't hang fenders from the guard rails for any length of time; attach them to a strong point, eg stanchion base, cleat or shroud.
- No rings to be worn at sea.
- When going up the mast, always wear a safety harness and clip on.
- Rig up the steamer scarer light in the cockpit during night hours.

COASTGUARD

RYA SafeTrx is an app that can be used to log your passage plan, with your emergency contacts receiving an SMS if you are 30 mins later than your planned ETA and have failed to report that you have arrived at your destination. You are warned 15 mins after your ETA, to either end or extend your ETA. On our cruise we would register our passage plan with the local coastguard. On the south coast, during weekends, the local Solent Coastguard became totally fed up with leisure craft requesting radio checks every two minutes. However, elsewhere the coastguard has more time, and by radioing in daily, they get to know you, ask what you are doing and are very helpful and friendly. At one point we had a problem with our VHF signal strength, which was very low. The coastguard was very helpful, switching to several different aerials to see if they could pick us up. It was with some regret that we would sign off from one coastguard, but exciting when we first picked up the next one.

FOG

While the gales reduce in the summer, the likelihood of fog increases as the warm moist air meets the colder sea. We encountered fog on ten days during our trip; it is inevitable. Therefore, you need the equipment to be able to make passage safely in such conditions. The key is to be seen and to see others.

Being seen

Plastic, GRP or wooden boats don't show up well on radar, therefore, to be seen you need to improve your radar visibility. For boats under 49ft (15m), SOLAS V guidance for recreational craft requires you to fit the largest radar reflector you can, as high as possible and to the manufacturer's instructions. Your visibility on radar is measured in two ways: radar cross section (RCS) and detection probability. Both need to be as large as possible. There is a current international standard (ISO 8729) specification. Part 1 covers passive radars and Part 2 covers active radars.

If you have the chance to cruise in company on a lumpy sea with another boat that has radar, ask them at what range they lose you as a target; it can be quite scary. However, it is not as simple as just mounting a reflector and checking your visibility with another boat. It is even more difficult for commercial vessels to see recreational vessels, for the following reasons:

- The differences between leisure and commercial radars give them different detection abilities. The technical differences are around the angle of sea clutter zone and the angle of beam width. Radar visibility is also affected by the height of the other vessels' antennae – a yacht and a ferry have very different heights of antenna.

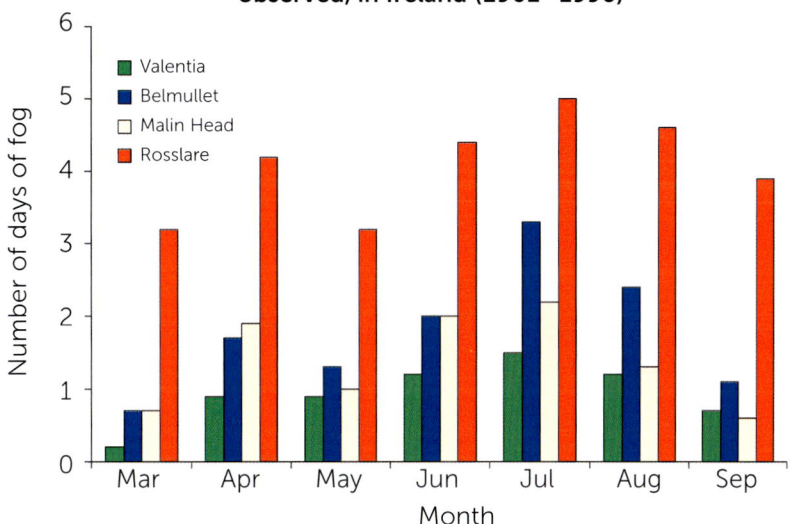

Average number of days per month that fog was observed, in Ireland (1961–1990)

Adapted from data supplied by the Met Éireann (see page 4 for more information)

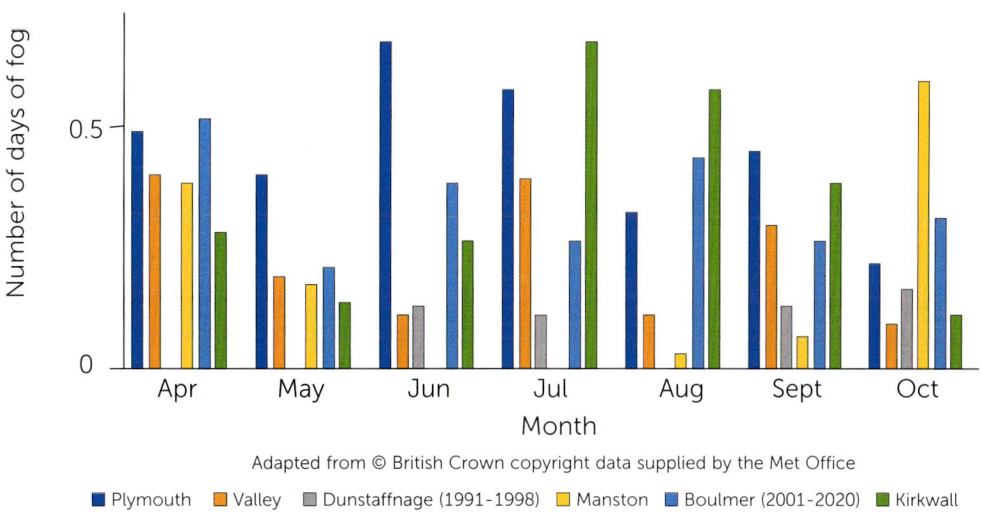

Average number of days per month where fog was observed at 0900, in the UK (1991–2020, unless otherwise stated)

Adapted from © British Crown copyright data supplied by the Met Office

- Marine radar operates on two bands: X-band and S-band. S-band improves the detection of large targets in bad weather and so requires a large scanner with higher power requirements, so is only fitted to large vessels. X-band is heavily affected by sea or rain clutter but has smaller scanner and power requirements, hence this is fitted to recreational boats. Large ships use both X- and S-bands, depending on the density of traffic and the sea state. There is no reflector available for recreational boats that operates effectively on S-band. Passive radar reflectors for recreational boats only offer a tenth of the performance on S-band compared to that seen on X-band.

- For a large vessel to pick up and track a ship on an Automatic Radar Plotting Aid (ARPA), it is not just the maximum size of the peak that is important but also the consistency of the return echo at different bearings. Too many zero readings and it will not be tracked. For this reason, the international standard recognises that the consistency of the response is more effective in raising the probability of detection than single peaks, and is defined as the Stated Performance Level (SPL). The response has to be maintained at 10° (for motor cruisers and sailing vessels such as catamarans with a small angle of heel) and 20° (for all other sailing vessels).

- The performance of radar reflectors from different manufacturers varies greatly, with cost not necessarily being an indicator of effectiveness. The performance of some has not matched the manufacturers' claims. A report commissioned by the Marine Accident Investigation Branch (MAIB), as a result of the loss of the *Ouzo*, has provided an independent assessment of the most popular radar reflectors, comparing them to the current and future ISO standards. This, along with other studies, helps to inform recreational boaters which is the most effective and appropriate systems. However, it advises 'in certain circumstances their craft may still not be readily visible on ships' radars and thus, they should always navigate with caution' (Report by QinetiQ, 'Performance Investigation of Marine Radar Reflectors on the Market'). The report is available from the MAIB or on its website at www.maib.gov.uk.

Combine these issues with the pitching and angle of heel and it is important that you do everything possible to make yourself seen and always be aware of the limitations of your system. You may consider doing an 'All ships' call when in fog. We were crossing the Pentland Firth in fog with radar and a Sea-Me active radar reflector fitted. Due to the nature of this stretch of water, all large vessels passing through have to radio into the coastguard. Two vessels radioed in; normally you don't get the luxury of knowing what is out there beyond your ship's radar range. We took the decision to contact the two vessels to check they could see us. Thankfully they could, which was reassuring.

There are two types of radar reflector:

Active radar reflector

This is a reflector which enhances a radar signal and then retransmits it when it receives it. This increases the detection range, the chance that you will be seen and results in a stronger signal around the full 360° azimuth. The Sea-Me and Echomax are examples of active reflectors; they exceed the requirement of both standards up to an angle of heel of 15°. Active radar reflectors were recommended by the MAIB report if power was available. Dual-band active radars (both X and S) are now available.

Passive radar reflector

The performance of this type varies greatly, from those considered not suitable, to higher-end performers which only just fail the two standards. The MAIB report makes essential reading when selecting a passive reflector.

SAFETY

Seeing others

It is also important to see others and not just rely on them seeing you. There are several options, which all have strengths and weaknesses.

Radar

Not all vessels have AIS fitted, therefore, having radar will ensure that you can see other vessels. From the Graphs (see page 143), you can see that you will encounter fog en route. However, radar does give you confidence to make safe passage, either using a stand-alone radar or integrated with a chart plotter. But I appreciate it is a significant investment. I do note that only 36 per cent of those recently surveyed had radar fitted.

Mini Automatic Radar Plotting Aid (MARPA)

Technology has now made assessing the course of other targets easier. If your radar is fitted with this, it calculates the speed, course and closest point of approach of acquired targets. However, as it is based on radar, its accuracy can be affected by the boat's pitching and yawing. It is worth testing it on boats in good visibility to see this effect. Be aware of its limitations and use features such as Electronic Bearing Lines (EBL) to track a vessel's course.

Automatic Identification System (AIS)

AIS allows you to be seen and see others who have AIS equipment fitted. All passenger vessels and commercial vessels over 300 tons are required, by law, to have an AIS installed. This equipment transmits key data every couple of seconds, such as the ship's name, MMSI number, position, speed, course and heading. AIS enables other vessels and port authorities to understand the movement of ships in their area. Some of the data is dynamic, so it is updated automatically and some has to be entered manually, eg your destination. Yachts and motor boats have no legal requirement to fit AIS but you can benefit from this technology if you choose to have the appropriate equipment installed.

Transmitting AIS data

To transmit data, an AIS transponder is required and there are two types of transponders:

- Class-A AIS transponder for those vessels legally required to carry AIS equipment. The frequency of data transmission depends on the speed of the vessel. Over 23 knots it is updated every 2 seconds, and at less than 10 knots it is every 14 seconds.
- Class-B AIS transponder designed for leisure craft and vessels that are not legally required to carry AIS equipment. This device has the same features as the basic AIS receiver, plus the capability of being able to transmit your vessel's data as well, which it does every 30 seconds.

Any other AIS-equipped vessel within range will be able to identify your vessel on their AIS system. On large vessels and commercial ships, where the AIS system is fully integrated to their navigation systems, an automatic alarm should sound if a potential collision situation is detected, thus enabling the watch officers to take appropriate action to prevent a dangerous situation developing.

Receiving AIS data

To receive the data, you need to have an AIS receiver. This will give you the ability to receive data but will not transmit your own boat's data. This information can be displayed either by:

- An AIS receiver which is interfaced with a PC-based charting software or a compatible chart plotter. You are able to monitor the positions and movements of any other AIS-equipped vessels. The range is limited by that of the electronic charting display.

- Stand-alone AIS receiver which displays the positions and movements of AIS equipped vessels on a simple LCD screen, similar to a radar display. Your vessel is located at the centre of the screen and you can zoom in or out, to locate any AIS equipped vessels at different ranges.

Limitations to AIS

In theory, AIS has the advantage over radar in that it provides accurate data which is not affected by the movement of the boat. However, there are several limitations:

- It only works if vessels have the appropriate receiver and transponder and it is switched on.
- Some of the data is entered manually; therefore, it is only as accurate as the operator.
- AIS is integrated to the ship's displays only on ships built after July 2008, so often on older ships it is difficult to see targets, or the equipment can only handle a limited number of targets.
- It operates on VHF band and class-B, and therefore does not have the same priority of data transmission as class-A, which means that sometimes it doesn't transmit.

Therefore, having a class-B transponder is no guarantee that larger vessels have spotted you.

DINGHY SAFETY

It is easy to invest time and money in safety equipment and routines for your boat, and then hop into your dinghy and cross open water with little thought about safety. Some key points to staying safe in a dinghy:

- Always wear a lifejacket; we used to padlock them in the dinghy once ashore, to avoid having to carry them around.
- Don't overload the dinghy.
- Carry a handheld VHF radio.
- Don't use a dinghy during periods of strong tidal flow; your outboard could fail and you will then be at the mercy of the tide.
- Always take oars with you.
- Secure your dinghy well above the tidal level on a rising tide. We saw a dinghy blow away on Holy Island due to this in 2.3 knots of tide.
- Always carry spare fuel with you.

Herring boats recycled on Holy Island

CHAPTER FOURTEEN

HAZARDS IN COASTAL WATERS

POTS AND NETS

Virtually half of the 61 people surveyed encountered problems with lines from pots or nets wrapped around their propellers, rudders or keels, though most said they were a nuisance even without propeller fouling. If you are contemplating a circumnavigation of the UK and Ireland, or extended cruising in coastal waters, it is essential that you plan how to cope with a fouled propeller or rudder.

Fishing pots

Fishermen's pots are a serious hazard for yachts around the coasts of the UK and Ireland. Many are so poorly marked that you need to be very observant to spot them from a yacht cruising at 5–6 knots, and even more difficult in a motor boat when you are cruising at 20 knots. Several times on the VHF we heard of boats being rescued as a result of fouled propellers. In Stonehaven, we had moored next to a German couple who had to be rescued off Rattray Head because the rope from a line of pots had fouled both their propeller and steering. We came across many pots along the east coast of the UK. The best marked pots were off Stonehaven as they were marked with flags and buoys, and the worst were off Peterhead/Rattray Head, those off the north-east coast of England, and Harwich. We saw every type of marker, from five-litre containers to a couple of plastic footballs in a net. It makes you think twice

Pot markers: the good, the bad and the ugly

about sailing at night and in fog in areas where pots are commonplace. In Scotland, thanks to the Cruising Association's Lobster Pot Campaign, legislation now exists to ban inappropriate items being attached to the ends of static fishing gear, it has to be marked with a proper buoy.

We had one more close encounter when we hit a pot, submerged about half a metre below the surface, right on the leading line into Helmsdale, but thankfully suffered no damage.

Pot bound off Orkney
27 June – Stromness to Pierowall

With weed starting to grow on the bottom of the hull, it was a sure sign that it was time to move on. To catch the end of the ebb, we bid farewell to Stromness at 5am but had to motor, as there was no wind. Out through Hoy Sound, with its dramatic landscape, we had the tide with us, carrying us parallel to the coast. We made good time and I decided to go down below to take a nap, but within minutes I felt the boat dramatically change course and Mags called me up on deck. I heard the panic in her voice. To my horror I saw we had a fisherman's buoy waterskiing behind us. I yelled at Mags to put the engine into neutral and to stop it. The buoy marked a lobster pot and, although Mags had steered well clear of it, there was a length of floating rope which was impossible to see. It then wrapped itself around the prop and potentially rendering the engine useless. Luckily, we managed to stop the engine before the rope did that. But it meant that we couldn't use the engine, and there was not enough wind to sail. We were about 2 miles off a rocky coast with an onshore wind, but we were lucky as it was very light, so we drifted in the tide. Leaning over I saw that we would not get the pot off by pulling, so I cut it loose but that still left the rope wrapped round the propeller. We had two options: call for a rescue as we couldn't sail out of danger or get into the water and cut off the rope. We had a wetsuit for exactly these kinds of emergencies. Mags donned the suit and I tied her to the boat. The water was bitterly cold and it took Mags about ten minutes to stop hyperventilating and get control of her breathing. Thankfully, the water was crystal clear so it made cutting the rope easier.

The rope had wrapped itself round the propeller and carefully missed the ropecutter. Mags needed to untangle the rope before cutting it, so decided to put the knife down; unfortunately, this was not the brightest idea in 100m of water! So she came up to get another knife, this time it was the bread knife, and then returned with it tied to her wrist.

It was a great relief when both Mags and the fisherman's rope were back on the boat. We carried on our way and fortunately had no permanent damage to the engine. Westray came into sight and we passed Noup Head, our most northerly point on the trip. We passed through Papa Sound, which was very benign, despite the warning of doom from the almanac. On arrival at Pierowall we were greeted by a very friendly harbourmaster, Tom Rendall.

HAZARDS IN COASTAL WATERS

Orkney fishing boat with pot markers

Pot tactics

- If you see a pot, always pass up tide and up wind of it, to miss any floating rope.
- Always make sure you brief your crew on what to do if you hit a pot or rope. If I had briefed Mags to put the engine into neutral and stop immediately, it might have prevented the rope wrapping round the propeller.
- Keep a full wetsuit on board, and a sharp knife, so that you can cut a rope loose if the conditions allow. In stormy weather, we would not have attempted it; there is a real danger of the bottom of the boat hitting the head of the crew member and then you have a casualty in the water, as well as a fouled propeller.
- When you cut off the buoy, keep hold of both ends of the rope, with some to spare if possible, so that you can cleat it off. Then at least you can try to untangle it but also, if you have tension on the line, then the swimmer can use it to pull themselves down to the propeller.
- Keep a long ladder onboard. We have a long swim ladder and short dinghy ladder. We nearly left the long ladder behind to save space, as we weren't planning to go swimming. We will never again consider leaving the ladder behind.
- Tie the knife on with a strop, or better still, keep it in a knife sheath strapped to your leg.

Nets

Drift nets are used to catch salmon in coastal waters. They are suspended either between two large conspicuous buoys or just one buoy with a boat (often called a coble) at the inner end. They can extend up to 1.5 miles in length and the nets usually have smaller floats along the line. They used to be common around Irish waters but the good news for leisure craft is that, from 2007, they were banned in order to protect the dwindling numbers of wild salmon returning to rivers. The Irish Government set up a fund for the fishermen who lost their livelihood; this appears to have had the desired effect of eliminating the drift nets, according to the Irish Central Fisheries Board. They have also been banned in Scotland

Pierowall Harbour

A fishing boat in Uist, Scotland

and so, in theory, the only place you could find them is between Whitby and Holy Island. In 2014, there were 44 licences for these in England. The cobles are recognisable either because they are speeding over to you with the fisherman waving his arms frantically, or by the tarpaulin tent covering in the bows of these small open boats. Steve Cooksey (*Gamaldansk*, Westerly GK29) got a net tangled around the rudder off Tynemouth while on his trip round Britain via the Caledonian Canal, he was able to clear it with a boat hook.

In Ireland, despite the ban, some illegal nets remain. A good place to find salmon is around headlands and estuaries, these were the favourite places for the nets; so it may still be prudent not to plot a course from headland to headland. Also, if you are travelling at night or in poor visibility, staying a minimum of 5 miles offshore should keep you clear. Ireland does still have a few draft nets left. According to the Irish Central Fisheries Board, they are only in a few locations such as Cork and Castlemaine, and only from 1 to 21 July. But elsewhere they were banned in 2016. These nets are smaller than drift nets in length, they have buoys at each end and usually have a team of two boats at either end.

SHIPS

You will see an increased amount of shipping around the major ports but there are some other areas to watch out for. Crossing the Humber keeps you on your toes; you are crossing three shipping lanes exiting the traffic separation scheme (TSS) roundabout. Some ports such as Humber, Harwich/Felixstowe and Portsmouth require entry via defined small vessel channels. From the Minch to the Pentland Firth, all large ships are required to radio in to the coastguard when entering and leaving this stretch of water, so you get advanced warning of what is out there. We encountered several types of ships en route:

- **Fishing boats** The majority of the other vessels we saw were fishing boats. AIS would not be of use for many of these fishing boats as they are below the size at which AIS is legally required.
- **Gas rig supply ships** On the east coast, you will see many gas rig supply ships. Watch out as their superstructure (bridge) is at the bow rather than the stern, as found on many coasters and vessels elsewhere.
- **Ferries** Dover and Portsmouth are busy with ferries. You need to obtain permission from the Dover Harbour Control to enter but with ferries entering regularly, sailing in this area is like crossing the M25 on a zimmer frame.
- **Container ships** As Felixstowe is a major container port, you will see some strange sights: massive container ships with what appear to be cranes on board. Remember that visibility from the bridge of container ships is very poor if you are close to them.

One of the saddest observations derived from our cruise was the realisation that the UK fishing industry has been completely decimated. We entered many fishing ports where, in the past, the volume of fish landed had been sizeable, yet now there were no trawlers at the quayside and their fish markets stood empty.

Submarines

You can find out which areas are being used by submarines for exercises by listening to the Subfacts broadcast issued by the coastguard on VHF and on NAVTEX. Submarine exercise areas and times of the broadcasts can be found in *Reeds Nautical Almanac* and in the Maritime Communication (NP 291 or NP289). Here is the official advice if you are sailing in an area where there are submarine exercises:

- Keep clear of any vessel flying the code flags NE2 (meaning that submarines are in the area).
- Run your engine or generator even when under sail. Submarine sonar equipment is designed to detect noise over a wide range of frequencies.
- Operate your echo sounder.
- At night, show deck level navigation lights on your pulpit and stern.

How will you know if you are being followed? You will see your depth reduce dramatically when, by checking the chart, you know that it should be reading much deeper If you alter course dramatically, the depth will return to normal. If a submarine is following you, the depth will reduce again, as it alters course to follow. According to the Faslane Operations Room, if they are following you, it will be no less than 20m below you. I say this because when we were screaming along down the Sound of Sleat, in a gale force 8, we experienced exactly this. But the depth reduced to 2m. I contacted the duty Submarine Operations Room and they confirmed there were no submarines in the area. 'Maybe it was a whale' they offered... or maybe it was Morag, Nessie's lesser-known cousin!

Drilling rigs

One of the strangest sights was seeing a rig being towed in the Moray Firth. It puzzled us on watch for a long time. They are serviced in the Cromarty Firth, so in fact it is a regular sight. Most of the North Sea rigs are well offshore, except those around the Humber and off the Norfolk Coast. You will pass close to these large beasts but you must stay at least 500m from them.

Wind farms

As of 2024, there are 50 offshore wind farms (operational or under construction) in UK waters. If all the windfarms that are contracted are built by 2030, then capacity is due to be 73GW. The blades are at least 22m above mean high water springs (MHWS), to ensure the safety of small recreational craft. As of 2024, you are permitted to navigate through most windfarms, notwithstanding the 50m exclusion zone around each pylon, though some farms do have a specified passage through them, such as the one at Foulger's Gat. Do monitor a windfarm's working VHF channel if available.

Scroby Sands wind farm

The MCA has carried out trials on the effects of wind farms on navigational aids and communication equipment. A summary of which is:

- GPS, magnetic compasses, VHF, DSC and mobile phones were not affected.
- Small vessel radar performance was affected, including difficulties in picking up stationary vessels or other turbines, because of blind and shadow areas. MARPA had difficulty tracking a vessel within the farm.

Wave and tidal power

The technology for harnessing the power of the sea is far less developed, with several types being trialled currently in UK waters. They are unlikely to impede your route as they are research and development locations that can easily be avoided.

MIDGES

Midges are *definitely* a hazard on the west coast of Scotland. There is now even a midge forecast updated daily (www.midgeforecast.co.uk), with a scale of low, medium, high and nuisance. However, I don't quite understand the subtle differences between high and nuisance. The worst times are at dawn and dusk, when there is no wind. You will soon notice them biting. We barbecued once on a beach but were savaged by the midges; after that we only barbecued at anchor. Do not think of visiting the west coast without insect repellent! You will soon develop your own avoidance tactics, such as only opening hatches and windows at night with the lights off.

Halfway down Neptune's Staircase

CHAPTER FIFTEEN

ENGINE MAINTENANCE

We were surprised about the amount of time we needed to use our engine and the survey has revealed that we were not alone. On average, 52 per cent of time at sea was spent motoring or motor sailing. This has several effects: you will need a bigger budget for fuel, and you will need to factor in time and cost for engine maintenance and spares. So remember that, whether you are in a motor boat or a sailing boat, your engine will be vitally important in achieving your cruising aims.

However, your engine is only one of many systems and pieces of equipment on board that needs to stand up to extended use. So you need to ensure:

- Timely preventative maintenance
- Good access and visibility
- Correct spares are on board
- Access to information, skills and tools

Timely preventative maintenance

Timely preventative maintenance and regular inspection are important to keep your boat working.

- Do engine checks as soon as you get into harbour; don't wait until you are about to leave. This way, if you have a problem,

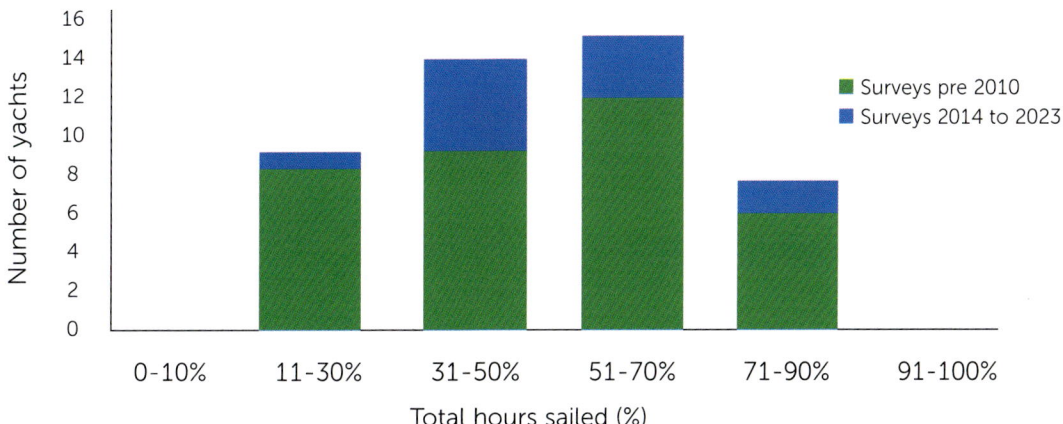

Hours sailed as a percentage of total hours, based on 45 yachts surveyed

there is a chance of getting it fixed without affecting your departure time. You will need to wait for the engine to cool to carry out some of the checks (such as oil level).

- Devise a maintenance routine of daily, weekly and monthly checks. Ours is shown below but each boat will need its own routine tailored to the systems on board.
- Use protective covers while in harbour, eg sail cover, instrument covers etc. We failed to put on our instrument covers during a gale in harbour. Moisture got in and one instrument failed. It was all the more frustrating, as it could have been prevented.
- Inspect your boat regularly for any potential equipment failures.
- Service equipment more regularly. Winches that you normally service annually need additional servicing en route.
- Service your engine regularly as prescribed in the manual.
- Prevent any chafing of equipment or material if possible.

	ENGINE – WHEN IN USE	GENERAL
DAILY	Check primary fuel filter for water or sediment Check fuel levels and note engine hours Check water level in expansion tank for fresh water system Check engine compartment for leaks Check oil level Check for oil leaks Check raw water pump for any drips Check water strainer Check tension on alternator belt Turn stern grand greaser half a turn every 4–6 hours Check stern gland	Check sails for any signs of wear
WEEKLY	Check nuts on transmission plate (due to a known problem)	Close and reopen all seacocks Check drinking water level Check paraffin level Walk round the boat and check standing rigging Grease rudder bearing (via stern greaser) Clean the heads with vinegar
MONTHLY	Check gearbox oil level	Test CO detectors
EVERY 100 HOURS	Change impeller Change primary fuel filter – unless you have a very rough passage, in which case every 50 hours Change oil and oil filter	

Note: as we have low-maintenance AGM batteries, there is no need for battery checks

Good access and visibility

If essential systems are difficult to access, you are less likely to check them or, in an emergency, you will find it difficult to carry out an urgent repair. Sometimes you can improve access or visibility:

- Our raw water strainer has a clear top and is easy to access both in harbour and at sea. If the engine overheats, the strainer can quickly be checked to see if it is blocked. Also we can easily see that it is clear on our daily inspection.

- Our primary fuel filter not only has a glass bowl to see debris or water, but we have a white patch painted behind it on the bulkhead, so that it contrasts against anything in the glass bowl to make it even easier to spot.

Correct spares on board

There is a balance between spares you carry, the space you have and the cost. It may be that in order to reduce the cost of spares, or to reduce the space required, that you reduce the spares you carry. The impact is likely to be increased time to source a spare, if not available locally, and possibly a higher cost, as you are making an emergency purchase. Prior to leaving, we spoke to an engineer who has regularly worked on our engine and sought his advice on what engine spares should be carried. Allow 20 per cent contingency budget for repairs en route. The spares we carried, plus those we wished we had carried, are shown in the table below:

SPARES CARRIED			
ENGINE		**ELECTRICAL SYSTEM**	
Fuel filters	Engine oil and empty engine oil container	Bulbs for navigation lights	Batteries
Oil filters	Gear box oil	Bulbs for cabin lights	Tinned electrical wire – assorted sizes
Impellers	Outboard spark plug	Selection of fuses	Terminal ends
Exhaust hose and various hoses	Outboard oil	Insulation tape	Crocodile clips
Alternator belts	Stern tube grease		
SAILING		**PLUMBING AND COOKING**	
Various shackles and blocks		Diaphragm pump spares	
Winch grease and oil for pawls		Heads kit	
Pawls and springs for winches		Baby oil to lubricate head pump	
Split pins and circular clips		White vinegar for heads to prevent build up of calcium in the pipes	
Line to make up either halyard/topping lift		Spares for cooker, eg spare gas regulator or paraffin cooker spares	
Sail spares: battens, batten ends, sliders			
Sails: carried old genoa. Stored old main with a relative which could be sent if needed			

GENERAL	
Spares for autohelm (belts, bracket)	Whipping twine – multiple colours
WD40	Varying sizes of elastic cord
Team McLube	Assorted stainless screws (marine grade)
Lithium grease spray	Assorted jubilee clips
Vaseline	Seizing wire
3-in-1 oil	Assorted nuts and bolts (marine grade)
Epoxy kit	Duct tape
Underwater setting sealant	Self-amalgamating tape
Sealant	Anti-rust paint
Wood glue	Miscellaneous, eg door catch
Marine catalogues	

SPARES WE WISH WE HAD CARRIED	COMMENTS
A complete water pump	The bearings on the water pump failed, which required specialist tools and the correct-sized bearings. Carrying a whole pump means you can replace it yourself and you don't have to wait for the bearings to arrive
Exhaust elbow	These fail about every five years
Car exhaust bandage	Temporary repair for a leaking exhaust elbow

RNLI and Coastguard in training

ENGINE MAINTENANCE

Access to information, skills and tools

The harbourmasters are a mine of useful information about local experts. They will know where to find the right expertise – often in surprising places. We had neither the tools nor the knowledge to remove a sheared and seized alternator bolt, but we found both at a local scallop gear manufacturer. Make sure you take all the equipment manuals with you. We were able to diagnose a problem and confirm that it could be left until later without any issue, by contacting the manufacturer over the phone. The manual will give you the contact numbers. These are all the tools that we took with us:

TOOLS AND REPAIR EQUIPMENT	
EASY TO ACCESS TOOLS	**RIGGERS TOOL KIT**
Screwdrivers (flat head and Phillips)	Bosun's chair
Adjustable spanner (small)	Knife
LED head torch and hand torch	Zippo lighter
Pliers	Lighter fluid
Scissors	Sail maker's palm
Tape measure	Several needles stored in oiled paper
Knife	Waxed thread
POWER TOOLS	**ELECTRICIANS TOOL KIT**
12V or mains drill	Multimeter
Drill bits (metal and wood)	Wire cutters
	Crimper
	Electrical testing screwdriver
GENERAL TOOL KIT	
Bradawl	Chisel
Metric and imperial socket set	Spanner for stern tube
Paint brush	Oil filter extractor
Epoxy kit	File
Hand saw	Sandpaper and sanding block
Multi-sized allen keys	Hammer
Multi-sized screwdrivers (flat head and Phillips)	Long-nosed pliers
Large adjustable spanner	Metal ruler
Flexible nut spanner	Any tools required for your cooker
Long grabber tool	Baby's nappies – excellent for cleaning up engine oil, cleaning the bilges etc

The last day
22 August – Dover to Gosport

We left Dover with the most spectacular sunrise over the white cliffs – it made getting up at 4:30am seem worth it. With a NW F4/F5, *Ituna* picked up her skirts and we were screaming along at 8.5 knots. We passed Dungeness power station (I wondered about writing a book: nuclear power stations we have passed... Windscale, Sizewell etc...) The wind soon died but at least it stayed NW – until about half way to the magnificent chalky cliffs of Beachy Head. We still had the tide with us, so at least we were making progress, despite the wind being dead on the nose. But then the tide turned... and we sailed depressingly slowly; it was at this point we started singing. We decided to press on and not go into Brighton, as the wind would be even stronger from the same direction the next day – so we would go even more slowly!

Portsmouth's Spinnaker Tower was visible for a long way out, like a beacon. At times it was depressing because it was so far away, yet welcoming as it was our finish line. It stands just inside the entrance of the narrow harbour, and at 2am when we passed it was swathed in purple light. We had very mixed emotions: elated that we had finished, yet tinged with sadness that our adventure was over. For me, there was also a touch of relief that we had arrived back safely – as skipper you are always responsible for whatever happens on board, and it was brought home by the mayday that we heard during the day. The body of a yachtsman had been found at sea, just south of where we were, with no sign of the yacht.

But for us this had been an amazing experience, something that we would treasure for the rest of our lives.

Sunrise over the White Cliffs of Dover and Portsmouth Spinnaker Tower – our finish line

CHAPTER SIXTEEN

TEN OF THE BEST!

Part of the joy of a circumnavigation is the spectacular places you have the opportunity to visit, but the challenge is knowing where they are! This section gives you ten of the best unmissable spots along the way in a range of categories. For each of the categories, I will explain the reasons I've chosen them. Do bear in mind that the information is not intended to replace that found in pilot guides, you will still need those, but hopefully some of this knowledge will help you to make the initial decision as to where to visit.

All locations are chosen because they are close to the standard cruising route, which is why you won't find places like St Kilda in the 'Remote anchorages' listings. Likewise, I could easily fill up all the 'Drop dead gorgeous' places with anchorages in the Outer Hebrides, the white beaches of Vatersay Bay are sublime but it is unlikely that many would be able to fit this in on the average three-month cruise. But if you do have time, you will be rewarded.

I have also balanced the locations around the coast in proportion to the number who complete each route. So, you will find more round the coast of Britain rather than Ireland because fewer go around the west coast of Ireland. They are not in order of preference and some locations could easily fit into several categories. Please feel free to suggest others at www.sailingwithcarra.com. The colour coding shows which route each location lies on:

All routes round Britain	Cape Wrath route	UK and Ireland

The spot that I have considered to be the split between all routes around Britain and the Cape Wrath route is Ardnamurchan Point; this is slightly north of the actual split at Lismore Island in Loch Linnhe, although as said before, do visit some of the wonderful places north of here even if you are on a 'Caley' trip.

One other comment: when those surveyed were asked what the best location they had visited was and why, some gave reasons such as 'it was the first place we visited in Ireland' or 'the people we met were so friendly'. Clearly, so much of what you enjoy about a place is not just what you find there in terms of beauty or attractions, but your actual experience. A beautiful place can be ruined by a bad experience or an ugly one can be made special by the friendliness of the people. The difficulty of entry is also marked on a scale of 1 to 5 (1 = easy; 5 = difficult).

10 CASTLE ANCHORAGES

CASTLE	LOCATION	DIFFICULTY	VISITING
Hurst	Hurst Point, Solent	1	£/EH
Torrisdale	Torrisdale Bay, Kintyre	2	N
Lochranza	Loch Ranza, Arran	2	Outside/HES
Duart	Duart Bay, Mull	2	£
Tioram	Loch Moidart	5	N
Kisimul	Castlebay, Barra	1	£/HES
Eilean Donnan	Loch Duich	2	£
Lindisfarne	Holy Island	4	£/NT (Priory EH)
Dunstanburgh	Newton Haven	3	NT
Townshend	Castletownshend	1	N

Being an island nation, our coast has been fortified for hundreds of years – but where are the anchorages with spectacular views of a castle? The best thing about most anchorages is that dropping your anchor is free.

Entry: N = no access; Y = visit free of charge; £ = entry fee; NT/NTS/EH/HES = member of National Trust, National Trust for Scotland, English Heritage or Historic Environment Scotland.

❶ Hurst Point

Hurst Castle was built to defend the western entrance of the Solent by Henry VIII in 1544, though it has seen service many times: during the Napoleonic Wars; when Charles I was imprisoned here prior to his trial and execution; and again, during the Second World War. The castle is built on a spit that provides two anchorages. The open anchorage shown here is often used by boats catching the early tide through the Needles. It is out of the main tidal streams but a strong current runs next to the beach. Inside the spit is Keyhaven and there is an anchorage in a small pool between the entrance and the fisherman's pontoon. You may be charged for the inside anchorage if the harbourmaster is being active.

❷ Torrisdale Bay

On the east coast of Kintyre Peninsula. You can either choose to anchor in view of the 19th-century Torrisdale Castle, which is visible through the trees, or tuck into the sandy Carradale Bay, which is more protected. In settled weather there is a beautiful lunch stop just south of Torrisdale

Hurst Castle with views to the Isle of Wight

Bay in Saddle Bay, where you will see Saddle Castle (see banner photo on page 162) and the beach made famous by Paul McCartney's video of his song 'Mull of Kintyre'.

❸ Loch Ranza
Located on Arran, Loch Ranza provides the ideal location to anchor and see the 13th- and 16th-century ruined castle walls bathed in the glow of the setting sun, it is a very scenic location. Beware of squalls funnelled down the hills. Its proximity to the Clyde-based yachts means it can be busy at weekends. Beyond the Castle is the distillery, just 30 minutes' walk and does a good un-peaty island malt. Mooring type: Anchor and mooring buoy. The mooring buoys will mean you avoid the weed and the gusts.

❹ Duart Bay
On the Isle of Mull, this is the location of Duart Castle. It stands on a crag that guards the Sound of Mull, and there are spectacular views in every direction. The 13th-century fortress castle is the home of the Clan Maclean, and is in remarkable condition thanks to the 26th chief who restored it at the beginning of the 20th century. Mooring type: anchorage suitable in settled weather but too good an opportunity to miss one of Scotland's best habitable castles. The Clyde Cruising Club (CCC) *Kintyre to Ardnamurchan Sailing Directions* give good advice on the anchorage. Then you can move into Loch Aline for a more permanent overnight stay.

❺ Loch Moidart
North-east of Ardnamurchan Point, it has a challenging entrance with a maze of rocks guarding it. Take the south entrance and once past the rocks, you are rewarded with wooded banks with rocky outcrops and white sands between them and turquoise water – quite beautiful. By the island of Riska you can anchor close to the ruins of Castle Tioram (pronounced 'Cheerum'). It was once home to the Clan Chief

Tioram castle, Loch Moidart © Robert Cronk

Allan of Clanranald, who ordered it to be burnt when he left to fight for the Jacobite rebellion in 1715, in order to prevent it falling into enemy hands. Antares Charts are recommended.

❻ Castlebay

This is the main village on Barra and gets its name from Kisimul Castle, which is situated in the bay. It has been the home of the MacNeils since 1427. The 46th clan chief handed over the castle to Historic Scotland for the annual rent of £1 and a bottle of Talisker whisky. Barra is the Outer Hebrides in miniature – white beaches bordered by machair (a carpet of flowers), beautiful scenery and empty roads. It can be explored by bus, by foot or by bike. It also claims to have the only airport in the world where planes land on the beach at low tide! The anchorage is north-west of the castle, avoiding the ferry routes, and there are also pontoons. The stunningly beautiful sandy bay of Vatersay close by is also worth visiting.

❼ Loch Duich

Possibly the most photographed castle in Scotland – Eilean Donnan. The 13th-century castle was destroyed in the Jacobite rebellion in 1719, when King George discovered that there were Spanish troops residing there to help the Old Pretender James. It was then restored in 1919. It is the epitome of a highland castle and consequently has been used for many films, including 'Highlander'. With views over Five Sisters of Kintail and along Loch Long, it is a stunning anchorage especially if the heather is in bloom. There is an anchorage opposite in the small bay of Ob Aoinidh (Totaig).

❽ Holy Island

An amazing harbour on the Northumbrian coast. Here you can see two castles from your anchorage: Lindisfarne and Bamburgh. Holy Island is one of the most important sites of Anglo-Saxon Christianity because of the priory and St Cuthbert, and still

Eilean Donnan

Lindisfarne Castle from the Priory

attracts pilgrims today. The Vikings sadly plundered many of its treasures, and then came the dissolution of the monasteries by Henry VIII, which saw the destruction of the Priory, the stones from which were then used to build Lindisfarne Castle. The castle was converted into a private house by Edwin Lutyens in 1903. Entry to Holy Island is via a narrow channel which is marked by a pair of impressive obelisks. Just off the Old Coastguard Station is the deep-water anchorage, but if you can take the ground, the Ouze provides the best shelter. Pick a spot adjacent to the upturned-herring-boat shacks just above the beach. (Also created by Lutyens, see photo on page 146) You are in a National Nature Reserve, so do explore in the dinghy at low water for an unforgettable experience: 200+ grey seals and rare terns nest here (you shouldn't land at the breeding sites). (See photo on page 89.)

⑨ Newton Haven

An anchorage on the beautiful Northumbrian coast just north of Craster. It epitomises this part of the coast: stunning white beaches and a castle. Two miles to the south is the spectacular 14th-century ruined Dunstanburgh Castle, with its two striking towers of the gatehouse. The anchorage is surprisingly sheltered and peaceful owing to the rocks offshore that are exposed for all but two hours either side of HW. The anchorage is close to the attractive 18th-century fishing village of Low Newton, with its cream-washed cottages round a neat village square.

⑩ Castletownshend

Located on the south coast of Ireland, this is a delightful little village in the natural harbour of Castle Haven. The castle was finished in 1720 and is still the home of the Townsend family. There is a single street which slopes steeply from the tiny stone quay in the harbour. In the middle of the street are two trees which visiting cars struggle to negotiate. Halfway up the hill you'll find Mary Ann's, a good seafood pub of some renown; booking is essential at weekends. The harbour is quite serene, with several anchorages, though it is popular in the summer. (See photo on page 101.)

10 WILDLIFE ENCOUNTERS

LOCATION/NEAREST HARBOUR	WILDLIFE	DIFFICULTY
Lundy	Lundy pony, razorbill, fulmar, oyster catchers	1
Skomer	Puffin, guillemot, razorbill, kittiwake, Manx shearwater, and grey Atlantic seal	3
Rathlin/Church Bay	Fulmar, guillemot, puffin, kittiwake, Manx shearwater	1
Loch Spelve	Sea eagle (white tailed) and golden eagle, otter, wild goat, deer	2
Lunga Treshnish Isles	Seal, guillemot, razorbill, puffin, kittiwake, fulmar, shag, skua	3
The Shiant Isles	Puffin, razorbill, Manx Shearwaters, storm petrels	1
Pierowall/Westray	Puffin, gannet, guillemot, kittiwake	1
Chanonry Point	Dolphin	1
Farne Islands/The Kettle	Puffin, guillemot, razorbill, sandwich tern, roseate tern, shag, cormorant, eider duck	3
Cape Clear/North Harbour	Manx shearwater, stormy petrel, auk, gannet, cormorant, fulmar, kittiwake, black guillemot, chough	2

Unsurprisingly, all bar one of these locations are islands, as the wildlife prosper in the unique protection that islands provide. Well known for their birdlife, many of these locations are RSPB (ISPB in Ireland) sites – though in any remote location, or while at sea, you will often see a range of birds, seals, dolphins and possibly whales. In 2023, there were 646 sightings of whales spotted in Irish waters, the most common species being minke, followed by humpback and fin whales. The wildlife is a real highlight of the trip. We saw less wildlife in the busy seas of the south coast but you can still see some if you are anchored in a quiet spot. On many of these islands you will get an ideal photo opportunity with the comical puffins, because on land they aren't frightened of humans. They breed from April to July, leave in early August and then spend the rest of their time at sea.

❶ Lundy

A granite outcrop that lies 12 miles off the North Devon coast, and is England's only Marine Nature Reserve. It has a diverse range of flora and fauna, eg the Lundy cabbage, which is unique to the island as is the Lundy pony. Being on a migration route, Lundy offers an abundance of birdlife to

The Landing Bay Lundy © Stephen Harries

see. With a history linked to piracy and smuggling for many centuries, the Marisco Tavern is named after a famous pirate. It was also home to the Barbary pirates, who would capture crews, cargo and ships and raid Devon and Cornwall's villages to take the villagers back to Africa as slaves. There are several anchorages to choose from and you are encouraged to anchor only in recognised ones, because of the delicate seabed wildlife. The Landing Bay is the best place to explore the island from. Mooring type: anchoring and visitors' buoys at Landing Bay.

❷ Skomer
Owned by the Wildlife Trust of South and West Wales. In May, you can see fantastic displays of bluebells, when the puffin chicks have hatched. There are two anchorages: North and South Haven. There is a fee to land which you can pay at the North Haven to the warden. Tides and the Wildgoose race can make entry challenging at springs. Mooring type: visitors' buoys and anchoring. Don't anchor shoreward of the visitors' buoys as it is prohibited due to a rare seagrass.

❸ Rathlin
Situated in an area of strong tides, which are compressed further by its position 5 miles off the Antrim coast and 12 miles from the Mull of Kintyre. The resulting overfalls and eddies mean that careful planning is required for a visit here. The island's dramatic cliff-lined coast is made up of black basalt and limestone. The basalt stretches from Giant's Causeway through to Staffa and Mull. The cliffs have many caves which are only accessible from the sea, including the fabled location of Robert the Bruce's Cave where he had his encounter with the determined spider. The main population of about

The Landing Seals basking in the sun in Church Bay, Rathlin Bay

100 is around Church Bay, which is also a good spot to see seals basking on a sunny day. The island has been inhabited since the Stone Age, and has a history of raids and massacres: first by the Vikings, then once by Scots and twice by the English. At the western end is Bull Point, part of the RSPB nature reserves, and in the summer a minibus runs between the viewpoint and Church Bay. Mooring type: anchor in the harbour or alongside at the pontoon protected by a breakwater.

❹ Loch Spelve

Located on Mull, it is completely enclosed with the exception of the narrow and tricky entrance channel with fast flowing tides – but once in, it offers shelter from any direction. It is beautiful and remote; there is an old disused pier and a few scattered houses at Croggan. It is well known for eagles, and the golden eagles breed in enormous eyries on the cliffs outside the entrance. Mooring type: anchoring.

Looking over the anchorage at Lunga, Treshnish Isles © Sandy Campbell

The Shiant Isles © Alan Kohler

❺ Treshnish Isles

These form an archipelago of several small uninhabited islands off the west coast of Mull. Settled weather is needed to explore, and the tide runs strongly between them. Fladda is known as the Dutchman's Cap due to its shape. Lunga is the largest island and has the highest hill (103m). Its archaeological history dates back to early Viking times. Designated as a site of special scientific interest, there is much wildlife to see. Advisable to have CCC *Sailing Directions*, and Antares Charts are recommended to visit. Mooring type: anchorage at the north end of Lunga.

❻ The Shiant Isles

A magical anchorage NE of the isthmus between Garbh Eilean and Eilean an Tighe, where you are surrounded by a huge seabird population. These privately owned, deserted islands are an important breeding site, with 10 per cent of the UK's puffins and 7 per cent of the razorbill population breeding here. Antares Charts are recommended. Owner Adam Nicolson's book *Sea Room* is his love story with these islands, and is essential reading.

❼ Pierowall

This is the largest community on Westray and is built around a bay lined with beautiful white sand. Pierowall has a plane that goes to Papa Westray, which claims to be the shortest scheduled flight in the world – just two minutes. The RSPB bird reserve is at Noup Head, but a trip to Castle O'Brien is a must to see the puffins roosting at night, arranged via the harbourmaster. Also, worth visiting by land are: Grobust Beach and Mae Beach, both with turquoise blue waters and white sand, Notland Castle, and the café in Pierowall for Westray shortbread. At the heritage centre you can see the recently discovered Westray Venus – the only neolithic carving of a human found in Scotland. Mooring type: very small marina and a free mooring buoy in the bay. (See photos on pages 40 and 150.)

Mae Beach, one of several stunning beaches on Westray

⑧ Chanonry Point

Located on the Moray Firth, this is reputedly the best place in Europe to see dolphins. The conditions of the fast-flowing river and the tide mean that the plankton are kicked up, providing a rich source of food for the dolphins. Also, dolphins love to play in the fast tides. The water deepens quickly from the shore, allowing the dolphins to come in very close, which is why you will see people watching the dolphins from the shore only feet away. Closest harbour: marina at Inverness (which is outside the canal). At Fortrose there are visitor moorings for boats up to 6 tons/12m or you can anchor close SW of Chanonry Point.

⑨ The Farne Islands

Made up of 28 islands, just off the Northumberland coast. All the buildings on the largest island, Inner Farne (NT), date back to the monastic period, as it was St Cuthbert's home for many years throughout his life, and he died there. The ruins of the Fishehouse near the landing jetty are the remains of his visitor's guest house. Then in the 14th century, a church was built dedicated to him. Pele's Tower was built in the 16th century to house monks, though it now houses the National Trust wardens. In Victorian times, Grace Darling and her father, the lighthouse keeper on Longstone, rowed to rescue nine survivors from a steamer that had run aground on the rocks. There are several anchorages – the most well-known being the Kettle – which will give you access to Inner Farne.

⑩ Cape Clear

A few miles off the West Cork coast and an important location for migratory birds. There is a bird observatory at North Harbour which is an inlet where the island's harbour is located. The harbour mainly serves fishing boats and the ferries, but you can lie afloat at the seaward end of the quay. There is also an anchorage in south harbour, which can be used in settled weather or in northerly winds. If you don't manage to visit the island, there is a ferry which runs several times a day from Baltimore and Schull.

Inner Farne

TEN OF THE BEST!

10 CULINARY EXPERIENCE

HARBOUR	ESTABLISHMENT	WEBSITE	DIFFICULTY
Dartmouth	Seahorse Rockfish	www.seahorserestaurant.co.uk www.therockfish.co.uk	1
Falmouth Restronguet Creek	Pandora's Inn	www.pandorainn.com	1
Padstow	Paul Ainsworth's The Mariners	www.paul-ainsworth.co.uk	2
Ardglass	Aldos	See Facebook page Aldo's Ardglass	1
Inverie, Loch Nevis	The Old Forge Pub	www.theoldforge.co.uk	1
Sound of Sleat	Duisdale Hotel Isle Ornsay Kinloch Lodge in Loch na Dal Doune Knoydart	www.sonascollection.com/our-hotels/duisdale www.kinloch-lodge.co.uk www.doune-knoydart.co.uk	1 1 1
Loch Dunvegan, Skye	The Three Chimneys	www.thethreechimneys.co.uk	3
Orford	The Crown and Castle	www.crownandcastle.co.uk	5
Pin Mill	Butt and Oyster	www.debeninns.co.uk/buttandoyster	1
Kinsale	Too many to mention!	Check trip advisor	1

This is an impossibly difficult list to compile, as personal taste is such a big factor. These are all places that won't disappoint. The criteria for selection are not only good food but whether they are within a ten-minute walk of the harbour. Some serve good pub grub and others are a special treat. Many of the expensive ones have cheaper fixed price menus for early bird meals.

❶ Dartmouth

It has a memorable entrance, as you enter the River Dart between two castles. The wooded banks give nothing away, until you pass a series of bends, then the picturesque towns of Dartmouth and Kingswear open up, with houses clinging to the steep slopes. The impressive Royal Naval College overlooks the harbour. The town is made up of quaint winding streets and lays claim to the Pilgrim Fathers setting off from here. Mitch Tonk's restaurants will cater for all budgets: Seahorse for that extra special celebration meal of seafood with an Italian twist, and Rockfish for delicious seafood at a cheaper price. Mooring type: two marinas, public pontoons or you can anchor in the middle of the river.

Looking over the entrance of the River Dart

❷ Falmouth

A large deep-water natural harbour, which found fame and prosperity as an international trading port. Pendennis Castle (EH) was built as part of Henry VIII's defences, as was its counterpart at St Mawes over the water. It has much to offer visiting yachtsmen and is now the departure point for those setting off for distant shores. There is a choice of where to anchor here depending on your need to access shore facilities.

Anchored in Ryan Creek

If you want to be close to the attractive town of Falmouth, with its long main street that threads through the town and a good selection of shops, supermarkets, pubs and restaurants, then anchor off the town or stay in one of the three marinas. Nearby is the Falmouth Maritime Museum which is worth a visit. A real favourite with many yachtsmen is Pandora's Inn, the 13th-century inn in Restronguet Creek; flagstone floors and low beams give the pub bags of character and the food has an excellent reputation. There is a pontoon directly outside the inn, or you can pick up a deep-water mooring. If you are looking for somewhere quieter and free to anchor, then head up the wooded River Fal and anchor in Ryan Creek. Before you get there, you will pass the incongruous sight of various large ships moored in a relatively narrow river, apparently a barometer of the global economy – the more ships moored, the worse the economy.

❸ Padstow

Located on the north Cornish coast and accessed over the ominously named Doom Bar, and up the Camel River, where you lock into Padstow's old stone inner harbour. Once over that, you have the narrowest part of the Strait, Belan Narrows – at less than 400m wide, the tides run very strongly here. It is a very attractive waterfront, lined with many listed buildings and narrow winding streets. This, coupled with the fame brought by TV chef Rick Stein, mean that it is often packed with tourists during the day, but early morning or evening is the time to see it in its full glory. There is a local fishing fleet providing fresh fish to the many places to eat. There are so many Rick Stein establishments here – catering for a range of budgets from his Deli, Fish and Chips, Café, St Petroc's Bistro and The Seafood Restaurant – that it is known as Padstein. All are relatively expensive, even the fish and chips. For more affordable but still amazing local food, try Paul Ainsworth's The Mariners. There is an enjoyable cycle along the Camel Trail to Wadebridge – you can hire bikes locally. (See photo on page 32.)

❹ Ardglass

A charming town in Northern Ireland, close to the entrance of Strangford Lough. The harbour is divided in two: an active fishing fleet in one part and a marina with some smart facilities in the other (Phennick Cove Marina). The town has the remains of several medieval buildings and is overlooked by Jordan's Castle and by the former Ardglass Castle. Aldos is a family-owned restaurant with fabulous food. Mooring type: marina

❺ Inverie

Located in Loch Nevis (which means Loch of Heaven) on the Knoydart Peninsula, is Inverie, which is incredibly remote with mountains that tower around you. Situated in the tiny hamlet, the Old Forge Pub is the remotest pub on mainland Britain as it is an 18-mile hike over a couple of Munros from the nearest road, or a 7-mile sea crossing from Mallaig. Community owned since 2022, this lively pub has become a real destination; free food for musicians and instruments on the walls mean that impromptu ceilidhs are the norm. It has won many awards, serving fresh local food, which is either grown or caught locally or comes in by sea. Mooring type: visitors' buoys with a donation requested.

❻ Sound of Sleat

Rarely do you get to pick your culinary experience based on the wind direction but with a few good restaurants on either side of the Sound of Sleat, it is entirely possible, or why not visit them all, in a gastronomic cruise! All have three things in common: good food focusing on fresh local produce, stunning scenery and free mooring buoys if dining. Duisdale Hotel, Isle Ornsay – an attractive village overlooks this natural harbour created by the small isle. Kinloch Lodge in Loch na Dal, was founded by the food writer Claire Macdonald, and has a peaceful anchorage. Doune Knoydart is off grid, accessed only by foot or by sea, in the small rocky Dun Ban Bay at the end of the Knoydart peninsula.

❼ Loch Dunvegan, Skye

Loch More on the west side of the scenic Loch Dunvegan, is perfect for the Three Chimneys. The historic croft, nestled on the shore, showcases the very best of Skye's natural produce, with exquisitely cooked dishes. The place for a special celebration, fine dining at its best but not at extortionate prices, though booking in advance is essential. Dunvegan village provides alternative mooring, both at anchor and on mooring buoys. The seat of the Clan Macleod Castle is nearby but not visible from the village moorings, though you can anchor in the scenic bay NW of the castle.

View from the Three Chimneys, Dunvegan

Crown and Castle, with Orford Castle in the distance

⑧ Orford

On the River Ore is a small Suffolk village with an impressive medieval castle and church, though only the Norman keep (EH) remains. The Crown and Castle, which is by the castle, does excellent food and is run by Ruth Watson of 'Hotel Inspector' fame. The long river which changes its name to the Alde halfway along, is protected from the sea by Orfordness, a 6-mile spit of shingle which extends all the way to the entrance. The Ore entrance has quite a fearsome reputation, due to the strong tides and shifting banks of shingle (see www.eastcoastpilot.com/downloads for latest information). In the middle of the Ore is Havergate Island, a bird sanctuary, with one of the largest breeding colonies of avocets in the country (landing is not permitted). There are several places to anchor in the river depending on whether you want to be close to Orford or have remote views over the marshes. Mooring type: anchoring and visitors' buoys.

The Thames barges of Pin Mill, overlooked by the Butt and Oyster Inn

❾ Pin Mill

A hamlet on the banks of the river Orwell. It is easy to travel back in time when you see the magnificent Thames barges sailing up the river. In June, there is the Pin Mill Barge match and the barge posts at the hard are still used regularly. Pin Mill had links to smugglers in the 19th century and was made famous as the setting for Arthur Ransome's 'We Didn't Mean to Go to Sea'. The 17th-century Butt and Oyster Inn has fine views of the river, and is named after the oysters, a major export which were harvested along the river, and a butt (the large wine cask that they were transported in). It serves traditional pub food and Adnams bitter and Broadside and it has a CAMRA historic pub interior. Live folk music on the first Sunday of every month. Mooring type: visitors' buoys.

❿ Kinsale

On the south coast of Ireland, this is an historic town and is known as the gourmet capital of Ireland. There are many great restaurants in its warren of winding streets: Crackpots, Jim Edwards, Fishy Fishy and Man Friday to name a few. But there are many more, and the compact nature of the town means that you can browse to find one that takes your fancy and suits your budget. It has a rich maritime history because its broad, sheltered harbour made it a place of strategic importance in Irish and English history. Charles Fort and James Fort in the harbour guard the east and west shores. The French Prison, or Desmond Castle to give it its proper title, is worth a visit; it used to hold up to 600 prisoners during the Napoleonic wars. It was off Old Kinsale Head in 1915 that the Lusitania was torpedoed by the Germans, killing 1,198. Mooring type: two marinas for visitors and also a couple of anchorages in the harbour.

The beautiful Kinsale

10 CHALLENGING TIDAL RACES

RACE	USEFUL HARBOUR	KTS AT SPRINGS	DIFFICULTY
Portland Bill	Weymouth, Brixham	8	5
Jack and Ramsay Sounds	Dale, Fishguard	7	5
Menai Strait	Caernarfon, Conwy	8	5
Strangford Lough	Portaferry, Ardglass	8	3
Mull of Kintyre	Campbeltown, Gigha	7	5
Cuan Sound	Toberonochy, Ardinamir, Craobh Haven, Puilladobhrain	7	3
Kyle Rhea	Kyle of Loch Alsh, Kyle Akin, Mallaig, Armdale, Isle Ornsay	8	2
Pentland Firth	Scrabster, Long Hope, Wick	12	5+
Rosts around Orkney	Kirkwall, Stromness, Westray	8	5
Barloge Creek	Barloge Creek, Baltimore	N/A	N/A

The tidal races you will encounter on your trip will certainly make things more interesting. Many can provide a useful short cut or tidal slingshot to speed you on your way. With careful planning, most will be benign when you pass through the challenging part at slack water. Some are more complicated, if for example there are several on one passage and passing at slack is not always an option; this is where local knowledge provided by cruising guides come into its own, as it is often possible to pick up useful back eddies. There are some tidal races which might give you a sleepless night, but the sense of achievement is tremendous when you can tick them off. This list shows races that can reach at least 5 knots. Given the strength of these tides, a healthy respect must be given for wind-over-tide situations, as many become dangerous when the wind is over a certain strength.

❶ Portland Bill

The Isle of Portland on Dorset's Jurassic coast is famous for the white hard limestone quarried there, Portland stone, which has been used in such buildings as St Paul's Cathedral and Buckingham Palace. The isle, really a peninsula, disrupts the flow of water in the Channel and, combined with a ledge of Portland stone extending further out to sea, causes the legendary race south of the Bill. It can be avoided by staying 3–5 miles offshore,

The Race at Portland Bill

but if you are planning to visit Weymouth then the inshore passage is much faster and shorter. But careful planning and the right weather are required for a safe passage and to avoid being drawn into the race. It remains an ambition of many yachtsmen to conquer the inshore passage. Harbours: Weymouth and Portland Harbour.

❷ Jack and Ramsay Sounds

These two races were created as the tide forces its way through the islands and reefs off the Pembrokeshire coast. They provide a useful shortcut, but can only be attempted in daylight. Jack Sound is only about 200m wide and Ramsay Sound is slightly wider but its narrowest point is less than 400m, being constricted at this point by ominously named rocks called The Bitches – a ledge of rocks that extends into the sound. With 7 miles between the two, you will arrive at the first at slack, but then by the time you arrive at the second, the tide has been running for an hour – so you will have a speedy passage through. Both Fishguard and Dale (Milford Haven) have all tide entry/exit, which does make planning easier. If the conditions don't allow for you to pass through the Sounds, then you have an alternative which goes outside the islands and the Bishops and Clerks, but is quite a bit further.

The Bitches, Ramsay Sound

The Swellies with the Menai Bridge in the distance, Menai Strait

❸ Menai Strait

The strait is a challenging narrow 14nm stretch of water between mainland Wales and Anglesey, and is guarded by the shifting sands of Caernarfon Bar. Once over that, you have the narrowest part of the Strait, Belan Narrows – at less than 400m wide, the tides run very strongly here. There are two 19th-century bridges that span the strait, Thomas Telford's Suspension Bridge and Robert Stephenson's tubular Britannia Bridge, and they bound the notorious rocky twisting passage, the Swellies. However, the work involved in negotiating strong tides, rocks, sand banks and mud flats is rewarded by the view of magnificent castles, stunning scenery, historic harbours and a real sense of achievement.

Useful harbours for timing a passage include Caernarfon Victoria Dock, and Conwy marina in the shadow of Conwy Mountain (and a 20-minute walk from Edward I's 13th-century castle). Caernarfon's harbourmaster has a guide for a safe passage through the Swellies.

❹ Strangford Lough

Formed out of debris left by ice age glaciers then flooded by the sea, forming drowned drumlins. This lough is a Marine Nature Reserve as it is the ideal habitat for wildlife and, if you have the time to explore the lough for a few days, you will be well rewarded. It has an extremely narrow 3-mile-long entrance called 'The Narrows' which is only 400m at its narrowest point. Entering on the flood is rarely dangerous, though the speed of the current can be impressive and you pass by a rotary eddy known as the Routen Wheel. There is only 15 minutes of slack water and 3 knots within an hour of this. The challenge is more apparent when you leave, as the sea conditions can't be

Looking across to Portaferry, Strangford lough

TEN OF THE BEST!

anticipated when you set off, and once on the tidal escalator there is no getting off. A useful harbour for timing your entry is Ardglass and, once in, Portaferry is a convenient marina. If anchoring, the River Quoile is a tranquil spot close to the narrows, or go further in to Ringhaddy Sounds.

❺ Mull of Kintyre
To yachtsmen and locals, it is known simply as 'The Mull' which means headland. It is at the end of the Kintyre peninsula and only 12 miles from Northern Ireland. While spectacular, it has a fearsome reputation especially when a west going tide meets any wind/waves from south or west, the combination of the weather, swell and strong tides that create overfalls and turbulent water. Anchoring at Sanda, if weather allows, is also a good option. Harbours: Campbeltown and Gigha.

❻ Cuan Sound
South of Oban is the stretch of water between Seil Island and Luing. Its challenges include negotiating a 270° bend, a few rocks and a ferry which crosses the sound. The narrowest point is only 140m, between rocks off Seil Island and Cleit rock (a rock identified by a yellow perch). Antares charts are recommended. The swirling currents and the 7 knots of tide do make it difficult to hold a steady course. Unlike many tidal patterns it reaches its greatest flow soon after turning. Useful harbours to time your passage through: going north, Toberonochy or Ardinamir (both on Luing) and Craobh Haven; going south, Puilladobhrain.

❼ Kyle Rhea
A narrow passage of water separating Skye from the mainland, Kyle Rhea. At its narrowest it is just over 500m. For many centuries, cattle drovers used to swim hundreds of their Highland cattle across every season to begin the trek south to the cattle fairs; though now you are more likely to see seals on the shore. It is also a well-known place to see otters, though you will probably be passing too quickly to spot them as they are quite shy. Lookout for MV Glenachullish, claimed to be the last manually operated turntable ferry in the world. Kyle Rhea is quite straightforward providing you have done your planning correctly and there is no adverse weather – though there is a ferry to add to the excitement. Harbours south going: Kyle of Loch Alsh and Kyle Akin. Harbours north going: Mallaig, Armdale and Isle Ornsay.

Cuan Sound, with Cleit Rock in the distance and 270° bend visible (top left)

Strangford Lough, with the tide streaming in

⑧ Pentland Firth

Tides here are legendary given that they are some of the strongest in the world – 16 knots close to the Pentland Skerries. The overfalls and races have even been named – the Merry Men of Mey, the Swelkie, the Duncansby Race and Liddel Eddy. Treat all crossings with respect both crossing and going with the tide. There is much advice available from the Clyde Cruising Club Sailing Directions and from local harbourmasters, particularly the harbourmaster at Scrabster. Heed the advice and don't go if the conditions aren't right. The Scrabster harbourmaster has been known not to charge for additional nights if the conditions are not right to cross, saying 'We never want small boats going through Pentland if the conditions are not right.' Useful harbours: Scrabster, Long Hope, Kirkwall, Wick. (See photo on page 122.)

⑨ Orkney

The islands have many challenging tidal races, not just the Pentland Firth, but Eyenhallow Sound, Westray Firth, Papa Sound, Hoy Sound and Stronsay Firth to name a few. Unsurprisingly, it is an important site for tidal energy generation.

Hoy Sound

The Rapids, Lough Hyne

Locally, tidal races are known as rosts and exist between most of the islands. So, the real challenge is that to go anywhere in Orkney, you need to work out how to cope with several tide races which appear to be going in different directions to your desired course. CCC *Sailing Directions* are invaluable for this. (See photo on page 122.)

⑩ Barloge Creek

At the entrance to Lough Hyne near Baltimore in County Cork, is Barloge Creek, and unlike the others in this category, this tidal challenge is not one that can be made in a yacht, but only in a dinghy. Lough Hyne is a unique sea-water lake which is cut off below half tide and is known as a half-tide lake, creating a unique ecosystem with 72 species of fish! It is the only inland sea lake in Europe and was Ireland's first marine reserve. The lough is accessed via a narrow stretch called the rapids, which go from a trickle to impressive rapids with each tide. The rapids make a fun ride in a dinghy. You can anchor in turquoise water in Barloge Creek in settled conditions.

10 WHISKY TASTING

HARBOUR	DISTILLERY	DIFFICULTY	WEBSITE
Campbeltown	Springbank	1	www.springbank.scot
Port Ellen	Bunnahabhain	1	www.bunnahabhain.com
Lagavulin, Islay	Lagavulin	3	www.malts.com
Craighouse	Isle of Jura	1	www.jura.whisky.com
Oban (Kererra)	Oban	1	www.obanwhisky.com
Carbost, Loch Harport, Skye	Talisker	1	www.malts.com
Eriskay/Acairseid Mhor	Am Politician	2	
Wick	Old Pulteney	1	www.oldpulteney.com
Crosshaven	Old Midleton	1	www.jamesonwhiskey.com
Portrush	Old Bushmills	1	www.bushmills.com

If you are a whisky fan ('whiskey' in Ireland) then this cruise will be a chance to savour a dram or two at some of the finest distilleries in Scotland and Ireland. Uisce beatha (pronounced 'ooshkava') as it is known in Gaelic, or 'water of life', has played an important role in the economy of both countries. Irish immigration, from 1740 to 1910, spread the popularity of Irish whiskey in the US, and the number of distilleries grew until 1920, when prohibition was introduced; as a result only a few remain today. Scotland didn't depend on the American market to the same extent and, while overproduction in the late 19th century closed many distilleries, there are well over 100 in operation today. All distilleries listed here produce a malt whisky and are within walking distance of the harbour, with the exception of Midleton, Bushmills. All offer tours, but note that some distilleries require you to book a few days in advance, so do check their websites.

❶ Campbeltown

This town lies in a magnificent setting at the head of Campbeltown Loch and in the shadow of Bengullion. Entry passes Davaar Island, which is accessible at low tide by foot; in a cave on the island, is a painting of Jesus. Campbeltown is home to three whiskies: Springbank, Hazelburn and Glen Scotia. At its peak there were over 30 distilleries and it once enjoyed the highest income per capita of any town in Britain – hence the song 'Campbeltown Loch, I wish you were whisky... for I would drink you dry'. Springbank Distillery is the oldest family-owned distillery in Scotland and is the only Scottish distillery to carry out the full production on site. There is a music festival usually in the third week in August and, while you won't get tickets on spec for any of the big groups, all the pubs have live Scottish music throughout the festival. Mooring type: pontoon or anchor in the Loch. (See photo on page 38.)

❷ Port Ellen

With nine distilleries on an island that is 25 by 15 miles, a fan of the island's distinctive peaty whiskies will want to spend time here. Islay is one of the five Scottish whisky regions, and hosts its own annual 'Festival of Malt and Music' (Fèis Ìle) at the end of May, with events and tastings. In the south, the whiskies are peatier, as the malt is heavy with peat and peaty water (see Lagavulin entry). If you are not a fan of peaty whisky then try Bunnahabhain, the lightest with a delicate flavour profile, the water being sourced from limestone springs. If anchoring, a dinghy and whisky tasting feels like too much excitement, then the security of a pontoon at Port Ellen is an alternative, with regular buses to the distilleries. Mooring type: marina.

❸ Lagavulin

Mill in the Hollow, as Lagavulin means, is on the south coast of Islay. First established in 1816, it is the middle of the three southern distilleries, Laphroaig and Ardbeg being either side, so with just a 2-mile walk you can cover all three. All have a strong peaty character. The conspicuous distillery is in a rocky bay, which is a natural harbour and will fit quite a few boats – up to 20 during the Classic Malt cruise, though local knowledge from a pilot book for entry is required. Mooring type: anchoring or visitors' buoys.

❹ Craighouse

On the eastern shore of Jura is the main settlement in a large bay, sheltered by some islands with views to the distinctive Paps of Jura. The distillery, Isle of Jura, is situated in Craighouse and was built in 1810 but it had become a ruin by the early 1900s. In 1950, a few people on Jura got together to restart the distillery and it reopened in 1963, providing much-needed employment for the island. There is a pontoon for dinghy landing. Mooring type: anchoring and visitors' buoys.

❺ Oban

Known as the 'Gateway to the Isles', because many of the Caledonian MacBrayne (or CalMac) ferries to the islands leave from Oban. It is a picturesque harbour, in beautiful surroundings, with a bay sheltered by the island Kerrera. There is a great view of the harbour from Pulpit Hill. Below McCaig's Folly, an imitation of Rome's Colosseum, is the Oban Distillery. It produces a rich, sweet malt whisky with a subtle hint of sea salt and peaty smokiness. The west highland flavour falls between the dry, smoky style of Scottish islands

Lagavulin © Adobe Stock/Martin M303

Oban with the distillery chimney visible below McCaig's Folly

and the lighter sweeter malts of the Highlands. Mooring type: marina or a visitor buoy on Kerrera. There is a short stay pontoon at the North Pier in Oban. There is a free ferry to Oban if you are in the marina. Trains and buses go to Glasgow, so it is a good place to leave your boat.

❻ Carbost

Loch Harport is home to Skye's only distillery, Talisker. Located on the west coast, Loch Harport is in a magnificent setting with the dramatic Cuillins of Skye close by. The distillery, which was founded in 1830, is on the south side of the loch, in the tiny Gaelic-speaking, crofting community of Carbost. The lease paid for the land is £45 and a 10-gallon cask of best-quality Talisker, presented to the Chief of the Macleod Clan in Dunvegan Castle. Talisker has a strong, smoky, peaty flavour somewhere between the lightness of the Highland malt whiskies and the heaviness of the Islay malts. Robert Louis Stevenson describes it as the 'king o' drinks' in a poem. Mooring type: anchoring or visitors' buoy.

❼ Eriskay/Acairseid Mhor

SS *Politician*, while not a distillery, has its place in whisky folklore guaranteed following Compton Mackenzie's book *Whisky Galore* and the subsequent films. The story is based on the wrecking of SS *Politician*, which ran aground off the coast of Eriskay in 1941 on the way to Jamaica. Her cargo included 22,000 cases of scotch whisky. Quickly, 40,000 cases were squirrelled away by the Islanders; in their eyes legitimate salvage, but as no duty had been paid, members of HM Customs and Excise took a different view and pursued and prosecuted those who had removed the whisky. Eriskay's only pub (which sadly is rather mundane) was named

A view of the Talisker Distillery along loch Harport © Adobe Stock/hardyuno

after the SS *Politician* and the Am Politician, has a couple of the famous whisky bottles. An ideal anchorage is Acairseid Mhor (big harbour) though it is a fair walk to the pub — use of Antares Charts is recommended. Mooring type: anchor.

❽ Wick

On the north-east coast of Scotland, Wick used to be one of the largest ports in the world for herring, which were also known as silver darlings. To give you an idea of the scale of the industry, 3,500 'fisher lassies' would gut 50 million fish in two days. Thomas Telford created Pulteneytown, as it was originally called, and the harbour for Sir William Johnstone Pulteney. It was during the town's heyday, in 1826, that the distillery opened and the town became known for silver (herrings) and gold (whisky). The Old Pulteney bottle incorporates a bulbous neck that reflects the shape of the stills – which don't have the traditional swan neck. Tradition has it that when the original stills were delivered, they didn't fit in – so they were cut down! Mooring type: marina in a former fish dock.

❾ Crosshaven

A quiet, peaceful village located where the Owenabue River enters the sea at the mouth of Cork Harbour. It is a big yachting and motor boat centre, so it is good for any marine services. Either stay in one of the three marinas, or head 2 miles upstream to the beautiful Drake's Pool where you can anchor west of the moorings mid-channel. It is next to a road, so it is not as peaceful as you might hope.

Drake's Pool was named after Sir Francis Drake, who eluded the Spanish Armada by sailing up the river. Closer to the distillery is the new marina, which has opened up in Cork city centre. Midleton Distillery was founded in 1740 but

The old distillery, Midleton

ceased distilling in 1975, when production was switched to the New Midleton Distillery. The visitor centre is based in the old distillery. There is the option of a guided tour which includes tutored tasting.

Midleton is 23 miles from Crosshaven and you can get there by bus, changing in Cork. If you decide not to go to the distillery you can go to Cronin's Pub and Restaurant in Crosshaven which has a fine selection of whiskeys. Mooring type: marina or anchor.

❿ Portrush

Old Bushmills Distillery is Ireland's oldest working distillery; James I granted a Royal licence to distil whiskey in the area in 1608. Bushmills managed to survive the American prohibition in the 1920s, by betting that it wouldn't last forever and, when repealed, reportedly was able to set sail with Ireland's largest shipment of whiskey. The whiskey is made from malted barley and the water drawn from the River Bush, which flows over beds of basalt rock. Bushmills is about seven miles from Portrush. See Giant's Causeway (page 226) for details of Portrush. Mooring type: marina.

10 HISTORICAL INTEREST

HARBOUR	ATTRACTION	DIFFICULTY
Caernarfon	Caernarfon Castle and Walls	2
Port Dinorwic	Bryn Celli Ddu	2
Bull Hole	Iona	3
Kirkwall	Skara Brae, Maes Howe, Stones of Stenness, Ring of Brodgar, Brough of Gurness, St Magnus Cathedral, Bishop's Palace, Earl's Palace	1
Berwick-upon-Tweed	Elizabethan Walls, three iconic bridges and picturesque Georgian buildings in the town	2
Amble	Warkworth Castle	1
Dover	Castle, Roman Painted House	1
Glandore	Drombeg	1
Dingle	Fahan and ancient monuments	1
Derry (Fahan, Coleraine)	Derry: City walls, murals and Free Derry Corner	1

Being island nations, there are a vast number of historic sites located all around the coast, many revealing our histories. The time span is also vast, from the sites of the earliest settlers through to those linked to very recent history. I have not included London, Dublin or Edinburgh – clearly historic – as most people know what they have to offer. Having said that, they can be explored on the trip, and recommended ports are: London, St Katharine's Docks; Dublin, Howth; and Edinburgh, Granton or Port Edgar. Indeed, some respondents have cited visits to the heart of a city as a highlight of their trip.

❶ Caernarfon

Located in North Wales, this is the ideal starting point for a trip through the Menai Strait. North Wales has some of the finest medieval castles in the world, but Caernarfon is perhaps the most remarkable in Britain. The location has been strategically important since Roman times. The present castle was started in the 13th century, though never actually finished. In more recent times it was the location for the investiture of Prince Charles. The fairy tale towers of the fortified town and castle overlook Victoria Dock, the small marina (with a sill). From Caernarfon you can get the Welsh Highland railway to the start of a walking route up Snowdonia. Mooring type: marina.

Caernarfon Marina overlooked by the impressive castle and walls

❷ Port Dinorwic

The Grade-II picturesque small marina is in the Menai Strait. It is tucked away behind the lock gates of the harbour that was built in 1763, for the world's second largest slate quarry, which is nearby. Close by (8 miles away) on Anglesey is the prehistoric (Neolithic) site and burial chamber of Bryn Celli Ddu. You can go into the burial chamber through a stone passage which aligns to the summer solstice sunrise and lights the back of the chamber. There is a reproduction of the 'Pattern Stone', carved with sinuous serpentine designs. Mooring type: marina.

❸ Bull Hole

Located on the Ross of Mull, a large peninsula extending south-west towards Iona, across the narrow Sound of Iona. Its west end is made up of pink granite with brilliant white sands, making the Bull Hole anchorage truly beautiful. You can anchor off Iona in settled weather, or in Bull Hole and take the ferry from Fionnphort (0.5 miles away). Iona is known as the Cradle of Christianity in Scotland, as it was the first place that St Columba landed after being banished from Ireland; his writing cell, and a collection of 180 medieval carved stones and crosses have been preserved. There is a spiritual atmosphere about Iona, and it is still a place of daily worship and retreats. It is busy with visitors during the day but early morning or late in the day is the best time to visit. Mooring type: anchor.

❹ Kirkwall

The capital of the Orkney Islands, Kirkwall is on 'Mainland', which is the largest of the 70 islands. It has a wealth of well-preserved ancient history and is a fascinating amalgam of its strong Scandinavian heritage, from the early Viking rulers, and its Scottish ancestry. It was first settled in 6,000 BC, and Skara Brae (HS) is the best-preserved Stone Age settlement. There are other ancient sites: Maes Howe, a chambered tomb (HS) with some Viking graffiti, the impressive stone circles at Stenness, the Ring of Brodgar and the ancient community of Brough of Gurness (HS). In Kirkwall, there are the 12th-century Bishop's Palace and the magnificent red sandstone St Magnus Cathedral, which hosts several concerts during the June classical music festival. Kirkwall is a busy market town, with a narrow paved main street that twists down to the harbour, and is lined with old stone houses, gift shops, cafés and restaurants. Mooring type: marina or anchoring.

The Broch of Gurness is an Iron Age broch village overlooking Eynhallow Sound, Mainland Orkney

❺ Berwick-upon-Tweed

Located at the mouth of the River Tweed, Berwick is the last town on the east coast of England, before the Scottish border. Owing to its location and relative wealth, it changed nationality 13 times following raids. The ramparts were repaired and reinforced in Elizabeth I's time and are still in good order and worth exploring. The town has many fine Georgian buildings from its time as a prosperous trading port. The three bridges that span the river are landmarks, and on the other side of the river from the town is the harbour. A new pontoon in Tweed Dock has made this accessible for most, as you can settle in soft mud. Just watch the unmarked sandbank covering most of the entrance. Speak to the harbourmaster for advice. Mooring type: pontoon.

❻ Amble

Warkworth Castle is a spectacular Northumbrian medieval castle, whose keep and outside walls are nearly all intact. It is perched on a hill with a commanding view over the River Coquet. Nearby, accessible only by boat, are the remains of a chapel known as the hermitage, carved directly out of the cliff rock. Amble, is a short walk along the river. A mile offshore is Coquet Island, with its distinctive lighthouse built on top of the ruined medieval tower that was the home of St Cuthbert when he was a hermit, before he became Bishop of Lindisfarne. It is now home to 35,000 nesting birds in the summer, including one of Britain's rarest seabirds, the roseate tern, 90 per cent of the UK's population is found here. Mooring type: marina. (See photo on page 131.)

❼ Dover

At the entrance to the English Channel, and with its proximity to France, Dover has always been of strategic importance – even as far back as Roman times. The port, at the base of the imposing white cliffs, is where Richard the Lionheart set off for the Crusades. Dover Castle (EH), the 12th-century castle, was built by Henry II but has been added to throughout history, including a network of tunnels added during the Napoleonic

Dover Castle

Looking towards Union Hall

Wars, which housed some 2,000 troops. It was from here that the evacuation of Dunkirk was directed in the Second World War. There is also the Roman Painted House and the museum has a Bronze Age boat. Mooring type: three marinas, two of which are locked, or anchoring off the beach in the outer harbour.

❽ Drombeg (Glandore)

This is the Bronze Age stone circle, made up of 17 stones which is also called the Druid's Altar, and is over 3,000 years old. It is about 25 minutes' walk west of Glandore, which is in a beautiful natural harbour. Nearby, Union Hall is a pretty, picture-postcard place, though a new development has sadly slightly changed its character. Entrance to the harbour is past two islands, hence the local phrase 'Avoid Adam, hug Eve'. Mooring type: anchor and mooring buoys.

❾ Dingle

On the stunningly beautiful Dingle Peninsula, Dingle is the most westerly town in Europe. The large natural harbour has a very famous resident, Fungi the dolphin – the natural performer has become a tourist attraction. The colourful town has houses, shops and over 50 pubs of every colour, ten of which have traditional Irish music almost every night (both organised and impromptu). West of Dingle, between Ventry and Slea Head, are many ancient monuments. At Dunbeg, there is an Iron Age fort and clochans – the stone beehive huts which were the dwellings of prehistoric farmers, cave dwellings, standing stones and approximately 500 crosses; the main group is at Fahan, and the tourist office in Dingle has a good map to explore them. Mooring type: marina.

Reconciliation – Hands Across the Divide, Derry

❿ Derry

With deep roots in the history of Ireland, Derry is a city which is full of optimism about its future, as the statue Reconciliation – Hands across the Divide so aptly captures. Although commonly called Derry, even its name has been contentious and so signs point to Londonderry/Derry, leading a local DJ to rename it 'Stroke City'. There is lots to visit: the city walls, which are the best preserved in Europe and Ferry Gate, where the Apprentice Boys gained notoriety when they closed the gates and started the siege. The more recent history of 'The Troubles' has been depicted on both sides of the conflict: in the murals around Free Derry Corner and the protestant murals close to the Ferrygate. You can moor at the pontoon in Derry but much nicer is the marina at Fahan (Lough Swilly) or the pontoon at Coleraine. Both have regular public transport to Derry.

10 TAKING THE GROUND

HARBOUR	DIFFICULTY	TYPE OF MOORING
Looe	1	Quay (drying)
Green Bay, Bryher	4	Anchoring (drying)
Tenby	1	Anchoring (drying)
Solva	1	Anchoring (drying)
Barmouth	3	Quay (drying) or anchoring (drying)
Castletown	1	Quay (drying)
Kippford	3	Dry out by pontoon or anchoring (drying)
Anstruther	1	Dry out in marina or against a wall
Wells-next-the-Sea	4	Dry out at quay, limited pontoons and the creek for longer term
Maldon	2	Dry out at pontoon or lock into a basin

If you can dry out, not only do you often have better access to shelter but you also have the opportunity to visit some truly stunning or picturesque villages.

❶ Looe

A picturesque fishing harbour, with an active fishing fleet serving local restaurants. The town, with its cobbled streets, winds up the hillside behind the harbour. The proximity of the beach does mean that this is a popular tourist spot. But don't leave without having possibly the best ever Cornish pasty at Sarah's Pasty shop. The limited visitor's berths dry to level firm mud, with access ladders to the quay.

❷ Green Bay

Located on the east coast of Bryher, the smallest of the five inhabited islands of the Isles of Scilly. It is a beautiful anchorage with a sandy beach and crystal-clear turquoise water, in the sheltered channel between Bryher and Tresco. The island's village is close by on the east side – the west side of the island is exposed to the full force of the open Atlantic. In a gale, the western coast can make the aptly named Hell Bay an awe-inspiring sight. Watch Hill has the best views over the island.

❸ Tenby

In Pembrokeshire is the walled seaside town of Tenby. The harbour, which dries to firm sand,

The colourful Tenby harbour

is lined with colourful Georgian and Victorian houses. The 13th-century medieval walls are still intact and there is the impressive Five Arches Barbican Gatehouse. The town has sandy beaches either side of it and hence it is popular at peak times. Just off the coast is St Catherine's Island, which is linked to the shore at low tide and is home to the prominent Palmerston Fort, built to defend Pembroke Docks. Slightly further offshore is Caldey Island, home to a Trappist monastery which sells chocolate and perfume. You can dry out alongside but space is limited and you need the permission of the harbourmaster, or you can anchor just outside the harbour. There is an anchorage north-east of Castle Hill if you don't want to take the ground.

❹ Solva

The crowded little harbour of Solva is located in a windy rocky inlet between Jack and Ramsay Sounds. The inner harbour, which dries to firm sand, is hidden by a dogleg entry, which provides good shelter. You can dry out against the small quay which has some good ladders. The Café on the Quay, which is also the local sailing club, does possibly the best bacon butties anywhere! The other facilities are in the village, which is a short walk away up the river.

Looking out to sea from Solva

Views over Screel across Urr Estuary, Kippford

❺ Barmouth

On the north-east coast of Cardigan Bay, Barmouth is at the mouth of the beautiful Mawddach Estuary, which is within the south-west corner of Snowdonia National Park. As the name suggests, there is a bar at the entrance, which is well known to many as the start of the Three Peaks Race. Barmouth is a seaside town with white sands close by and the old town, with its slate roofed cottages, nestles in the craggy hills.

❻ Castletown

The ancient Manx Capital is a gem not to be missed if you are visiting the Isle of Man. The medieval castle, which is thought to be 10th century, dominates the harbour and the small picturesque town. There are many fine buildings, winding streets and ancient quays, and it was once home to the Parliament in the House of Keys. You can lie against the wall outside Cain Bridge (the first bridge) or you can moor within the drying harbour. The old heritage harbour, with its attractive stone walls, reflects the importance of the town and is built around the river. At low tide, you will be among the herons and egrets that fish there.

❼ Kippford

Kippford overlooks the Urr Estuary and in the distance is an imposing hill called Screel. In years gone by, the river saw commercial vessels taking granite from the local quarries further afield, but now the attractive village is a focal point for sailors, artists, tourists and walkers. The estuary has strong tides and the meandering channel is marked with poles and unlit buoys. You can dry out at the yacht club pontoon. Walk past the beaches made up entirely of cockle shells and walk out to Rough Isle along the wrack, but check the tides, as they come in very quickly over the mud and sandbanks.

Anstruther © Felicity Chancellor

The Albatross, Wells © Matt Turner

The magnificent Thames barges at Maldon

⑧ Anstruther

On the East Neuk of Fife, Neuk meaning 'corner' in Scots, is Anstruther. It's an attractive old fishing town with an inner and outer harbour, both of which are drying. The inner harbour has a small marina, though you can also dry out against the wall. It has an attractive waterfront, with its row of neat houses, and the town is a maze of cobbled streets. Anstruther is also the home of Scotland's secret bunker – it was operational until the end of the Cold War in 1993 and is now a major attraction.

⑨ Wells-next-the-Sea

A beautiful town on the north Norfolk coast, though not as close to the sea as the name suggests, being about a mile inland. Wells, as it is known locally, has been a port for over 700 years and was a major one in Tudor times. It is in an area of outstanding natural beauty, and entry is over a bar then via a shallow channel that winds through the changing sandbanks.

The harbourmaster will always advise about entry and if available will escort you in. Nearby is Holkham Beach, which has miles of golden sands, strewn with shells and backed by knurled pines. A permanent feature at the quay is the Dutch sailing ketch *Albatross*, which smuggled Jewish refugees out of Denmark during the Second World War.

⑩ Maldon

On the river Blackwater in Essex, lovely old houses crowd the main streets of Maldon, many of which are Georgian. The waterfront at Hythe Quay is home to the largest fleet of Thames sailing barges in the UK and there are still about 10–15 whose home port is Maldon. But Maldon is probably best known for the sea salt which has been produced here since 1882, which is made from salt crystals from the marshes that border the river. Visitors can moor on the pontoon by the quay, though check with the harbourmaster as this pontoon has suffered from silting. Alternatively, you can lock into Heybridge Basin at the canal's entrance.

10 BEAUTIFUL RIVERS AND ESTUARIES

HARBOUR	DIFFICULTY	TYPE OF MOORING
Chichester	2	Marina, anchoring, drying and buoys
Dittisham	1	Buoy or anchoring
Newton Ferrers	1	Anchoring, river pontoon or buoys
Helford	1	Buoys in the Pool and limited anchoring avoiding the oyster beds
Milford Haven	1	Dale: anchorage and an isolated pontoon
Kirkcudbright	2	Pontoon
Findhorn	5	Anchoring and buoys
Walton Backwaters	1	Marina and anchoring
Pyefleet	1	Anchoring
Lough Swilly	1	Anchoring and marina

We have a huge diversity of rivers and estuaries, and on this trip you will see the full range, from wide-open estuaries to narrow winding rivers, rocky estuaries to the sandy or muddy rivers where the scenery becomes far more tranquil and rural.

❶ Chichester Harbour

A large natural harbour and area of outstanding beauty. Once over the bar, this large expanse of water is an important environment for birdlife, mainly waterfowl and wading birds. There are several anchorages: East Head has a lovely sandy beach, but is crowded in the summer, though the anchorage in the Thorney Island channel is usually much quieter. The other options are to dry out at Bosham, a beautiful old harbour, or there are several marinas: Chichester, Birdham, and Northney.

❷ Dittisham

Upstream, away from the bustling Dartmouth harbour, the pace of life slows, as you proceed up the tree lined River Dart. You can anchor downstream of the Anchor Stone or proceed to the visitors' buoys in the bend by the village. Close by is Agatha Christie's Georgian House, Greenway, whose garden and woods sweep down to the river and the boathouse – which features in *Dead Man's Folly*. You can also go further up to Stoke Gabriel or Bow Creek if water allows.

Peaceful Dittisham

❸ Newton Ferrers

It is a delightful place in Devon that time forgot, and sits on the unspoilt and secluded River Yealm. There is an anchorage in Cellar Bay which is just over the bar that guards the river – it is a tranquil spot with a beach. From here you would never guess the character of the river upstream, as it twists and turns to become densely wooded with many boats snugly moored on buoys. Further upstream the houses of the small villages of Newton Ferrers and Noss Mayo cling to the banks. There is a walk out to Yealm Head along part of the coastal path. (See banner photo on page 211.)

❹ Helford

A special place for many, and one of the loveliest places in Cornwall. The distinctive pine trees of Durgan Bay, which is also an anchorage, greet you as you enter the Helford River. The wood-clad shores of Helford Passage and beyond inspired Daphne du Maurier's 'Frenchman's Creek'. Sub-tropical Trebah Gardens are close to Durgan, and the thatched Shipwright Arms in the tiny village of Helford is packed full of character, and does good food.

Cellar Bay anchorage at the entrance to the River Yealm

Durgan, Helford River

⑤ Milford Haven

A massive estuary, where you could easily spend a couple of days exploring this area of outstanding beauty. It is also home to Milford Haven Refinery, which provides some contrasting views: in one direction, the beautiful Pembrokeshire Coast and in the other, the refinery. Milford Haven has numerous places to moor or drop anchor. There are several marinas including Milford Haven (entry via a lock) and Neyland. Dale is a very useful passage anchorage for this trip, being close to the entrance, and it is a delightful one at that.

⑥ Kirkcudbright

Pronounced 'Ker-coo-brie'. This is at the top of the narrow, shallow and winding River Dee. Proceeding up the river, the scenery changes from rugged coast to the softer fields and undulating hills of this delightful part of south-west Scotland. In the centre of this attractive town is the 16th-century Maclellan's Castle, but it is better known as the Artists' Town because, in the late 19th century, it was home to a group of artists called the Glasgow Boys. There are several galleries and the area still attracts many artists.

⑦ Findhorn Bay

A natural sheltered anchorage on the Moray Firth. The formerly busy fishing and trading harbour is now a peaceful little village. With miles of sandy beaches, it is an attractive spot though there is a tricky entrance with a shallow bar more reminiscent of the east coast rivers. See http://www.rfyc.co.uk for latest navigational advice.

Kirkcudbright

Sunset over Walton Backwaters

⑧ Walton Backwaters

The inspiration behind *Secret Water*, as every good Arthur Ransome fan will know. But even if you aren't a fan, this maze of low-lying islands is a peaceful spot to drop anchor, though during the weekends it does lose some of its tranquillity, as it is a popular destination. As you enter you will pass the sunken Thames barges, which form part of the sea defences protecting the vulnerable ecosystem that has formed. It is a great place to watch marsh birds.

⑨ Pyefleet Channel

Also known as Pyefleet Creek, it is off the river Colne just north of Mersea Island and opposite Brightlingsea Creek. It is a lovely quiet anchorage, though on a Saturday it can get busy as it is a favourite of east coast sailors. If you are lucky, with the big skies of Essex, you will have a stunning sunset and with the reflections on the water, it makes it quite memorable.

⑩ Lough Swilly

A busy sailing and diving centre on the north coast of Ireland. Many sandy beaches line this beautiful estuary. There are several anchorages of note; on the west side these include Portsalon and Macamish. Portsalon has more facilities, while Macamish is particularly attractive, with a Martello tower and rocky inlets interspersed with sandy beaches. At Fahan there is a marina, convenient due to its proximity to Derry and the airport. There is a bus into Derry and the airport is 14 miles away, which makes it a useful place to leave your boat if staging your trip or if you want to explore Derry. Near the marina is Lough Swilly Yacht Club, which has showers (only open at limited times).

Lough Swilly

10 GLORIOUS GARDENS

HARBOUR	GARDEN	DIFFICULTY	WEBSITE
Weir Quay	Garden House, Buckland Monachorum, Yelverton	1	www.thegardenhouse.org.uk
Fowey	Eden Project and Lost Gardens of Heligan	1	www.edenproject.com www.heligan.com
New Grimsby Sound	Tresco Abbey Gardens	4	www.tresco.co.uk/enjoying/abbey-garden
Portpatrick	Logan Botanic Garden	3	www.rbge.org.uk/visit/logan-botanic-garden/
Ardminish Bay Gigha	Achamore House	1	www.visitgigha.co.uk/Achamore-Gardens
Loch Ewe	Inverewe Garden	1	www.nts.org.uk/visit/places/inverewe
Scarborough	Scampston Garden	1	www.scampston.co.uk
Brightlingsea	Beth Chatto Gardens	1	www.bethchatto.co.uk
Glengarriff	Illnacullin and the Bamboo Park	1	www.bamboo-park.com
Portmagee	Glanleam House	1	www.glanleam.com

With the Gulf Stream bathing much of the west coast, there are a few good exotic gardens to explore, many created by the Victorians' new-found ability to travel to the southern hemisphere. Most require a short journey by bus or taxi to get to the garden. Garden openings times are April–September, and are daily unless otherwise stated.

❶ Weir Quay

An unspoilt corner of rural Devon, set in an area of outstanding beauty, about 6 miles from Plymouth Sound up the river Tamar. The Tamar forms the border between Cornwall and Devon. The Garden House has been described by Rachel de Thame 'as perhaps the most-breathtaking of all gardens in Britain'. The 8-acre garden was originally created by the Fortescues over 40 years, in the romantic cottage style, until they bequeathed the house and garden to the charity which now maintains them. Inspirational planting creates spectacular vistas of colour in all of the 13 gardens, including the Long Walk, the South African Gardens and the Cottage Garden to name a few. It is 5 miles from Weir Quay, and can be reached by taxi; it lies between the villages of Crapstone and Buckland Monachorum. Mooring type: visitors' buoys and a small pontoon for loading.

❷ Fowey

A popular sailing harbour, but also a busy commercial port, exporting large quantities of china clay. It is an attractive small town with steep narrow streets. It is 6 miles from the unique Eden Project with its biomes, which are gigantic greenhouses each with its own climate: one tropical and one Mediterranean, and all set in an abandoned clay pit. This incredibly ambitious garden is worth seeing even if you have just a passing interest in all things green. It is also a big hit with children. Go early to get the best experience – after 11am the biomes get very busy. It is 1 mile out of St Blazey near St Austell. To get there by bus, first go to St Austell and there is a bus to the Eden Project from there. The Lost Gardens of Heligan are also worth visiting and only 14 miles away. Mooring type: visitors' buoys.

New Grimsby Sound

it is a beautiful and popular spot. A short walk away are the famous sub-tropical Tresco Abbey Gardens, which were created in the early 19th century around the old ruined medieval priory. The high walls and hedges of the gardens protect the 20,000 exotic plants from the Atlantic winds. It has been described as 'Kew with the roof off', because many of the plants only grow elsewhere in Britain under glass, but prosper in Tresco due to the milder winter and the increased hours of sunshine. Mooring type: anchorage and visitors' buoys.

Gig racing at the Fowey Regatta

❸ New Grimsby Sound

Located between Tresco and Bryer, two of the 48 islands that make up the archipelago of the Isles of Scilly, the narrow Sound has one of the most protected anchorages in the islands. With its white sand and crystal-clear turquoise water,

❹ Portpatrick

A picturesque port hidden in what appears to be an impenetrable rocky coast, which has seen many shipwrecks. You need to pass through the narrow rocky entrance, which is only 35m wide at LW, followed by a sharp turn to the left, revealing the small inner harbour. The harbour is lined with brightly coloured houses but it is also home to one of Scotland's rarest seabirds, the black guillemot. Lean over the inner harbour wall (April–mid-July) and you will see them as they breed in holes in the walls. Logan Botanical Gardens are 10 miles

Portpatrick

from Portpatrick and are claimed to be Scotland's most exotic gardens. Nearly half the plants are collected from the southern hemisphere. Majestic tree ferns, gum trees, flowers from South Africa, plants from central and South America, a massive gunnera bog garden and a Tasmanian glade all grow in the walled and woodland gardens. From Portpatrick take the bus to Stranraer and change there for a bus to Portslogan; ask the driver to stop at the gardens. Mooring type: wall.

❺ Gigha (pronounced Gee-a)

A small community-owned island just west of Kintyre, which is the southern-most island of the Inner Hebrides. It has beautiful bays, breathtaking sunsets and stunning views over Islay, Jura and Kintyre. It was named by the Vikings and means 'the Good Isle' or 'God's Isle' and you can see why. Because it is low-lying, it has a drier and warmer climate than that normally associated with the west coast. Achamore House has 54 acres of garden, which were laid out from 1945 by Colonel Sir James Horlick, and are home to his rhododendron collection. There is also a walled garden and woodland walk. You can hire bikes on Gigha at the post office and there is a music festival in May/June. Ardminish Bay is a useful anchorage when rounding the Mull of Kintyre. Mooring type: visitors' buoys, pontoon and anchoring.

Ardminish Bay, Gigha © Sandy Campbell

❻ Loch Ewe

Located on Wester Ross, it is located 4 miles from the major headland of Rubha Reidh (pronounced 'roo-a-ree'). The sense of isolation and stunning views characterise this part of Scotland. The great Arctic convoys of the Second World War were assembled here before leaving for the ports of northern Russia. There are several anchorages but if you wish to visit the gardens at Inverewe, and the wind allows, then the anchorage at Pool Ewe is the most convenient. The 50-acre sub-tropical garden (NTS) was created by Osgood Mackenzie in 1862. It is an oasis of exotic plants, bursting with vibrant colour. Rhododendrons from the Himalayas, eucalypts from Tasmania, olearia from New Zealand and other species from far-flung places such as Chile and South Africa all flourish here. Mooring type: anchoring.

❼ Scarborough

Close to the Yorkshire Moors, this has been an east coast seaside resort since the 17th century. With fine sandy beaches and a Victorian promenade, its skyline is dominated by the attractive 11th-century Scarborough Castle (EH) high up on a rocky promontory. There are two harbours, one dries and the other – the old harbour – has a marina where you can lie afloat. Scampston Garden is famous for its walled garden, set within the 18th-century original kitchen garden for the hall. There are also the traditional gardens surrounding the house and the park, designed by Capability Brown. Scampston Garden is in Malton, about 25 miles from Scarborough. Mooring type: marina.

❽ Brightlingsea

A town on the east coast located on Brightlingsea Creek close to the mouth of the Colne Estuary. The waterfront is lined with coloured beach huts and distinctive timber-framed buildings, though the traditional waterfront view has been changed with the new marina development. The marina has improved the number of visitor berths. The Betto Chatto Gardens are at Elmstead Market, 6 miles from Brightlingsea. The original site was a gardener's nightmare: areas of poor gravel soil, deep shade and a soggy bog. Over 40 years she turned this 5-acre wasteland site into a famous gravel garden, woodland area with shade-loving plants and a water garden with huge gunnera. Take a taxi. Mooring type: marina or pontoon in creek – water taxi available.

Beach huts at the entrance to Brightlingsea Creek

After the rain, Glengariff

⑨ Glengariff

Situated at the head of Bantry Bay. The tree-lined shores and islands are surrounded by the mountains at the head of the bay, which form a natural bowl and create a microclimate. In 1910, the owner of Illnacullin (Garinish Island) turned the barren rocky island into an oasis of exotic plants from every corner of the globe, with the help of dynamite, boat loads of top soil and 100 men. There are several parts to the garden: an Italian garden overlooking a formal pool, Happy Valley with a lily pond and bog garden, a walled garden, and all are themed around a classical pavilion. There is also a Bamboo Park about 800m out of the village towards Bantry, and in Bantry itself is also the house and gardens. Mooring type: several anchorages around the bay and some visitors' buoys.

⑩ Portmagee

A small picturesque fishing village on the south-west coast of Ireland; its brightly painted houses are very typical of Kerry. It is just south of Valentia Island on which the Glanleam Garden is located. There are several mooring options that are closer than the village, depending on conditions: there is an anchorage opposite the garden south of Harbour Rock and a marina in Knightstown on Valentia. The 40-acre sub-tropical garden was created in the 19th century by the 19th Knight of Kerry, with plants sent back by collectors from all over the world, particularly Australasia. The exotic plants are planted among the natural habitats in wild profusion. Paths wiggle through luxuriant growth past cordylines, bamboo forests, beschorneria yuccoides, groves of tree ferns, embothrium and its own variant of myrtle 'Glanleam Gold'. Mooring type: Portmagee anchorage either side of bridge, visitors' buoys.

10 PICTURESQUE MARINAS

HARBOUR	DIFFICULTY	MOORING TYPE
Yarmouth	2	Marina and wall
Weymouth	1	Marina long pontoon and wall
Carlingford	2	Marina or anchor
Glenarm	1	Marina
Ballycastle	1	Marina and anchoring
Tarbert, Loch Fyne	1	Marina
Ardfern	1	Marina, buoy and anchorages further out on the loch
Craobh Haven	1	Marina
Stornoway	1	Marina
Lawrence Cove	1	Marina

While on this trip, you may actively want to avoid marinas, but sometimes they are very welcome for all the facilities and convenience they bring. So, if you need to use marina facilities, which ones offer the usual advantages of a marina but provide the most picturesque view from your boat?

❶ Yarmouth

A small village with an extremely attractive harbour at the mouth of the River Yar. It is one of the earliest settlements on the Isle of Wight; the narrow little streets were laid out by the Normans and the castle (EH) was built by Henry VIII to defend the Solent. The pier, which is the longest wooden pier in England, was built by the Victorians in 1876. The challenge is that at the weekends the harbour fills up very quickly but there are visitors' buoys outside and a good water taxi. The ferries, strong cross tides and narrow harbour entrance always mean it is an exciting entry for the new visitor.

❷ Weymouth

While there is a more convenient marina at Portland, there is nothing quite like the atmosphere of the charming harbour of Town Quay Marina, with distant views to the Jurassic coast. It is overlooked by the coloured houses with their bay windows, which glow in the evening sun. The large mooring rings on the stone quay are reminiscent of its former life. There is still a buoyant fishing fleet that supplies the town's many fish restaurants.

TEN OF THE BEST! 207

Weymouth's bustling harbour

❸ Carlingford

The Irish border runs through Carlingford Lough with Northern Ireland and the Mourne Mountains to the north and to the south, Ireland, the Cooley Peninsula and the Cooley Mountains. Carlingford Marina, being located on the south side, has spectacular views over the Mourne Mountains and the Lough. The town of Carlingford is about a mile's walk away; it is a well-preserved medieval town which enjoyed prosperity as a trading port in the 14th to 16th centuries.

❹ Glenarm

The small village on the Antrim coast dates back to Norman times. The picturesque main street of colour-washed buildings leads to Glenarm Forest. There is a lovely route up through the forest, providing fine vistas of the castle and village. At the centre of the village is the Barbican Gate, which leads to the castle. The distinctive limestone walled harbour dates back to the 15th century, when it was used by monks as a fishing harbour and to export lime. It has recently been restored and now is home to a lovely little marina. You just need to avert your gaze from the two rather ugly former lime-works, which I am sure in time will be improved.

Carlingford Marina, overlooking the Mourne Mountains

Ballycastle and Fairhead, with Kintyre just on the horizon

❺ Ballycastle

The bay, with its long sweeping beach, is dominated by the dramatic Antrim coast. The marina has views over Rathlin and the coast, in particular the distinctive Fair Head some 600ft (183m) high, and on a good day you can see the Mull of Kintyre. Ballycastle is a busy market town with a prosperous feel to it. Coloured houses and shops line the seafront and Quay Road leads up the hill to the town's heart. If there isn't the weather to sail to Rathlin, then you can get the ferry from here.

❻ Tarbert

On Loch Fyne, this is a natural harbour with an attractive waterfront. Although it still has a small fishing fleet, it is sadly in decline. The harbour is extremely well sheltered with a large area of pontoons, overlooked by the ivy-covered ruin of Robert the Bruce's 14th-century castle. Tarbert means isthmus, which is why you will find lots of Tarberts in Scotland, though each one states its location to prevent confusion, eg Tarbert Harris or Tarbert Jura. (See photo on page 37.)

Tarbert, Loch Fyne

❼ Ardfern

Situated in an idyllic spot at the head of Loch Craignish is Ardfern. Hills to the east give the loch a magnificent setting. It is a popular yachting centre and useful harbour if you can't go through the Dorus Mor tidal gate. It is also very convenient for the Crinan Canal. Good boatyard and chandlery, Galley of Lorne pub and great coffee shops, plus lovely walks.

❽ Craobh Haven

Pronounced 'Croove'. This is about halfway between Oban and Crinan. The sheltered harbour was created by linking three islands together. Its situation is stunning, with long views over to Mull. It is a long way from any villages or towns, though on site there is a holiday village with tastefully built houses and cottages.

Ardfern, Loch Craignish

Craobh Haven, with views to Mull

which then became Stornoway. The idyllic inner harbour, lined with colourful houses and overlooked by Lews Castle and its woods, affords good shelter and lies at the heart of the town. The harbour perfectly combines the needs of the visiting sailor, with a working harbour providing all the facilities you could want. With time being short on a circumnavigation, it is the ideal spot to hire a car and explore Harris and Lewis.

❾ Stornoway

The largest town in the Outer Hebrides, it was named by the visiting Vikings 'Steering Bay',

❿ Lawrence Cove

On the tiny Bere Island in Bantry Bay. The marina is in a sheltered bay with views of the mountains of Slieve Miskish and the Caha Mountains of the Beara Peninsula. The island has a population of 200 though it was over 2,000 before the great famine. If you don't fancy the marina you can anchor in the remote Lonehort Bay on the other side of the island. There are looped walks to the various sites on the island. The marina is a 10-minute walk to village shop, post office and pub.

Stornoway Marina overlooked by Lews Castle

10 REMOTE ANCHORAGES

HARBOUR	DIFFICULTY	TYPE OF MOORING
Worbarrow Bay	1	Anchoring at either end of the bay
Sanda	2	Anchorage on north of island near the pier
Loch Tarbert, Jura	3	Anchoring
Tinker's Hole, Mull	3	Anchoring (mooring rings on rocks)
Loch Scavaig	3	Anchoring
Acairseid Mhor, Rona	3	Anchoring and a visitor buoy
Tanera Beg	1	Anchoring
Loch Eriboll	1	Anchoring
Derrynane	3	Buoys and anchoring
Keem, Achill Island	1	Anchoring

There are many candidates for remote anchorages around the coast, but these ones are particularly special, beautiful locations or useful remote passage anchorages; there are, however, many others that could equally have made it onto the list. There are no facilities unless otherwise stated.

❶ Worbarrow Bay

A beautiful deep-water bay on the outstanding Jurassic Coast, where the land seems to fold with outbursts of brilliant white limestone. The bay is lined with a narrow strip of stony beach at the bottom of the crumbling chalk cliffs which are interspersed with greenery. Each side of the bay has an anchorage which gives you a choice depending on the wind direction. A short walk from Mupe Bay, just past the Second World War observation post, is the fossil forest, where stumps of prehistoric trees can be seen. The only drawback of Worbarrow Bay is that it is in the middle of the Lulworth Gunnery Range, so you can only visit outside firing times.

Worbarrow Bay, the Jurassic Coast

Sanda © Alan Kohler

❷ Sanda

Off the southern tip of the Kintyre Peninsula is Sanda, which is privately owned. It is a useful break in a passage from Campbeltown to Gigha or Ireland. There are strong tides, so careful planning is required to make a visit. It has associations with Robert the Bruce, and ashore you will find the ruins of an old chapel and an unusual lighthouse, consisting of two stepped-stone towers and the lighthouse – known as 'the Ship'. The island is a breeding site for shag, fulmar, kittiwake, guillemot, Manx shearwater, storm petrel and puffin. Consequently, it has SSSI status and is also a bird observatory.

❸ Loch Tarbert

The loch is located on Jura, one of the islands of the Southern Inner Hebrides. It is recognisable by the three distinctive hills, called the Paps of Jura, and is described as one of Scotland's last wildernesses; its population of just over 200 is outnumbered by the 5,500 deer. Loch Tarbert practically bisects the island and is littered with rocks, which means that navigation is challenging, though made easier by a series of beacons, so you will need a pilot guide to proceed. Antares Charts are recommended. The outer loch has several great anchorages. Navigate past the first patch of rocks, and you come to an anchorage at Cuan Mor Bay, the most popular anchorage. Proceed past a further patch of rocks and you are into the inner loch, which has an anchorage at Cruib Bothy. If you are feeling brave, then Cumhann Beag is reached via a series of extremely narrow passages, which leads to the hidden jewel, an anchorage in the magical inner sanctum. It was described by one crew surveyed as having 'peace, remoteness and stags that overlooked us at dinner'.

❹ Tinker's Hole

To the west of the Ross of Mull on the small Isle of Erraid. The pink granite, white sand and turquoise water ensures this is a very attractive and memorable anchorage. It is worth walking over the rocky hill to the beautiful Traigh Gheal beach. From the hill you will see views over to Iona and the Paps of Jura. It also is one of the driest and sunniest places in western Scotland. Erraid is featured in Robert Louis Stevenson's *Kidnapped*.

❺ Loch Scavaig

Located on Skye, this is considered to be one of the most spectacular and dramatic anchorages on the west coast, tucked in beneath the Cuillins that tower above. There is a rewarding short walk over to Loch Coruisk to see the stunning scenery and views of the ridge; you are likely to see deer and possibly sea eagles. However, the anchorage has a disadvantage in that the impressive scenery can be matched with equally impressive squalls and katabatic downdraughts at night, though they are fewer as you get further out. The inner harbour at Soay Harbour, which is close by, is an overnight option. Antares Charts are recommended.

Tinker's Hole © Nick Nottingham

Acairseid Mhor, Rona © Derek Lumb

❻ Acairseid Mhor, Rona

Also incorrectly called South Rona. This is a small island between Skye and the mainland. The anchorage has a feeling of total isolation, and once inside you won't want to leave. The population of one is in a marked contrast to the 180 that used to live here in mid-19th century, many of whom lived in the village at Acairseid Thoriam. The ruins of the houses and the old school are still visible and the Mission House has been restored. On the north side of the anchorage is the small Rona Lodge. There is an iconic view from the viewpoint Meall Acairseid. There are also some mooring buoys.

❼ Tanera Beg

The Summer Isles, so called due to the summer grazing, are an archipelago of islands and skerries at the mouth of Loch Broom. Tanner Beg is a convenient stop in this remote NW corner of Scotland, whose vast scenery is magnificent and raw. With several anchorages, shelter can

Tanera Beg, Summer Isles © Stephen Salter

be found from most wind directions. Tanera Beg's anchorage is remote and beautiful and at low water the shores are tinged with pink coral from the nearby bank. Tanera Mor's anchorage has been used since Viking times, it's the largest island and is inhabited. It operates its own private postal service printing its own stamps since 1970.

⑧ Loch Eriboll

A deep loch on the north coast of Scotland close to Cape Wrath which was used as a naval anchorage. HMS *Hood* spent her last days on shore leave here and in 1935 the crew created the name Hood in stones on the hillside on the opposite side of the Loch to Ard Neackie. The local school now maintains this memorial. It is a very picturesque and rugged loch with several anchorages; an attractive anchorage exists either side of Ard Neakie (a narrow spit with two identical curving sandy beaches).

⑨ Derrynane

Pronounced 'Derry-naan', located on the south west coast of Ireland, is a stunning natural harbour, with wide sandy beaches, backed by sand dunes and turquoise water. There is a tricky entrance but once inside it is sheltered in all winds. Even in a westerly gale, a yacht will lie quietly, though leaving is not an option! Entry at night is not suitable for first-time visitors. A short walk away is the house of Daniel O'Connell, who is one of Ireland's great historic figures. His house and gardens are open to the public.

⑩ Keem

On the west of Achill Island in County Mayo, is a horseshoe bay with a fine sandy beach, a natural amphitheatre formed by the cliffs of Benmore, a dramatic spur called Moyteoge to the west and the Croaghaun Mountain to the east. On a sunny

Derrynane. Top: the day after a gale. Below: a peaceful spot even when outside the waves are crashing on the rocks

day the clear waters turn turquoise and it provides a useful and beautiful passage anchorage in an offshore wind, though the ever-present swell may be uncomfortable.

10 TASTY TREATS

HARBOUR	TASTY TREAT	DIFFICULTY	MOORING TYPE
The Cove St Agnes	Turks Head Fish and Chips	2	Anchor
Howth	Dublin prawns	1	Marina
Peel	Queenies	1	Marina, buoys or anchor
Canna	Canna Bay Platter	2	Anchor or buoy
Stromness	Orkney Fudge	1	Marina
Lossiemouth	Rizza's Ice-cream	1	Marina
Arbroath	Arbroath Smokies	1	Marina
Southwold	Adnams Ale	4	Low quay
Cork	Cork Boi and Irish soda bread from the English Market	1	Pontoon
Bantry	Gubben, Durrus and Milleens Cheese	1	Pontoon, buoy or anchor

There is nothing quite like celebrating reaching your next harbour with a run ashore, which can be made all the more special, if you can find a local tasty treat to reward yourself with. Plus, you have the satisfaction that you are supporting smaller producers of local food, and that precious few food miles were involved in serving up the treat.

❶ The Cove St Agnes

Turks Head Fish and Chips. On this trip, you will have the opportunity to sample many award-winning fish and chips, so I would never claim that these are the best. However, there is something about lying at anchor in The Cove, which is often your first landfall on the Isles of Scilly, with its aqua blue water and its bar of white sand that joins St Agnes and Gugh. It's a short stroll to the pub, to eat fresh fish and chips and, if you are lucky, you will be able to watch gig racing, between the Islands. The home advantage being that they don't have far to get to the start line, but have quite a journey home after the race!

❷ Howth

Dublin Bay Prawns. Howth is a traditional fishing village with an active fishing fleet, ensuring that fresh seafood is readily available. Besoffs Market is the place to head for the local delicacy Dublin Bay Prawns. With its restaurant, café and seafood market, it ensures that all budgets are catered for. The local yacht club runs the well-appointed marina. With great local walks, the Howth Cliff Loop walk provides great views of the rugged coastline and being only 30 mins by train from Dublin, there is much to keep you occupied.

❸ Peel

Queenies. Peel, on the Isle of Man, is a harbour which comfortably fits in to any number of top ten categories. Guarded by the striking Peel Castle on St Patrick's Isle, it is connected to the town by a causeway. The 11th-century castle and fortifications were built of local red sandstone, though most of them are ruined with the exception of the outer walls. The Isle of Man's national dish is Queenies (Queen Scallops) and Peel is the perfect place to taste them, either at a little food shack by the harbour bridge or at the Boatyard Fish Restaurant. The marina depth is maintained by an automatic flap gate, there are four buoys outside the harbour or you can anchor beyond the outer breakwater.

❹ Canna

Seafood. Canna is the most westerly, and has the most sheltered anchorage, in the Small Isles. It is a very scenic, green and fertile island, and rising behind the farmland are the basalt cliffs, some 60 million years old. The surrounding waters and land are a rich source of ingredients for Canna Café. The dish not to miss, is the Canna Bay platter: whole local lobster, whole crab and at least one other item from the day's catch — langoustine or octopus (min two people). Pre-order only on 01687 482488 (there is no mobile signal on Canna). The café also listens on VHF Ch08. Canna is designated as a site of special scientific interest and special protection area; it is renowned for sea eagles, golden eagles and puffins.

Peel Castle

❺ Stromness

Orkney Fudge. This is a wonderfully creamy fudge that is made in Stromness. It is now made by Argo's Bakery, but is still as good as I remember it when growing up. Stromness has been an important trading port for centuries, the Hudson Bay Trading Company and later many of the herring fleets and whaling expeditions, would find their crew from here. The small town oozes character, clustered around the long narrow main street with its flagstones and no pavement. The harbour houses have their own piers, from which the merchants would trade, with beautiful views across Hoy Sound. It is a lively town, with a great little marina, and an ideal first stop when visiting mainland Orkney. (See photo on page 125.)

❻ Lossiemouth

Rizza's Ice-cream. Lossiemouth, or Lossie as it is known locally, is a former fishing harbour. The two attractive former fishing basins have now been converted into a marina. Across the river from Lossie are the most incredible sandy beaches, with big sand dunes, which were created using old railway carriages to protect the town from the heavy seas. Just by the old harbour, is the location of the winner of our national ice-cream survey; Rizza's Ices, which has been making Italian ice cream since 1914 and are now owned by the fourth generation of the family.

The sand dunes of Lossiemouth

Arbroath Smokies

❼ Arbroath

Arbroath Smokies. These are prepared using traditional methods dating back to the late 1800s. Haddock are salted overnight, then left to dry. They are smoked over a hardwood fire in a sealed barrel, covered with wet jute sacks. The humid, smoky conditions giving the Smokie it's characteristic taste. With protected status, they can only be made within a range of 5 miles of the town, and are readily available in the town's cafes, restaurants or in local fishmongers. If you want to learn more, you can follow the Arbroath Smokie Trail to learn about its history. The outer harbour dries, but you can lay afloat in the inner harbour at pontoons as it is behind the tidal gates.

❽ Southwold

Adnams Ale. This has been brewed in Southwold for over 150 years. The earliest record of beer being brewed here is from 1345. 'Ale wife' Johanna de Corby and 17 others were charged by the manorial court for serving illegal measures. Southwold is the quintessentially English seaside town, traditional coloured beach huts, a sandy beach and a wooden pier. The harbour, at the mouth of the river Blyth, is entered over a shingle bar, and is a step back in time with the old wooden stagings protruding into the river. The ebb can reach 6 knots, so you need to have adequate springs and shore lines. Opposite the visitors' staging is the Harbour Inn, where you can

The old wooden staging in Southwold, with the lighthouse in the distance

enjoy some locally caught fish and chips, washed down with a pint of Adnams. You can taste their ales (and lagers, cider and gin) at most of the pubs in Southwold and Walberswick, take a tour of their brewery or you can visit their shop in the town.

❾ Cork

The 18th-century covered English Market. This is full of local delicacies. Try third generation sausage maker O'Flynn's Gourmet Sausages Cork Boi sausage, made from locally sourced Pork & Beef, onions, fresh thyme and Cork's famous Murphy's Irish Stout with some traditional Irish Soda Bread from the Alternative Bread Company, to create your own sausage butty. Lunch at Café Marius is a good place to taste some of the local cheeses (see Bantry). The Customs House pontoon, at the head of Cork harbour is in the heart of the historic city; it is secure and a short walk from the main shopping street. Ideal for exploring the city or a crew change.

❿ Bantry

Cheese. West Cork is a must for any cheese lover; with lush green pastures and free roaming cattle, combined with the old artisanal methods, the small-scale farmhouse cheese making produces some wonderful cheeses. Gubben, Durrus and Milleens are three cheeses produced not far from Bantry, and the Friday Market is an ideal place to sample them and others. The lively regional town has a small popular marina. Other non-cheese related highlights of Bantry include a music festival and a literary festival.

10 ICONIC LIGHTHOUSES

LIGHTHOUSE	OPERATIONAL DATE	INTEREST
Berry Head	1906	Smallest, highest and deepest in the British Isles
Eddystone	1st 1698 4th 1882	Old toll gate
Longships	1st 1795 2nd 1873	Key turning point
Hook	Approx. 1240	World's second oldest operational
Mull Kintyre	1st 1788 2nd 1820s	Key milestone
Ardnamurchan Point	1849	Most westerly on mainland Britain
Cape Wrath	1828	Key turning point
Bell Rock	1810	World's oldest sea washed lighthouse
Dover	AD 1	Roman
Fastnet	1854	Ireland's teardrop

Since Roman times, lighthouses have kept sailors safe, although it wasn't until international shipping trade significantly increased in the 18th century, and later, that the lighthouses we see today were constructed. There are more than 348 lighthouses in the UK and Ireland. Many are built in spectacular but hazardous places, and they are a testament to the ingenuity of the engineers, resilience of their builders and the bravery of those that operated them. On this voyage you will pass too many to mention but here are a few iconic ones. If you are lucky, you will see them on a beautiful day.

❶ Berry Head

Berry Head claims to be home to the smallest, highest and deepest lighthouse in the British Isles. The smallest because on its tip toes it is only 5m high, the tallest because it is perched on the limestone headland of Berry Head and hence is 58m above sea level. The deepest because the optic was turned by a weight falling down a 45m shaft, though it has since been replaced by a motor. It is a great walk from the marina, through a nature reserve, with spectacular views over Brixham in Torbay.

❷ Eddystone

This is perhaps one of the most well-known lighthouses you will pass – but there were three lighthouses before the one you see today. The first lighthouse was lit from 1698, and was the world's first open ocean lighthouse, but it only survived

Eddystone lighthouse

many bodies of water meeting, it should always be treated with respect. The first lighthouse, built in 1795, was only 12m tall (24m above sea level), hence it was often obscured by the waves and so was replaced by the current lighthouse in 1873, which is 24m taller. There are a few modern additions: a helipad perched on its top and it is now powered by solar panels, that surround the lower half of the lantern additions, including solar panels surrounding the lower half of the lantern, and a helipad. (See photo on page 76.)

❹ Hook

This is up there with the most remarkable of all lighthouses, as one of the oldest in the world and the second oldest operational one. The lighthouse, which has stood for an incredible 800 years, was built sometime in the early 13th century and was first shown as operational on a map of 1240. The black and white banded lighthouse was operated by monks for its first 400 years and stands on the isolated peninsula at the mouth of Waterford Harbour. Fuels over the years have included coal, whale oil, gas and paraffin oil, and it was electrified in 1972.

❺ Mull of Kintyre

The name was immortalised by Paul MacCartney's chart-topping song, though that relates to the headland rather than the lighthouse. First built in 1788, and rebuilt in the 1820s, it proved to be a difficult site to build on, being inaccessible by sea or road, so material had to be carried overland on horseback, across the rough moorland. Even today it is easier to access on foot; if travelling by car you need nerves of steel and good brakes. The barren headland was also the scene of one of the worst Royal Air Force peacetime disasters, resulting in the loss of 29, when a Chinook helicopter crashed into the hill.

for five years. The second acted as a toll gate, charging for every ton that passed. The third one stood for 120 years, and only failed because the rock it was built on developed cracks and hence the lighthouse was moved to Plymouth Hoe as a testament to Smeaton, its designer, though its base can still be seen next to the current one.

❸ Longships (Land's End)

For most this will be another great milestone, a turning point, either going north or east for the first time. It is a beautiful sight at sunrise, but with

❻ Ardnamurchan Point

A significant milestone on your cruise is rounding mainland Britain's most westerly point. Tradition dictates that, after rounding the point, you are entitled to put white heather on your pulpit or in your hat. The lighthouse was designed by Alan Stevenson, one of the notable Stevenson family, prolific engineers and lighthouse builders of their day; Alan was the uncle of Robert Louis Stevenson. Part of the peninsula is actually a collapsed inactive volcano. The lighthouse is built out of pink granite from Mull, and stands 35 metres tall and soars 55m above the sea. If you want to visit, anchor at the beautiful Sanna Bay, then it is a 5km hike to the visitor's centre and tea rooms, or take the ferry from Tobermory. (See photo on page 52.)

❼ Cape Wrath

A major milestone on your route and appropriately Cape Wrath is Norse for turning point. You will pass it with a real sense of achievement and, if you are lucky, you will see it! However, it has suffered from the same challenge ever since it was built in 1828 by Robert Stevenson; due to the height of the light, which is 122m above sea level, which means it is often obscured by low cloud or fog. Initially, the solution to this was to add an additional low light, involving tunnels, though the First World War ended this and work has never restarted.

❽ Bell Rock

Off the East coast of Scotland, this is Scotland's oldest sea washed lighthouse, which stands on the Bell Rock. Built by Robert Stevenson in 1810, it took three years to build, the challenge exacerbated as it was covered with water every day for 20 hours. It operated in tandem with a shore station, the Bell Rock Signal Tower, at the mouth of Arbroath harbour, and used to send signals to the lighthouse keepers. An expectant father would learn of the sex of his new born, depending whether it was trousers or a dress that were hoisted from the signal tower. It now houses an interesting museum about the history of the lighthouse.

Cape Wrath, looking east along the North Coast © Alan Kohler

The Bell Tower, Arbroath

❾ Dover

The Roman lighthouse that dates back to the year AD 1; this ancient octagonal lighthouse was built by the Romans and can be found in the grounds of Dover Castle. Originally, it was 24m-tall, and the fire in its crown served as a beacon for ships crossing from Gaul into the port of Dubris (Dover). It is one of the best preserved lighthouse anywhere in the world. Its survival was helped because it was repurposed as a bell tower to the 11th-century church built close by. The upper stonework is mainly medieval.

❿ Fastnet

The most southerly Irish lighthouse. For many sailors, it is famous for the race of its name, and the tragic race of 1979; but for many it was the last part of Ireland that Irish emigrants saw when they sailed to North America, hence it was known as Ireland's teardrop. The second lighthouse to be built here holds many records, it is the most southerly point of Ireland, it holds the highest wind gust record, 119mph (2017) and is the tallest and all of its 48m height was covered by a rogue wave in 1985.

10 SEA SHORE GEMS

HARBOUR	SEA SHORE GEM	DIFFICULTY	MOORING TYPE
St Michael's Mount	Castle and Church	2	Anchor or drying out
Conwy	Britain's Smallest House	1	Marina and buoy
Douglas	Laxey Wheel	1	Marina
Portrush	Giant's Causeway	1	Marina
Staffa	Fingal's Cave	3	Occasional anchorage
Colonsay	Machair	1	Anchor, buoy and local quay
Lamb Holm/Kirk Sound	The Italian Chapel	2	Anchorage
Woodbridge	Sutton Hoo	4	Marina and buoys
Inishbofin (Galway)	Traditional Irish Music	2	Anchor
Tory Island	Most of the Island	2	Local quay or anchor

Like exquisite shells half-buried on a beach, they are so easy to pass by if you don't know where to look. Close to our shores, there is a rich tapestry of special places that make for a unique experience. These little gems are on, or close to, the sea shore and you wouldn't want to miss them. Some are natural, others the result of craftsmanship but all worthy of being called Sea Shore Gems.

❶ St Michael's Mount (NT)

This is instantly recognisable with its strong resemblance to the Mont St Michel. A tiny tidal island in Mount's Bay, crowned by a medieval church and castle connected by a granite causeway. It was an important place of pilgrimage until the dissolution of the monasteries by Henry VIII. But the castle only saw action in the English Civil War. Since Roman times, the harbour has been important in the export of tin, but now it is a beautiful and peaceful place to take the ground, once the tourists have left! Mooring is free because there are no facilities. In settled weather you can anchor to the south-west of the entrance.

❷ Conwy

The old harbour lies at the base of the historic walled market town, and is dominated by the imposing castle walls. Conwy is an UNESCO World Heritage site for its late 13th- and early 14th-century military architecture. By the harbour, against the scale of the large walls is Britain's smallest house; the 16th-century house is painted in post box red. The floor area is only

The UK's smallest house, Conwy

Laxey Wheel

1.8m and its last occupant was a 1.8m fisherman, who couldn't stand up straight in his own house! The harbourmaster has some river moorings off the town, with a water taxi run by North Wales Cruising Club, but if none are available, Conwy marina is a convenient alternative.

❸ Douglas (Laxey Wheel)

The Laxey harbour is only accessible to those who can take the ground. Douglas will be the harbour that most use to get to the Laxey Wheel. The Victorian Manx electric tram will take you along the beautiful coast to Laxey. The wheel is the world's largest operating waterwheel. The local mines extracted lead, copper, silver and zinc, but needed water to be cleared from the mines. With no coal on the Isle of Man, the water powered wheel was used to pump water out of the mines. Douglas is a very sheltered harbour accessed via the sill and lifting bridge. There are some fabulous cycle/walks along Marine Drive that overlooks the coast.

❹ Portrush (Giant's Causeway)

This impressive UNESCO World Heritage Site is made up of 40,000 red basaltic prisms or columns as a result of an explosion some 60 million years ago. Local legend has it that this was the Giant Finn McCool's bridge, which he built to settle a dispute with a Scottish Giant. It is just 8 miles from Portrush which is a typical seaside town, with numerous caravan parks and a beautiful beach backed by dunes. A bus goes to both Bushmills and the Giant's Causeway.

❺ Staffa

Fingal's Cave is on the uninhabited island of Staffa. The towering hexagonal basalt columns, similar in structure to the Giant's Causeway, rise up and support the cathedral-like roof. With its natural acoustics, it has been the source of inspiration for poets and musicians alike: Keats, Wordsworth, Sir Walter Scott and Mendelssohn to name a few. In calm weather, you can land and enter the cave. There is only a temporary anchorage off the east side, which is only tenable in calm weather; it is advisable to leave a member of your crew on your boat, as the holding is questionable and Antares Charts are recommended. If you aren't blessed with calm weather, you can take a day trip from Tobermory.

❻ Colonsay

Machair is the Gaelic word meaning fertile, low-lying grassy plain, and it is a mosaic of grassland filled with wild flowers which only occurs on the exposed west-facing shores of Scotland and Ireland. See the banner picture. Common flowers interspersed with rarer species, such as orchids, provide the ideal habitat for two of Britain's rarest birds: Colonsay's most famous residents, the corncrake and the red billed chough. Head towards the beautiful, iconic, crescent-shaped Kiloran Bay, to see the machair. Anchor NW of ferry pier, alongside the north side of the the pier with a fender board, or the six visitors' moorings in Loch Staosnaig/Queen's Bay. Although the machair is found on many of the Hebridean Islands, it is easier to access from the sea on the smaller islands (Uist, Tiree, Coll and Barra).

❼ Lamb Holm/Kirk Sound (The Italian Chapel)

The Churchill Barriers were built by Italian prisoners of war in the Second World War to protect the strategic harbour of Scapa Flow. At their camp, they also created the remarkable Italian chapel. Built from two Nissen huts and concrete; the inside is painted as a trompe l'odeil. It is so well crafted that it deceives with ease and you can't believe it is not real; it is quite beautiful and unique. Anchor north of the chapel for temporary anchorage.

The Giant's Causeway

Italian Chapel Lamb Holm

Woodbridge © Paul Galley

⑧ Woodbridge

Sutton Hoo on the banks of the Deben at Sutton Hoo (NT), is the burial site of the Anglo Saxon King of East Anglia, who died around AD 625. A 40-oar ship, contained the coffin, the magnificent helmet and other finds which are now in the British Museum. Replicas are displayed at Sutton Hoo and show the extraordinarily intricate craftsmanship of the time. The story, made famous by the Film *The Dig*, is well told in Edith Pretty's former house. Woodbridge is an historic Suffolk market town at the head of the River Deben. There is a challenging entrance to the river, which changes frequently (see www.debenestuarypilot.co.uk for up-to-date information). On the way up is the popular waterhole, the Ramsholt Arms at Ramsholt. The marina is by the picturesque Tide Mill.

⑨ Inishbofin (Galway)

Nothing quite creates an atmosphere like a bar filled with traditional Irish music. Inishbofin has a vibrant local traditional Irish music scene, and on most nights in the season (June – August) you will be able to find a lively trad session; local musicians will often strike up in a spontaneous session. Beautiful shell strewn beaches, with crystal clear waters, fresh seafood and an excellent natural harbour overlooked by the ruined Cromwellian Barracks are the other reasons to visit.

⑩ Tory Island

A sea shore gem, mainly because it could fit into so many of the Ten of the Best categories: it has formal and informal music sessions, corncrakes, spectacular walks, and one of only two Tau crosses in Ireland, indicating possible farming links to the Christians of Egypt. This fascinating island is less than 2 sq miles in area, and is Ireland's remotest inhabited island, with its own King; as voted for by its 141 Irish speaking inhabitants. It has a small community of artists, the most famous was its last King, Patsy Dan Rodgers who reigned for 38 years, until his death in 2018. For intriguing tales listen to the BBC podcast, *The House That Vanished*.

10 MARITIME HISTORY

HARBOUR	DIFFICULTY	MOORING TYPE
Portsmouth	1	Marina
Beaulieu	1	Marina, river pontoons, buoys and anchoring by river entrance
Plymouth	1	Marina
Charlestown	1	Wall or buoys
Dublin	1	Marina
Belfast	1	Marina
Scapa Flow	3	Buoys or anchor
Whitby	1	Pontoon
Hartlepool	1	Marina
Greenwich (Limehouse Basin)	1	Marina

The histories of the UK and Ireland are inexorably connected to the sea. As island nations, many of their peoples have set sail on voyages of discovery, naval conflict, trading routes (including slavery) and tragic events. It is the stories behind these acts of courage, seamanship, ingenuity and inhumanity, that bring these voyages to life. Many are well told in the maritime museums and dockyards around our shores.

❶ Portsmouth

This has been a port of strategic importance for hundreds of years; the approach is guarded by the imposing Napoleonic forts. Of particular interest to most are the Historic Dockyard and its ships: on show are HMS *Victory* and HMS *Warrior*. The *Mary Rose* consists of an amazing

Victory, one of the Historic Ships

collection of artefacts which were preserved by the mud, untouched since she sank off the entrance to the harbour in 1545. There are many marinas in Portsmouth Harbour, but to continue the historic experience, use Royal Clarence Yard. In Nelson's day, Portsmouth was used to load the ships with ammunition, and Royal Clarence Yard on the Gosport side, was for victualling. The old buildings still exist: the granary, the abattoir, the cooperage and Flagstaff Green, where the Admirals lived.

❷ Beaulieu

The village, and its river, have had a connection with the sea for years. Since Elizabethan times, many warships have been built at Buckler's Hard Shipyard from the oaks of the nearby New Forest. Several of Nelson's ships were launched here and the museum traces their history. While the shipyard is barely visible now, the site is brought to life by the hamlet of shipyard workers' cottages and the Master Builder's House. A 3-mile walk up the river is the attractive hamlet of Beaulieu, with quaint Georgian cottages and the occasional New Forest pony wandering through. It is also the home of Lord Montague, with many attractions to visit: the Palace, the Motor Museum and Beaulieu Abbey.

❸ Plymouth

Well known for Drake's game of bowls on Plymouth Hoe, prior to defeating the Spanish Armada. The Hoe has magnificent views of the Sound, and is also the location of Smeaton's lighthouse. Plymouth's importance as a strategic naval base, and its close connection to the sea, has continued to the present day. The old Sutton harbour, in the Barbican area, was the departure point for the Pilgrim Fathers bound for the New World as well as all three of Captain Cook's voyages. Close by is where Sir Francis Chichester and Robin Knox Johnston started and finished their historic voyages. There are several marinas but they are often full, so phone ahead to check availability. There are anchorages off Cawsand and Kingsand if you want to anchor close to the Sound's entrance, but visiting Plymouth from there isn't an option without a long trip.

The east end of Plymouth Breakwater – the basket was so that shipwrecked sailors could climb to safety

❹ Charlestown

A working Georgian port, constructed between 1791 and 1801, which exported tin and copper, but predominantly china clay, until 1999. With several traditional sailing vessels moored there, the smell of tar will take you back in time and make your stay memorable in the historic locked inner harbour. With its historic charm it is often used as a film location: *Poldark* and *Hornblower* to name just two. Accessed only on spring tides, you may need to stay on one of the mooring buoys outside, as they tend to only open the lock gates for those staying longer than a few days.

❺ Dublin

It is thought that one million people fled the Irish Famine in the late 1840s. In the heart of Dublin's Docklands is an authentic replica ship of the original *Jeanie Johnston*, built to remember and honour Ireland's famine emigrants. It tells the story of the desperate families fleeing, in the hope of a better life in North America, as 2,500 undertook the treacherous voyage aboard the *Jeanie Johnston*. You can moor near the city centre at Poolbeg Yacht and Boating Club, or further out at Dun Laoghaire with good access via the DART railway.

Jeanie Johnston © EPIC Museum

Titanic Belfast

❻ Belfast

The ill-fated voyage of RMS *Titanic* is well known, but the Titanic Belfast museum covers the entire story from the building of the ship, through to images of her watery grave. A moving place to visit, which deals with the sinking with reverence following the tragic death of so many. The marinas at Bangor and Carrickfergus give you access to Belfast via train or bus if you don't want to travel the extra distance down the Lough into the city. Alternatively, you can moor in the heart of the city, in the Titanic Quarter at Abercorn Basin, close to the museum.

❼ Scapa Flow

This natural harbour, which has been a safe haven since Viking times, when longships anchored here. In the 17th century, when France was at war with England, it was on a route that enabled shipping to miss the English Channel. After the First World War, the German Fleet was scuppered here and their wrecks have created a unique marine habitat, and a popular diving site. The First World War saw the tragic sinking of the HMS *Royal Oak* with the loss of 835 men, as the result of an audacious attack by a German U Boat. The construction of the Churchill Barriers followed, to prevent future attacks, but now provides essential road links to the surrounding islands. The Scapa Flow visitor centre is at Lyness on Hoy.

❽ Whitby

At the mouth of the River Esk, surrounded by the beautiful Yorkshire Moors, lies Whitby. Its skyline is dominated by the 13th-century Whitby Abbey (EH) on the east side, where the old town of cobbled streets and picturesque houses are nestled beneath the cliffs. Whitby has a long maritime history; alum and coal were traded through here, a whalebone arch commemorates the once large whaling industry, and the town still retains a fishing industry. Captain James Cook, the 18th-century explorer, navigator and cartographer, served his apprenticeship under a local shipowner, whose house is now the Captain Cook Memorial Museum. All of his ships were built in Whitby, and a replica of *Endeavour* still sails from the port. It is a popular seaside resort, so an early morning exploration is needed to capture the atmosphere of old Whitby.

❾ Hartlepool

The fully-serviced marina is in a locked basin. Close to the marina is the National Museum of the Royal Navy; its star attraction is HMS *Trincomalee*, whose canons are fired daily. Built in India in 1817, at the end of the Napoleonic

The Whalebone Arches at Whitby overlooking the harbour and abbey

wars, HMS *Trincomalee* is one of two surviving frigates from this period. She is the oldest warship still afloat in the UK and is docked in a recreated 18th-century quayside. She has travelled over 100,000 miles; though she never saw combat, she undertook duties that included policing, protection, and exploration.

❿ Greenwich (St Katharine's Docks)

There is so much naval history in Greenwich that you could easily spend a week there. But head to the Royal Observatory, which dates back to 1675, to see the exhibition about longitude and all four of Harrison's revolutionary timepieces, all set in the splendid Royal Observatory; the site of the meridian line and the red time ball, which when it drops allows mariners and anyone else who can see it, to set their clocks to 1pm. You can moor in St Katharine's Docks.

10 'DROP-DEAD GORGEOUS' PLACES

HARBOUR	DIFFICULTY	MOORING TYPE
Studland Bay	1	Anchoring
Porth Dinllaen	1	Anchoring and buoys
Puilladobhrain	2	Anchoring
Tobermory	1	Anchoring, buoys and marina
Arisaig	4	Anchoring and buoys
Plockton	2	Anchoring and buoys
Gallanach Bay, Muck	2	Anchoring
Stonehaven	1	Wall and drying out
Adrigole (Bantry Bay)	1	Anchoring and buoys
Roundstone	1	Anchoring and buoys

These are picturesque spots either to drop your anchor, pick up a mooring buoy or moor next to a wall. Some are villages, some remote anchorages, but all are drop-dead gorgeous. If you are lucky enough to see them when the sun is shining then you are in for a real treat. Those with a view to the west will treat you to a spectacular sunset as you eat your dinner in the cockpit.

Part of the Jurassic Coast – Old Harry Rocks in Studland Bay

TEN OF THE BEST!

❶ Studland Bay
A magnificent setting with a golden beach and chalk cliffs with distinctive rock formations, and it extends to its furthest point at Old Harry Rocks. The area is a nature reserve and also the start of the South West Coast Path. It is busy at the weekends with boats from Poole but on weekdays it can be a tranquil anchorage.

❷ Porth Dinllaen
A picturesque old fishing harbour on the north Welsh coast. The village, which is owned by the National Trust, is nestled on a thin strip of shore between the blue sea and cliffside with stunning panoramic views across the Llŷn Peninsula.

❸ Puilladobhrain
Meaning 'Pool of the Otter', Puilladobhrain is just south of Oban on Seil Island. With spectacular views over Mull framed by the rocks of the pool, the sunsets from here are unbelievable. Consequently, in the summer and at weekends it is a very popular anchorage, but in early season you can enjoy it practically undisturbed. Half a mile over the hill and you come to the Clachan Bridge, known locally as 'Bridge over the Atlantic', and the 18th-century inn Tigh an Truish, which means House of the Trousers. After the 1745 Jacobite Rebellion, wearing Highland dress was banned, so the kilt-wearing islanders would change into trousers before going to the mainland. Note that Puilladobhrain is not named on charts but is 0.3nm south east of Eilean Duin. Antares Charts will enable you to find alternatives close by, if the pool is full. (See photos on pages 15 and 90.)

❹ Tobermory
The largest town on Mull is Tobermory. The harbour is well known for its colourful houses and, ever since the popular BBC series *Balamory*, it has been gripped by toddler tourism. It is also a useful port for rounding Ardnamurchan Point. From Tobermory you can go on a trip to see sea eagles and, if the weather is against you for sailing there, get a bus and ferry to see Iona, Staffa and Fingal's Cave. (See photos on pages 39 and 192.)

Overlooking Porth Dinllaen

Sheep grazing in Arisaig

❺ Arisaig

This has a challenging entrance, which can only be attempted with knowledge from a pilot guide showing the poles placed by the Clyde Cruising Club, though the comment stating that 'some may be missing due to storms' does little to reassure the nervous skipper. Antares Charts are also recommended. See page 117. Once in, not only do you have a sense of achievement but the views to Rum and Eigg are beautiful; and where else can you see sheep grazing on the beach? North of here are the Silver Sands of Morar, just a train stop away. (See photos on pages 117 and 119.)

Plockton

Gallanach Bay, Muck © Alan Kohler

❻ Plockton

This is a very picturesque National Trust of Scotland conservation village, with most houses dating from the 18th or 19th century. It is in the sheltered bay of Loch Carron, surrounded by a bowl of hills which create a micro climate; hence the bay is lined with palm-like cabbage trees. Plockton Brewery beers are available locally in the stores and hotel.

❼ Gallanach Bay, Muck

With white sand bordering the bay, and views across the Small Isles and Skye, it is an extremely attractive anchorage. Antares Charts are recommended to help with the tricky entrance because of the reefs. An ideal anchorage in southerly winds. There is a restaurant at the nearby Gallanach Lodge.

❽ Stonehaven

A gem of a harbour on the north-east coast of Scotland. The harbour is nestled into the cliffs of Downie Point, though it is difficult to see the entrance when approaching. The drying inner harbour is lined with attractive old houses and is overlooked by Stonehaven's oldest building, the

Overlooking Stonehaven's inner harbour

The dramatic Adrigole

Tollbooth. You can lie afloat in the outer harbour but it does need settled weather, as shelter is poor. A 2-mile walk along the coast is 9th-century Dunnottar Castle in its dramatic location, three sides of which are sheer cliff, with a gruesome history. (See photo on page 85.)

❾ Adrigole

A beautifully atmospheric anchorage in Bantry Bay. It is overlooked by the awe-inspiring Caha Mountains of the Beara peninsula, one of which is Hungry Hill, made famous by Daphne Du Maurier's novel of the same name. It is arguably one of the best anchorages in south-west Ireland.

❿ Roundstone

With good shelter in all bar a SSE, it is a welcome safe anchorage on the north shore of Galway Bay. The picturesque artisans' village is surrounded by beautiful mountains and seascapes, its waterfront of coloured houses overlook the small drying harbour, all of which make this more than just a convenient passage anchorage. Close by, you will find spectacular beaches with crystal clear water, and in the village there are some fantastic craft shops, several cafés and pubs/restaurants where you can eat the local catch of the day. There are also visitors' moorings SE of the harbour.

MAPS

To make it easier to plan your trips the locations are organised graphically in the maps below.

240 UK AND IRELAND CIRCUMNAVIGATOR'S GUIDE

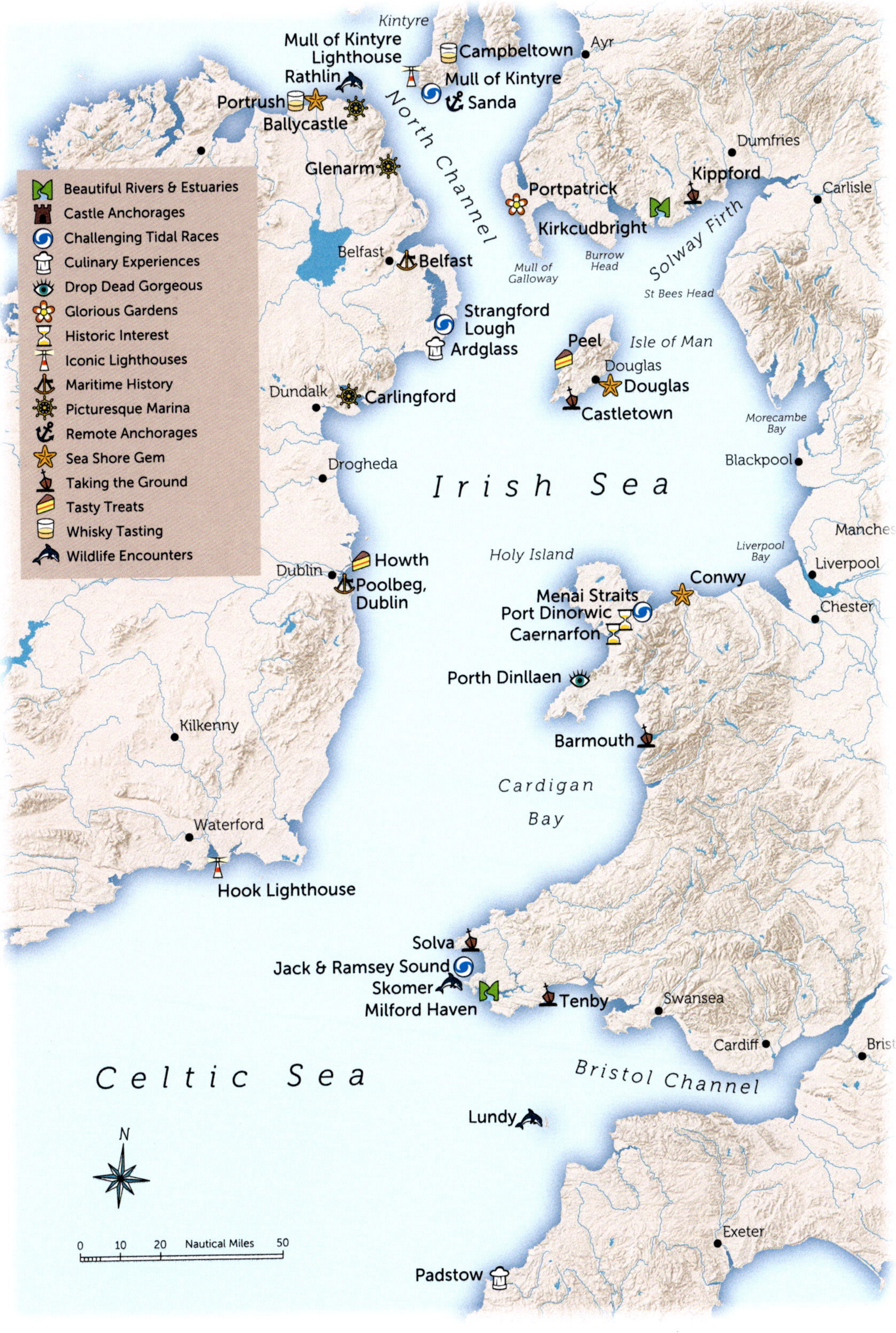
Beautiful Rivers & Estuaries
Castle Anchorages
Challenging Tidal Races
Culinary Experiences
Drop Dead Gorgeous
Glorious Gardens
Historic Interest
Iconic Lighthouses
Maritime History
Picturesque Marina
Remote Anchorages
Sea Shore Gem
Taking the Ground
Tasty Treats
Whisky Tasting
Wildlife Encounters
Kintyre
Mull of Kintyre Lighthouse
Campbeltown
Ayr
Rathlin
Mull of Kintyre
Portrush
Sanda
Ballycastle
North Channel
Dumfries
Glenarm
Kippford
Carlisle
Portpatrick
Kirkcudbright
Solway Firth
Belfast
Belfast
Mull of Galloway
Burrow Head
St Bees Head
Strangford Lough
Ardglass
Peel
Isle of Man
Douglas
Douglas
Dundalk
Carlingford
Castletown
Morecambe Bay
Drogheda
Blackpool
Irish Sea
Manches
Howth
Holy Island
Liverpool Bay
Dublin
Liverpool
Poolbeg, Dublin
Conwy
Menai Straits
Port Dinorwic
Chester
Caernarfon
Porth Dinllaen
Kilkenny
Barmouth
Cardigan Bay
Waterford
Hook Lighthouse
Solva
Jack & Ramsey Sound
Skomer
Tenby
Swansea
Milford Haven
Cardiff
Brist
Celtic Sea
Bristol Channel
Lundy
N
0
10
20
Nautical Miles
50
Exeter
Padstow

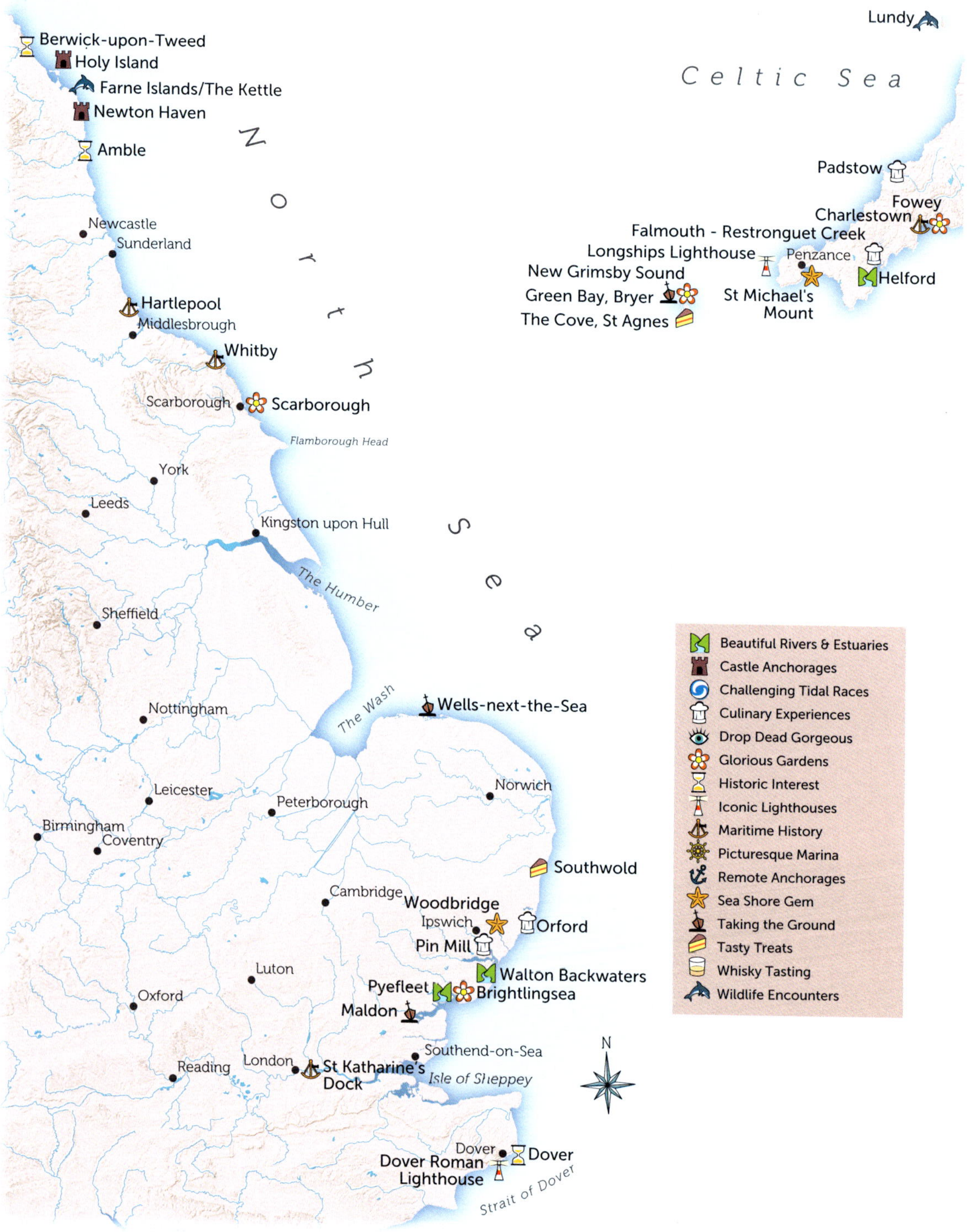

Berwick-upon-Tweed
Holy Island
Farne Islands/The Kettle
Newton Haven
Amble
North Sea
Newcastle
Sunderland
Hartlepool
Middlesbrough
Whitby
Scarborough
Scarborough
Flamborough Head
York
Leeds
Kingston upon Hull
The Humber
Sheffield
Nottingham
The Wash
Wells-next-the-Sea
Leicester
Peterborough
Norwich
Birmingham
Coventry
Southwold
Cambridge
Woodbridge
Ipswich
Orford
Pin Mill
Walton Backwaters
Luton
Pyefleet
Brightlingsea
Oxford
Maldon
Southend-on-Sea
Reading
London
St Katharine's Dock
Isle of Sheppey
N
Dover
Dover
Dover Roman Lighthouse
Strait of Dover
Lundy
Celtic Sea
Padstow
Fowey
Charlestown
Falmouth - Restronguet Creek
Longships Lighthouse
Penzance
New Grimsby Sound
Helford
Green Bay, Bryer
St Michael's Mount
The Cove, St Agnes
Beautiful Rivers & Estuaries
Castle Anchorages
Challenging Tidal Races
Culinary Experiences
Drop Dead Gorgeous
Glorious Gardens
Historic Interest
Iconic Lighthouses
Maritime History
Picturesque Marina
Remote Anchorages
Sea Shore Gem
Taking the Ground
Tasty Treats
Whisky Tasting
Wildlife Encounters

APPENDIX 1

MARINAS IN NORTH-WEST IRELAND AND SCOTLAND

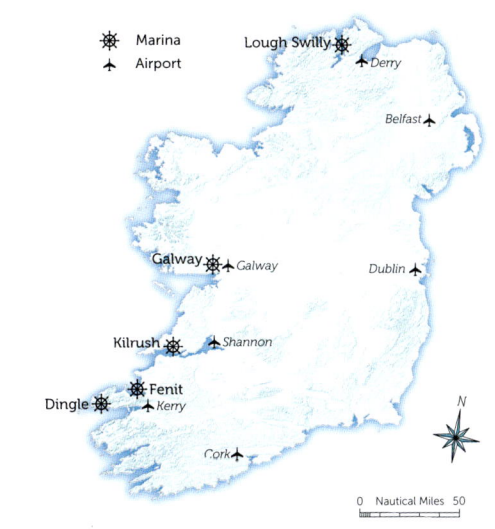

North-west Ireland

Cruising north-west Ireland and Scotland will need careful planning if you intend to leave your boat in a marina for the winter.

South, east and north-east coasts of both Ireland and Scotland are well served for marinas and hence omitted from the map.

MARINA LOCATION	FACILITIES	TRANSPORT
Lough Swilly Marina www.loughswillymarina.com	Storage Ashore	Approx 10min drive from Derry airport to marina. Daily flights from East Midlands, Glasgow, Liverpool and London Stansted to Derry airport
Galway Marina www.theportofgalway.ie/marina	Storage ashore	Short taxi ride from Galway airport to marina. Daily flights to Dublin, Luton, Manchester, Edinburgh to Galway airport
Kilrush Marina www.kilrushmarina.ie	Storage ashore (some under cover)	Approx 1hr drive from Shannon Airport to marina. Daily flights from low-cost operators to Shannon from London (Heathrow, Stansted, Luton and Gatwick), Liverpool, Nottingham, Manchester and Glasgow (Prestwick)
Fenit Harbour Marina www.visitfenit.ie	Afloat only	Approx 45min drive from Kerry airport and Dingle is 1hr away. Flights from low-cost operators to Kerry airport from Dublin, London, Liverpool or Manchester
Dingle Marina www.dinglemarina.ie	Afloat only	

244 UK AND IRELAND CIRCUMNAVIGATOR'S GUIDE

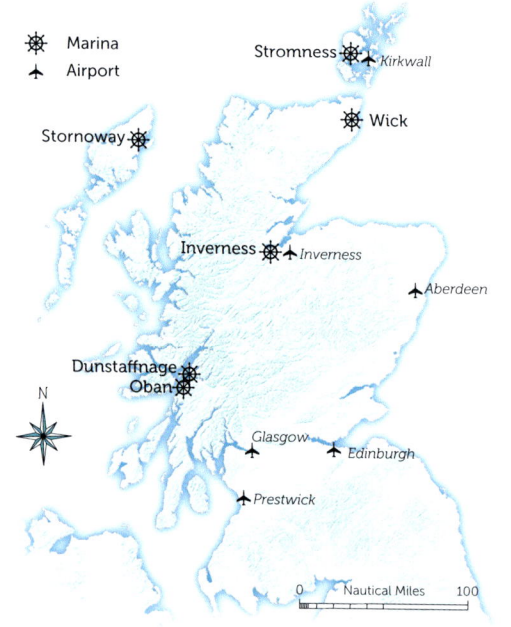

North-west Scotland

The coast below Oban is well served with Ardfern marina and the many marinas in the Firth of Clyde. In between Oban and the Orkneys there are buoys and some pontoons, including single pontoons at Loch Gairloch, Loch Inver and Kyleakin but these are often crowded. The north-east coast is well served with Wick, Inverness and Peterhead.

Barra Airport © Colin Hall

MARINA LOCATION	FACILITIES	TRANSPORT
Oban Marina: Located on Kerrera (an island opposite Oban) www.kerreramarina.com	Storage ashore (some under cover)	Approx 3hrs by train or bus from Glasgow airport. Low-cost operators fly to Glasgow and Prestwick. Some buses go from Glasgow airport to Oban. Distance: 100 miles to Glasgow, 200 miles to Carlisle. Oban Marina run a regular ferry service to and from Oban. There is a seaplane that operates straight to Oban from Glasgow. Berth holders get 25% discount; see www.lochlomandseaplanes.com
Dunstaffnage Marina (3 miles from Oban) www.dunstaffnagemarina.co.uk	Storage ashore	
Stornoway Marina www.stornowayportauthority.com	Some storage ashore	Flights from Aberdeen, Inverness, Edinburgh and Glasgow
Orkney Marinas: Kirkwall, Stromness www.orkneymarinas.co.uk	Afloat facilities only	Logan Air operates to Kirkwall from Glasgow, Edinburgh, Inverness and Aberdeen. Ferries from Wick, Scrabster and Aberdeen arrive at Stromness
Inverness: Inverness Marina www.invernessmarina.com In the canal: Seaport Caley Marina www.caleymarina.com	All facilities except Caley Marine are afloat	Regular flights from most main UK cities to Inverness
Wick www.wickharbour.co.uk	Some storage ashore	Regular flights to Wick airport from many UK cities

APPENDIX 2

FUEL AVAILABILITY

Table showing quayside availability of petrol in 2024. If you require petrol please check that these ports still have petrol as the availability will gradually reduce.

	WATERSIDE REFUELLING
S Coast England	Fairly regularly available; with careful planning, refuelling only at waterside is possible
W Coast England	Conwy, Pwllheli, Portishead
W Coast Scotland	Largs, Holy Loch Marina,
Ireland	Dun Laoghaire, Malahide, Howth
Northern Ireland	Bangor
N & E Coast Scotland	–
E & NE Coast England	Ramsgate, Gillingham, Bradwell (R Blackwater), Levington (R Orwell), Newcastle (Royal Quays)

Stromness waterfront

Loch Lochy from Laggan locks

APPENDIX 3

PILOT BOOKS AND SAILING DIRECTIONS

Our route was as follows:

Gosport – Yarmouth – Dartmouth – Salcombe – Falmouth – Helford – Penzance – Padstow – Dale – Neyland – Dale – Fishguard – Holyhead – Kirkcudbright – Campbeltown – Torrisdale Bay – Tarbert – Ardrishaig – Bellanoch Bridge – Crinan – Tobernochy – Puilladobhrain – Kerrera – Tobermory – Arisaig – Kyleakin – Loch Gairloch – Loch Inver – Kinlochbervie – Stromness – Pierowall – Calf Sound (Eday) – Stronsay – Sanday – Shapinsay – Kirkwall – Wick – Helmsdale – Inverness – Lossiemouth – Whitehills – Peterhead – Stonehaven – Arbroath – Eyemouth – Holy Island – Amble – Blyth – Newcastle – Whitby – Lowestoft – Pin Mill – Walton Backwaters – Dover – Gosport

Charts taken for our route can be found at www.sailingwithcarra.com. Pilot books and sailing directions are in the table below, we didn't take all of the pilot books due to cost, much will depend on the time you are spending in an area.

REF.	TIDAL ATLASES	AREA
NP 27	*Channel Pilot*, Admiralty	Scilly Isles, Cape Cornwall to Bognor Regis
NP 28	*Dover Strait Pilot*, Admiralty	Bognor Regis to Southwold
NP 54	*North Sea (West) Pilot*, Admiralty	Southwold to Rattray Head
NP 52	*North Coast of Scotland Pilot*, Admiralty	North and north-east coast of Scotland, Orkneys, Shetland, Faeroe Islands and Caledonian Canal
NP 66	*West Coast of Scotland Pilot*, Admiralty	Mull of Galloway to Cape Wrath
NP 37	*West Coast of England and Wales Pilot*, Admiralty	South-west Scottish Cape, Cornwall to Mull of Galloway including the Isle of Man
NP 40	*Irish Coast Pilot*, Admiralty	Coastal waters around Ireland
	The Yachtsman's Tidal Atlas Western Channel, Michael Reeves Fowkes	Western Channel, Southwest Ireland, Wales up to Bardsey Sound
	Central Channel and the Solent Tidal Atlas, Michael Reeves Fowkes	Newhaven to Lyme Bay
	Southern North Sea and Eastern Channel, Michael Reeves Fowkes	Wash to Solent

PILOT BOOKS AND SAILING DIRECTIONS

SEA AREA	OTHER PILOT BOOKS AND OTHER USEFUL PUBLICATIONS	COMMENTS
UK, Channel Islands and Ireland	*Reeds Nautical Almanac*	Provides all the data required to navigate Atlantic coastal waters around the UK, Ireland, Channel Islands and selected parts of Europe
Ireland	*South and West Coasts Ireland Irish Cruising Club (ICC) Sailing Directions*	Carnsore Point (SE) to Bloody Foreland (NW)
	East and North Coasts of Ireland ICC Sailing Directions	Carnsore Point (SE) up to Bloody Foreland (NE)
Irish Sea	*Lundy Irish Sea Pilot*, David Taylor (Imray)	Land's End to Portpatrick including Lundy and Isle of Man. This doesn't cover the Irish or Northern Irish coast
	Cruising Anglesey and Adjoining Waters, Ralph Morris	Anglesey, and the Menai Strait, Liverpool to Pwllheli
Scotland and the North of Ireland	*Welcome Anchorages*	www.welcome-anchorages.co.uk
West coast of Scotland	*Firth of Clyde Clyde Cruising Club (CCC) Sailing Directions*	Whitehaven to Mull of Kintyre to Upper Loch Fyne, Bangor to Rathlin Island, Isle of Man
	Isle of Mull and Adjacent Coast, Martin Lawrence	North Sound of Jura to Ardnamurchan Point and from Tiree across to Fort William, includes only Corpach sea lock of Caledonian Canal
	Kintyre to Ardnamurchan CCC Sailing Directions	Mull of Kintyre to Ardnamurchan including the islands of Islay, Jura, Colonsay, Mull, Tiree, Coll and Gigha
	Clyde to Colonsay, Martin Lawrence (Imray)	Mull of Galloway to Islay to Colonsay to Crinan to Upper Loch Fyne. Includes Crinan Canal, most of Jura bar (very northern corner) but excludes Northern Irish ports
North-west coast of Scotland	*Ardnamurchan Point to Cape Wrath CCC Sailing Directions*	Ardnamurchan Point to Cape Wrath, including Inner Hebrides north of Ardnamurchan; excludes Outer Hebrides
	Skye and Northwest Scotland Martin Lawrence (Imray)	
Western Isles	*Outer Hebrides CCC Sailing Directions*	Outer Hebrides from Butt of Lewis to Barra Head includes St Kilda Group
	The Western Isles, Martin Lawrence (Imray)	

Region	Publication	Coverage
Northern Isles	*Shetland Islands CCC Sailing Directions*	Covers Shetland Islands and Fair Isle
North and north-east Scotland	*North and East Scotland*, Martin Lawrence (Imray)	Blyth to Cape Wrath including the Caledonian Canal, Forth and Forth Canal, Union Canal, Farne Islands, Firth of Forth and Pentland Firth; excludes Orkneys
	N and NE Coasts of Scotland and Orkney Islands CCC Sailing Directions	Cape Wrath to Peterhead, includes Orkneys Islands, rounding Cape Wrath and Caledonian Canal
East Coast	*Humber to Rattray Head Royal Northumberland Yacht Club (RNYC) Sailing Directions*	Humber to Rattray Head: Available from RNYC E-mail: admin@rnyc.org.uk
	Forth, Tyne, Dogger, Humber, Henry Irving (Imray)	Blakeney to St Abbs
	East Coast Pilot, Colin Jarman, Garth Cooper, Dick Holness (Imray)	Lowestoft to Ramsgate
	East Coast Rivers, Jack Coote	Southwold to the Swale
East Coast	Suffolk Rivers Deben and Ore	The latest sketch maps showing the entrances to the Rivers Ore and Deben can be downloaded from www.eastcoastpilot.com.
South Coast	*The Shell Channel Pilot*, Tom Cunliffe	From Ramsgate to the Isles of Scilly, and from Dunkerque to L'Aber-Wrac'h
	Yachting Monthly West Country Cruising Companion, Mark Fishwick	Portland Bill to Padstow including Isles of Scilly
Isles of Scilly	*Royal Cruising Club Pilotage Foundation: The Isles of Scilly Pilot*, Robin Brandon, John and Fay Garey (Imray)	The Isles of Scilly

APPENDIX 4

BOOKS AND WEBSITES

Circumnavigations

England and Lowland Scotland via Forth and Clyde Canal
The Cruise of the Kate, EE Middleton

Round Britain via Cape Wrath
Around the Island: Britain in a Hundred Days, Stan Lester
Around these Islands in 12 Ports, Jonathan Winter
A Voyage Around Britain in a Small Yacht, Mark Evans
Blue Star Adventure, Mike Goodwin and Roger Colmer
Island Race, John McCarthy and Sandi Toksvig
Ninety-nine Days, Cate and Irving Benjamin
One Summer's Grace, Libby Purves

Round Britain via Caledonian Canal
Coasting, Jonathan Raban
Taking on the World, Ellen MacArthur
Walking on Water, Geoff Holt

UK and Ireland
Harbours and their Master, Mark Ashley Miller (in writing at time of publication)
Round Britain Windsurf, Tim Batstone
Sailing around the UK and Ireland, Roger Oliver
UK Circumnavigation, Ray and Margo Glaister

General
The 12 Volt Bible for Boats, K Brotherton
The Adlard Coles Book of Anchoring, Bobby Schent
Boatowner's Mechanical and Electrical Manual, Nigel Calder
Kids in the Cockpit: A Pilot Book to Safe and Happy Sailing with Children, Jill Schinas
'Performance Investigation of Marine Radar Reflectors on the Market', Report by QinetiQ, commissioned by the MAIB
Reeds Maritime Flag Handbook, Miranda Delmar Morgan
Staying Put! The Art of Anchoring, Brian Fagan

Tourist and wildlife guides
Attention all Shipping, Charlie Connelly
Coastal Britain, Stuart Fisher
Exploring Scotland's Islands, Terry Marsh
The RSPB Guide to British Birds The Rough Guides, Hilary Burn, Peter Holden and JTR Sharrock
The Scottish Islands, Hamish Haswell-Smith
Whales, Dolphins and Seals, Hadoram Shirihai and Brett Jarrett

Weather
Instant Weather Forecasting, Alan Watts
RYA Weather, Chris Tibbs
The Sailor's Book of the Weather, Simon Keeling
Skipper's Cockpit Weather Guide, Frank Singleton
Understanding Weatherfax, Mike Harris

Safety

First Aid at Sea, Colin Berry and Douglas Justins
Heavy Weather Sailing, Martin Thomas and Peter Bruce
The Liferaft Survival Guide, Frances and Michael Howorth
Reeds First Aid Handbook, Martin Thomas and Olivia Davis
Sea Safety, RNLI
Sea Survival Handbook, RYA
Skipper's Medical Emergency Handbook, Dr Spike Briggs and Dr Campbell Mackenzie

Websites

I have set up www.sailingwithcarra.com to provide additional resources and any new information about the routes. You can find a list of websites covering other circumnavigations, plus a role of honour – so if you have completed a circumnavigation, all I ask is that you complete a survey and you too will be added. You can also follow me on Facebook @doorstepsailing and follow our current adventures at www.carratidings.com.

Talks

Mags and I are available to give talks about the planning of a circumnavigation, coupled with an entertaining account of our trip round Britain. This talk should whet your appetite to set off – our coastline is stunningly beautiful. If you wish to book a talk please contact me through www.sailingwithcarra.com. You will also find a list of our future talks. We don't charge for these talks, but we do ask for a donation to the Ellen MacArthur Trust.

'Sam Steele and Mags Campbell gave an excellent talk at the Cruising Association, drawing a record attendance. The lecture is well illustrated and very entertaining, being both an account of a most interesting trip around the coast of Britain and a wealth of practical advice for those planning their own voyage. Highly recommended.'

Cruising Association

INDEX

Acairseid Mhor 214
Adrigole 238
almanacs 116
Amble 189
anchorages, remote 211–15
anchoring 88–90, 82
AngelNav App 124
Anstruther 196
anticlockwise route 24–5
Ardfern 209
Ardglass 173
Ardnamurchan Point 223
    to Cape Wrath 38–9
Arisaig 236
audit, electrical 59–61
automatic identification system (AIS) 145–6
autopilot 66

Ballycastle 208
Bantry 220
barbecues 65
Barloge Creek 182
Barmouth 194
batteries 71
Beaulieu 230
Belfast 232
Bell Rock 223
Berry Head 221
Berwick-upon-Tweed 189
    to Dover 42–3
bikes 65, 71
blogs 114
boat insurance 53
books and websites 71, 251–2
Brightlingsea 204
Bull Hole 188
buoys, mooring 85

Caernarfon 181
Caledonian Canal 48–9, 52
Campbeltown 183–4
canal locks 86–7
canals 45–52, 86–7
Canna 217
Cape Clear 170

Cape Wrath 223
    to Wick 40
Carbost 185
Carlingford 207
castle anchorages 162–5
Castlebay 164
Castletown 194
Castletownshend 165
chafe guards 88
Chanonry Point 170
charity, raising money for 56–7
Charlestown 231
chart datums 119, 121
chartering boat and skipper 28
chart plotters 121
charts 53–4, 119–21, 248–50
Chichester harbour 197
children, sailing with 133
clockwise route 24
clothes 64–5
coastal cruising 101–4
coastguard 142
cockpit tent 65
Colonsay 227
communications 105–15
contaminants, reducing 80–2
Conwy 225–6
cooking fuel 75
Cork 220
courses, attending 62
Cove St Agnes 216
Craighouse 184
Craobh Haven 209
crew 26–7, 131–2
Crinan Canal 47
Crosshaven 186
    to Portrush 33
Cuan Sound 179
culinary experiences 171–5
current, prevailing 20

Dartmouth 171
Derry 191
Derrynane 215
diesel 74–5

digital logs 126
digital navigation 123–5
dinghies 13, 91, 146
Dingle 191
disabilities, overcoming 14
documents 71
Douglas 226
Dover
   to Gosport 160
   to Land's End 44
   lighthouse 224
drilling rigs 153
drinks/provisions 72–3, 128–9, 183–6
Dromberg 191
Duart Bay 163
Dublin 231

Eddystone 221–2
electricity 59–61, 71
electronic charts *see* charts; digital navigation
emergency position indicating radio beacon
   (EPIRB) 137
emergency situations 135–46
engine maintenance 155–60
entertainment 129–31
equipment 59–62, 64–71
   emergency 135–42
Eriskay 185
experience, recommended 16

Falmouth 172
the Farne Islands 170
Fastnet 224
fender board 86
finances 53–7
Findhorn Bay 199
first aid 66
fishing 73
fishing pots 147–50
flags 134
flares 141
fog 103–4, 142–6
food 72–3, 128–9, 171–5, 216–20
Forth and Clyde Canal 46
fossil fuels, reducing 77–8
Fowey 202
fuel 56, 74–5, 247

Gallanach Bay, Muck 237

galley equipment 65
gardens, public 201–5
gas 75
goal setting 13
greener travel 77–83
Gigha 203
Glandore 191
Glenarm 207
Glengariff 205
grab bag 139–41
Green Bay 192
Greenwich 233
ground tackle 88–90

harbour fees 55–6
harbour planning 125–6
Hartlepool 232
hazards, coastal water 147–54
heating 66
heavy weather sails 65
Helford 198
historical sites 187–91
   maritime 229–33
   see also Holy Island
Holy Island 164–5
Hook 222
Howth 216–17
Hurst Point 162

Imray charts 119
Inishbofin 228
internet connection 105–8
Inverie 173
Irish Sea, passage through the 35

Jack Sounds 177
Jet Stream 97

katabatic winds 102–3
kayaks 13
Keem 215
Kinsale 175
Kippford 194
Kirkcudbright 199
Kirkwall 188
Kyle Rhea 179

Lagavulin 184
Lamb Holm/Kirk Sound 227

INDEX 255

land breezes 102
laptops/PC 122–3
Lawrence Cove 210
lifejackets 141
liferaft 137–8
lighthouses, iconic 221–4
Loch Duich 164
Loch Dunvegan 173
Loch Eriboll 215
Loch Ewe 204
Loch Moidart 163–4
Loch Ranza 163
Loch Scavaig 213
Loch Spelve 168
logs 126
Longships 222
Looe 192
Lossiemouth 218
Lough Swilly 200
Lundy 166–7

mail 114
Maldon 196
man overboard 138–9
maps for route planning 239–44
marinas
    North-West Ireland and Scotland 245–6
    picturesque 206–10
mast steps 65
medicines 66
Menai Strait 178
Met Éirean 95
Meteorological (Met) Office 95
midges 154
Milford Haven 199
mini automatic radar plotting aid (MARPA) 145
mobile phones 122–3
mooring 85–8
motorboats 13, 25, 84
Mull of Kintyre 179
    to Ardnamurchan Point 37
    lighthouse 222

navigation 116–26
Navtex 100
nets 150–1
New Grimsby Sound 202
Newton Ferrers 198
Newton Haven 165

night sailing 116
North Sea haar 103–4

Oban 184–5
offshore breezes 102
Orford 174
Orkney 40, 182
    and Shetland tides 117–18

Padstow 172–3
paper charts 54
Peel 217
Pentland Firth 182
Penzance to Padstow 31
Penzance to St Davids Head 32
petrol 74
photography 111–12
Pierowall 169
pilot books 53–4, 116–17, 248–50
Pin Mill 175
Plockton 237
Plymouth 230
Port Dinorwic 188
Porth Dinllaen 235
Portland Bill 176–7
Portmagee 205
Portpatrick 202–3
Portrush 226
Portsmouth 229–30
power cables 71
preparations 58–63
presenting your trip 113–14
pre-trip costs 53–4
project management 58–63
provisioning 72–7
publications 71, 248–50
    see also charts
Puilladobhrain 235
Pyefleet Channel 200

racing 11–12
radar reflectors 144
radar 145
Ramsay Sounds 176
Rathlin 167–8
remote working 108
repair costs 56
RIBs 13, 26
rig, loss of 138

rivers and estuaries, beautiful 197–200
rock hopping 118
Roundstone 238
route planning 28–31, 125–6
   see also maps for route planning
routing programs 126
rubbish 75, 83
rules, boat 141–2

safety 135–46
sailing directions 248–50
sails 65
St Michael's Mount 225
Sanda 212
Scapa Flow 232
Scarborough 204
schedule, planning a 29–30
sea breezes 101–2
sea condition forecasts 100
sea shore gems 225–8
search and rescue transponder (SART) 137
seasickness 127–8
shake-down cruise 63
Shiant Isles 169
shipping 152
shower facilities 131
skills to have 62
skipper, chartering 28
Skomer 167
snubbers 88
social networking 110, 112
Solva 193
Sound of Sleat 173
Southwold 219–20
spare parts, engine 157
sponsorship 56–7
Staffa 226
stages, travel in 18–19
starting point 24
Stonehaven 237–8
storage space 67–70
Stornoway 210
Studland Bay 235
Strangford Lough 178–9
Stromness 218
   to Pierowall 148
Studland Bay 235
submarines 152–3

Tanera Beg 214–15
Tarbert 208
Tenby 192–3
tidal atlases 117–19, 248
tidal races, challenging 176–82
tide, catching the 31
timing your trip 16–20
Tinker's Hole 213
Tobermory 235
Torrisdale Bay 162–3
Tory Island 228
Treshnish Isles 169

videos, producing 112–13
villages and towns, picturesque 192–6

Walton Backwaters 200
warps 88
watchkeeping 127
water supplies 75
wave and tidal power 154
weather 92–104
weather forecasts
   accessing/receiving 100–1
   coastal cruising 101–4
   forecasts 93, 95–7
   local observation 92–3
   sources of 94–5
Weir Quay 201
Wells-next-the-Sea 196
Weymouth 206
wetsuits 66
whisky tasting 183–6
Whitby 232
Wick 186
   to Eyemouth 41
wildlife 82, 129–30, 166–70
wind farms 153
winds 101–3
   prevailing 20–3
windsurfers 13
Woodbridge 228
Worbarrow Bay 211

yachts 13, 25, 84
Yarmouth 206